CONTEMPORARY INTERSECTIONAL CRIMINOLOGY IN THE UK

Examining the Boundaries of Intersectionality and Crime

Edited by
Jane Healy and Ben Colliver

I0136011

BRISTOL
UNIVERSITY
PRESS

First published in Great Britain in 2024 by

Bristol University Press
University of Bristol
1-9 Old Park Hill
Bristol
BS2 8BB
UK
t: +44 (0)117 374 6645
e: bup-info@bristol.ac.uk

Details of international sales and distribution partners are available at bristoluniversitypress.co.uk

© Bristol University Press 2024

British Library Cataloguing in Publication Data
A catalogue record for this book is available from the British Library

ISBN 978-1-5292-1594-6 hardcover
ISBN 978-1-5292-1595-3 paperback
ISBN 978-1-5292-1596-0 ePub
ISBN 978-1-5292-1597-7 ePdf

Cover design: Liam Roberts
Front cover image: istock/filo

Contents

List of Figures and Tables

Notes on Contributors

Ben Colliver is the Course Lead for postgraduate Criminology and a lecturer in Criminology at Birmingham City University. His research interests focus on hate crime, gender and sexuality, and he broadly investigates the role of gender and sexuality in relation to victimization. His PhD research focused on transgender people's experiences of hate crime and he has published in the areas of hate crime, online hate speech and the representation of lesbian, gay, bisexual, transgender and queer people in video games. He is also a member of the British Society of Criminology 'Hate Crime Network' as a steering group member.

Melindy Duffus is a lecturer in Criminology and Deputy Course Leader of Criminology, Policing and Investigation, and Security Studies, at Birmingham City University. Her main areas of research are around the topics of desistance, rehabilitation, substance use, prisons and probation. Melindy is currently completing her PhD whereby she is focusing on support within the community to encourage desistance from offending and substance misuse, having a particular focus on alcohol-related offending.

Emma Finnegan is a PhD student at Northumbria University. Her research interests include victimization against older people, gender-based violence, safeguarding and intersectionality. At the time of writing this is her first publication, but it is anticipated that the findings from her research will be published in 2022. She is also a volunteer at her local Citizens Advice Bureau, working on a specific project that seeks to improve the life chances of those that are 50 and over.

Jane Healy is Deputy Head of the Department of Social Science and Social Work and a lecturer in the Sociology of Crime and Deviance at Bournemouth University. Jane's research interests lie in the fields of victimology and hate crimes and she completed her PhD on the experiences of victims of disability hate crimes within the Criminal Justice System. Jane is on the Editorial Board of the *Safer Communities* journal and her work has been published in *Disability & Society* and *Criminology & Criminal Justice*.

Josh Hepple is an activist, researcher and writer. He has severe cerebral palsy and has taught and written about disability equality for many years. He is particularly interested in the social model, sex and disability. He has contributed to *The Guardian* newspaper on his own experiences and has worked as a disability equality trainer with many organizations including the Edinburgh Fringe Festival. Josh is particularly interested in contemporary constructions of disabled people's sexual identity and the decriminalization of sex between men.

Zoë James is Professor of Criminology at the University of Plymouth, UK. Her key research interests lie in examining hate from a critical perspective with a particular focus on the harms of hate experienced by Gypsies, Travellers and Roma. Zoë's research has explored how mobility, accommodation, policing and planning have impacted on the lived experiences of Gypsies, Travellers and Roma. Zoë is Co-Director of the International Network for Hate Studies and has published and presented her work nationally and internationally, most recently authoring a monograph, *The Harms of Hate against Gypsies and Travellers: A Critical Hate Studies Perspective.*

Jade Levell is a lecturer in Criminology and Gender Violence at the University of Bristol, School for Policy Studies. Her research focuses on the relationship between masculinities, violence and vulnerability, using music elicitation as a narrative research tool. Jade is on the editorial board for the *Journal of Gender-Based Violence.* Prior to her research career Jade worked in charities that work to end gender-based violence, including working in policy and training for a domestic violence charity, and front-line support work in sex-working women outreach projects, domestic violence refuges and rape crisis.

Hannah Marshall is a PhD candidate at the Institute of Criminology, University of Cambridge. Her research explores the processes by which young people involved in county lines identify, and are identified, as victims of criminal exploitation in the context of the youth justice system. Hannah's wider research interests include human trafficking, critical victimology, relational sociology, youth justice and participatory research. She has also worked as a researcher on projects exploring trauma-informed practice, outcomes for care leavers and rural youth crime. Her work has been published in *Economic Anthropology* and *Youth Justice.*

Katie McBride is a lecturer in Criminology at the University of Plymouth, UK. Before joining academia, Katie was an equality and human rights practitioner working within the public and third sectors on the development and delivery of policy and practice designed to address inequalities and discrimination experienced by marginalized communities. Her research interests lie in examining hate from a critical perspective with a particular focus on the harms of hate experienced by trans individuals. Katie's research utilizes deep ethnographic participatory methods as a tool to redress the balance of power in research and academia. Her research has explored how adverse childhood experiences, communities of support and structures of governance have impacted on the lived experiences of trans individuals.

Saabirah Osman is a lecturer and the Programme Lead of Criminology and Policing at Leeds Trinity University. Prior to her current role, Saabirah worked within the youth offending services in Birmingham and other higher education institutes. Saabirah is currently completing her PhD at Liverpool John Moores University, where she is exploring the experiences of asylum seekers who have been victims of sexual violence through their travels in seeking safety. While pursuing her academic role Saabirah continues to work closely with various agencies within the Criminal Justice System in Leeds and Birmingham in providing support to service users and building opportunities for students.

Lisa Overton is a senior lecturer in Politics at Middlesex University. Her PhD examined the intersections of youth, sexualities and gender in post-Katrina New Orleans where she fell in with a band of drag kings and gender performance artists. Since then, Lisa has worked on a range of crisis events with a wide lens. From the 2018 lecturer strikes, to the trappings of queer relationships, to gender and international development agendas, from Sri Lanka to Louisiana to the UK, she works from the view that crisis events are subjective and lived experiences.

James Pickles is a lecturer in Criminology at the University of Brighton, specializing in anti-LGBT+ hate crime. A former youth worker, he has an interest in research on 'youth' and young people. His current research focuses on criminal and social justice, in particular experiences of victimization in LGBT+ people.

Melsia Tomlin-Kräftner is a unit director and lecturer on the MSc Management and Organisation unit in the Management School of the University of Bristol, and lecturer in Qualitative Research Methods in the School of Management, University of Bristol. Previously she was a lecturer in Criminology and Policing, and a Seminar Tutor on Social Exclusion, Deviance and Criminology. Melsia is currently a member of the Cente for Gender Violence research at the University of Bristol. With over twenty years of Caribbean genealogical study of the various diasporas, Melsia's PhD research focused on the exploration of the intersections of race, gender, class and colourism, as they relate to mixed-heritage people, in the British colonial pre-post slavery emancipation period. Her research interests explore gender, kinship ties, family history and colourism, within the enslaver–enslaved dichotomy. The disciplines of human geography, sociology, anthropology, criminology, psychology, consumer behaviour and management intertwine to explore decoloniality, and the multiple diasporic movements that shaped Caribbean people's lives leading up to the Windrush period.

1

Introduction to this Collection

Jane Healy and Ben Colliver

The idea for this book originated in a panel session discussion at the British Society of Criminology's annual conference in summer 2019. Several papers were presented that year that drew upon the benefits of intersectionality to criminology, garnering a lot of discussion, though limited in number. The first author (Healy) presented one paper, subsequently published in the conference journal, where she submitted that there was a lack of intersectionality in hate crime research, and an underappreciation of it in UK criminological research generally. Healy concluded with a rallying cry: she wanted to teach students more about the advantages of using intersectionality as a methodology within criminological studies, but there was a paucity of UK-based academic literature to enable this. While acknowledging that articles and book chapters exist within UK publications, she could identify no single book based on UK studies that could be used for teaching UK students. This was effectively a call for action, that an 'intersectional criminology' has for too long been marginalized in UK criminology, essentially relegated to a subcategory within feminist criminology. Healy and Colliver had a conversation and realized they shared a desire to showcase what so many UK researchers have to offer, in drawing on intersectionality in contemporary criminological and criminal justice research studies, and so early discussions on this book began.

Intersectionality as a term first entered mainstream academic literature in the groundbreaking work of Kimberlé Crenshaw (1989; 1991). Subsequent chapters in this book will elaborate on Crenshaw's and others' contributions; suffice to say that intersectionality as a concept had existed long before it had this label. Crenshaw's work demonstrated how black women's experiences were marginalized and distorted in a legal system that functions through a 'single-axis' framework, resulting in the erasure of black women's perspectives because of a failure to accept that the 'intersectional experience' of 'race' and gender 'is greater than the sum of racism and sexism' (p 140). Consequently, she exposed how black women were (and are) marginalized and discriminated against in structural, political and representational ways. She describes their experiences as such; 'because of their intersectional identity as both women *and* of color within discourses that are shaped to respond to one *or* the other, women of colour are marginalized within both' (1991, p 1244).

What intersectionality offers, therefore, is an analytic approach to address a range of complex social issues and problems, and it is particularly relevant to examining how power relations are mutually constructed and intersect. Hill Collins and Bilge (2016) define intersectionality as:

> a way of understanding and analyzing the complexity in the world, in people, and in human experiences. The events and conditions of social and political life and the self can seldom be understood as shaped by one factor. They are generally shaped by many factors in diverse and mutually influencing ways. When it comes to social inequality, people's lives and the organization of power in a given society are better understood as being shaped not by a single axis of social division, be it race or gender or class, but by many axes that work together and influence each other. Intersectionality as an analytic tool gives people better access to the complexity of the world and of themselves (p 2).

Crenshaw acknowledges that this concept of intersectionality 'is not being offered here as some new, totalizing theory of identity' (p 1244) but rather demonstrates how a focus on race and gender (in her work) illustrates the need 'to account for *multiple grounds of identity* when considering how the social world is constructed' (p 1245, emphasis added). Subsequent academics have challenged this broader application of intersectionality to aspects of identity beyond race, gender and class, and some of these arguments are set out within this book (see Chapter Two), but Crenshaw acknowledges its wider applicability beyond its original usage. Likewise, Hill Collins and Bilge (2016) encourage its utility beyond any particular 'segment of the population' (p 30); rather they persuade us to use it to its fullest, to examine a range of topics related to social justice, social inequality and power relations. This is the approach this book has taken.

Thus, intersectionality offers us the opportunity to investigate and interpret the major axes of social division, those at the heart of discrimination, inequality, marginalization and subordination, such as race, ethnicity, gender identity, religion, ability, age, social class, sexuality and gender, not simply through a single-axis lens but through their intersections and interactions together, not as mutually exclusive, but as interactive and mutually constitutive.

Consequently, this publication is of value to many criminology students and researchers, but we believe it will also be of interest to activists and advocates. Hill Collins and Bilge (2016) rightly acknowledge that intersectionality is a 'polyglot', speaking to activists, communities, academics, institutions and young people, through publications, programmes and popular culture. Intersectionality is in vogue, broadly speaking, and we are aware it risks becoming the 'buzzword' that Davis (2008) warned us of, but this book showcases a variety of ways in which intersectionality can and does contribute to contemporary criminological studies.

Audre Lorde expressed that 'there is no such thing as a single-issue struggle because we do not live single-issue lives' (1984, p 138). Lorde was writing about the intersections of structures of racism, sexism and classism long before Crenshaw called it 'intersectionality'. We feel intersectionality is strikingly relevant to criminological studies, given so many of us are focused on experiences within a Criminal Justice System that relates to these forms of social division. We are delighted so many contributors came forward to consider how they are using – or will be using – intersectionality within their own criminal justice-related research and we encourage our readers to consider this concept, this tool, this buzzword as a method to enable a greater understanding of the complexity of individuals, communities and societies.

Synopsis of book and overview of chapters

The overall aim of this book is to contribute to and advance social scientific understandings of intersectional criminology. In these chapters, we showcase some of the innovative and critical research being conducted within criminology that utilizes intersectionality as a framework. This edited collection offers a range of empirical and conceptual chapters that investigate key aspects of victimization, harm and offending. The key thread running throughout the chapters is that adopting an intersectional framework enhances our understanding of these topics and provides a more nuanced conceptualization of people's lives and narratives.

The book is organized into three thematic parts. In the first part, 'Examining the Theoretical and Conceptual Contributions of Intersectionality to Criminology', contemporaneous and historic developments of intersectionality are explored, within an international context, as well as its contribution to our conceptualization of the harm of identity-based violence and abuse. This part offers a comprehensive overview of intersectionality and how it has, and can be, utilized within criminology. Appreciating the development of intersectionality as a concept, deriving from black feminist thought, this part engages with some of the key debates around how, and why, intersectionality is used. The chapters in this part offer a strong, conceptual grounding that contextualize the empirical chapters later in the book and are complimentary to each other, as outlined next.

In Chapter Two Jane Healy charts the emergence of the concept of intersectionality, from its origins in black feminist studies through to its global embrace within feminist academic literature, research and activism. Having first acknowledged its contribution to black feminist activism, Healy considers conflicting debates surrounding its use, including the argument that black women's experiences have been 'disappeared', as intersectionality became a 'feminist commodity' (Bilge, 2020, p 2) and a 'travelling' theory (Knapp, 2005, p 249). Healy then considers what intersectionality can offer to the field of criminology, highlighting how its approach to researching marginalized groups offers much in our constructions and interpretations of the meaning and consequences of multiple, structured and overlapping experiences of those touched by the Criminal Justice System.

In Chapter Three Melsia Tomlin-Kräftner offers a critical exposé of British colonial rule and its relationship with the development of slave societies in the Americas. This chapter provides a narrative of the British triangular slave trade in African people to the Americas and subsequent migration to the UK. Tomlin-Kräftner offers a detailed and fascinating insight into 18th-century British colonialism and imperialism, charting the impact of slavery from then through to the arrival of the 'Windrush generation' and contemporary society. She reflects on the intersecting and coalescing experiences of slavery with poverty, cultures, religion, childbirth, age and social class.

The central theme explored in Chapter Four is identity-based harms. James Pickles stresses the importance of adopting an intersectional framework when investigating issues of identity-based violence and notes the potential for intersectional analysis to aid the healing from such violence. Pickles examines some of the emotional, spiritual and psychological trauma that have been inflicted on people as a result of their identity. He argues that criminology as a discipline has a responsibility to raise the critical consciousness of marginalized groups and to actively resist structures that perpetuate oppression and exclusion. Adopting a broad understanding of identity, Pickles' conceptual paper has resonance with many different areas of criminological enquiry and illustrates the importance of considering complex identities when contemplating the impact and harms experienced as a result of identity-based violence.

The second part of the book, 'Crime, Harm and Criminal Justice Systems: Intersectionality's Engagement with Crime and Deviance', considers the application of intersectionality to specific elements of the Criminal Justice System, such as the probation service and prisons. Containing both conceptual and empirical chapters, various forms of victimization and offending are considered within intersectional frameworks, including domestic violence, substance misusers, gang violence and the criminal exploitation of children. Dominant narratives within criminology often position individuals in binary positions as either a victim or an offender. These chapters demonstrate how there is significant overlap in individuals' lives in which someone may be both a victim and an offender simultaneously. By adopting an intersectional framework, these contributions offer a more nuanced overview of how individuals experience crime, harm and the Criminal Justice System.

In Chapter Five Melindy Duffus draws upon empirical data collected with probation officers and service users to address the ways that gender and class impact on people's experiences of engaging with the probation service. In doing so, the author has a specific focus on the probation service within the context of substance use. Drawing upon both a class and gendered analysis, Duffus contends that service users from lower class backgrounds are considerably more likely to engage with the Criminal Justice System for longer, and this can be compounded for women who have experienced gender-based violence and have engaged in sex work. By adopting an intersectional analysis, Duffus illustrates the unique challenges and barriers that may be faced for women and those from lower class backgrounds when engaging with the probation service.

The focus of Chapter Six is on young people involved in county lines, and Hannah Marshall offers a critical analysis that recognizes the ways in which young people's perceptions of, and involvement in, county lines are shaped by multiple identities and various intersecting aspects of their lives. Utilizing intersectional analysis enables her to illustrate the way young people's varying relationships with power shape their experiences. As such, she challenges one-dimensional narratives that have dominated county lines discourse. Marshall presents an original and nuanced understanding and representation of young people's experiences, acknowledging the complexity of their involvement. Utilizing empirical data collected with young people affected by county lines, she argues that an intersectional approach can enhance our understanding of county lines, and specifically why young people may find the term 'victims of exploitation' problematic.

In Chapter Seven Jade Levell critiques the notion of the 'ideal victim' to investigate the experiences of young men who are 'on-road' and gang-involved. Through her analysis of empirical data collected with young men, Levell explores how race, class and gender intersect in particular contexts and spaces to create an archetypal image of a 'dangerous' working-class man. Levell examines the fragility of the concept of an 'ideal victim' by demonstrating how an individual may occupy both 'victim' and 'perpetrator' positions simultaneously. With a strong focus on identities, Levell also identifies why blanket labels that are imposed on young people may be problematic and contribute to a simplistic conceptualization of unique, individual experiences. By adopting an intersectional perspective, she is able to consider and interrogate interlocking oppressions that limit young men's abilities to seek help.

The focus of Chapter Eight is the prison service within England and Wales. Saabirah Osman introduces the chapter with an overview of some of the contemporary issues affecting the prison service, drawing upon issues of privatization to interrogate whether the prison service is indeed in 'crisis'. In this conceptual chapter, Osman provides an overview of existing literature that explores issues of gender, race and rehabilitation within the prison service, identifying that existing research primarily adopts a single-axis framework. She then argues that as a result of cultural invisibility and 'gendered pains', black, Asian and minority ethnic women are likely to experience the prison service in compound ways that are different to white women and black, Asian and ethnic minority men. Resultantly, this chapter calls for further empirical work to be conducted in which intersectionality is embedded throughout the research process.

In the final part, 'New Frontiers in Hate Crime Research', intersectional frameworks and methodologies are utilized to develop our understanding of hate crime, discrimination and abuse. Hate crime scholarship often operates in a 'silo' fashion (Mason-Bish, 2018), primarily based around the five monitored 'strands' and considered in isolation of each other. Arguably, this often results in a simplistic understanding of how 'hate' manifests and is experienced. The chapters in this part demonstrate how experiences of hate, discrimination and abuse are not experienced homogenously; rather, people experience hate uniquely, and these experiences may be compounded by multiple marginalization on the grounds of race, gender, religion, disability, age and other identity characteristics.

In Chapter Nine Ben Colliver considers the concept of 'master identity' and how this may be imposed upon transgender people, regardless of how their identities are perceived. He achieves this by interrogating the ways in which transgender people of faith experience exclusion and Othering from both religious and faith-based spaces as their trans identity is imposed on them, and how they are perceived to be transgender before they are considered religious. Consequently, and concurrently, transgender people of faith may experience exclusion from trans-friendly or trans-centred spaces in which their religion or faith is imposed on them, as the central feature of their identity. Colliver argues that this may lead to trans people concealing aspects of their identity in order to be accepted and to access certain spaces, and this may have negative consequences for their mental health. As such, supposedly 'inclusive' spaces operate on notions of 'exclusivity'.

Chapter Ten of this book explores the experiences of both transgender, and gypsy and traveller communities. McBride and James introduce a 'critical hate' perspective, informed by ultra-realism, in which they emphasize the importance of understanding hate within a contemporary, neo-liberal, capitalist society. Drawing upon empirical data collected with trans and gypsy and traveller communities, they develop discussions around hate beyond existing conceptualizations of prejudice, which are often based on a singular identity. As such, they adopt an intersectional approach to provide a discussion around the lived experiences of their participants. McBride and James enthusiastically engage with key tensions that exist between dominant theoretical perspectives within hate crime scholarship and discuss the impact these tensions may have on communities.

Chapter 11 considers how intersectionality can be beneficial for hate studies, drawing upon empirical data with disabled people as a case study. Through research with disabled men and women, Jane Healy explores how oppressions based on gender and disability intersect to create unique, gendered experiences of disablist hate crime. Offering a critique of 'strand-based' approaches to hate crime, Healy provides a complex reading of identities and argues that adopting an intersectional framework is essential in developing hate crime scholarship. While the focus is on disablist hate crime, the author offers an insight into how an intersectional framework can enhance hate crime scholarship more broadly.

In Chapter 12 Emma Finnegan provides a conceptual examination of how an intersectional framework can enhance our understanding of elder abuse. Despite a wealth of research exploring various forms of hate crime and abuse, age is often ignored as a contributory factor, and this chapter offers a critical exposé of how future research can adopt an intersectional framework to consider the role of age in older people's experiences of abuse. As a conceptual chapter, Finnegan details the social history of older people in the United Kingdom (UK) before applying critical elements of intersectionality to elder abuse. Drawing on age, gender and class, she demonstrates the different ways in which older people may experience abuse, and calls for further research to be conducted to truly appreciate the unique experiences of older people who are harmed.

Chapter 13 of this book exposes issues of safety, inclusion and exclusion more broadly, with a specific focus on sexualities and disability. By drawing upon empirical data collected in New Orleans, and autoethnographic data, Lisa Overton and Josh Hepple present original and intriguing insights into the roles of sexuality, gender and disability when navigating social spaces. They argue that social spaces play a central role in queer identity formation; however, these spaces are arguably not as 'inclusive' as expected. Rather, Overton and Hepple interweave our understanding of access, safety and inclusion within queer spaces, but also within 'heteronormative' spaces that surround and border them. Overton argues that in New Orleans, queer spaces may be understood as unproblematic, while the surrounding area is characterized by fear, danger and risk. Hepple's autoethnographic account offers an alternative reading of queer spaces, conceptualizing them as exclusive, as a result of which similarly created fear, danger and risk emerge in internal spaces for disabled patrons. As such, the dualistic nature of queer spaces is interrogated.

Finally, the conclusion (Chapter 14) of this book reflects upon the contributions of the writers and considers some of the essential and underlying themes that run across the chapters. In doing so, this chapter highlights how six core ideas of intersectional frameworks, as outlined by Hill Collins and Bilge (2016), have been incorporated throughout this collection. The chapter deliberates upon the ways in which intersectional frameworks can be utilized in criminology, and calls for further research that enhances our understanding of issues relating to crime, victimization and offending. By embracing intersectionality within criminology, we demonstrate how academics and researchers can extend beyond simplistic and one-dimensional approaches to identity, to engage in more nuanced interpretations and evaluations of our research that are more reflective of people's lived experiences.

References

Bilge, S. (2020) 'The fungibility of intersectionality: an Afropessimist reading', *Ethnic and Racial Studies*, [online] DOI: 10.1080/01419870.2020.1740289.

Crenshaw, K. (1989) 'Demarginalizing the intersection of race and sex: a black feminist critique of antidiscrimination doctrine, feminist theory and antiracist politics', *University of Chicago Legal Forum*, 1(8): 139–67.

Crenshaw, K. (1991) 'Mapping the margins: intersectionality, identity politics, and violence against women of color', *Stanford Law Review*, 43(6): 1241–99.

Davis, K. (2008) 'Intersectionality as buzzword: a sociology of science perspective on what makes a feminist theory successful', *Feminist Theory*, 9(1), 67–85.

Hill Collins, P. and Bilge, S. (2016) *Intersectionality*, Cambridge: Polity Press.

Knapp, G.-A. (2005) 'Race, class, gender, reclaiming baggage in fast travelling theories', *European Journal of Women's Studies*, 12(3): 249–65.

Lorde, A. (1984) *Sister Outsider: Essays and Speeches,* Trumansberg, NY: The Crossing Press.

Mason-Bish, H. (2018) 'Beyond the silo: rethinking hate crime and intersectionality', In: N. Hall, A. Corb, P. Giannasi, J. Grieve and N. Lawrence (eds) *The Routledge International Handbook on Hate Crime*, London: Routledge, pp 24–33.

PART I

Examining the Theoretical and Conceptual Contributions of Intersectionality to Criminology

Intersectionality and Criminology: Uncomfortable Bedfellows?

Jane Healy

Introduction

Intersectionality is arguably one of the most significant and certainly one of the most talked about concepts developed in recent times. Its foundations were grounded in the experiences of black women (Crenshaw, 1989; Crenshaw, 1991; Hill Collins and Bilge, 2016) but it has since been expanded and co-opted and is now considered a prominent feminist concept that generates a large amount of debate and discussion (Anthias, 2014). This chapter considers the development of intersectionality, from the early work of black critical race scholars to its global embrace as a feminist approach to research and epistemology. It explores how criminology has yet to fully endorse its application, despite the significant contribution that intersectional analysis can offer to understanding experiences and impacts of crime and harm. Its application to researching marginalized groups offers significant advantages in the interpretation and construction of meanings and consequences of multiple, structured and overlapping categories of identity, difference and disadvantage. This chapter acknowledges the groundbreaking contributions from black feminist academe but explicitly applies an expanded interpretation of intersectionality, to include research outside of black women's experiences and areas of marginalization and privilege (Potter, 2015).

Contextualizing intersectionality

Crenshaw (1989; 1991) is credited with the conceptualization of intersectionality, through her groundbreaking work on black women's experiences of employment discrimination. Crenshaw demonstrated how black women experienced racial discrimination and gender discrimination combined, but were constrained within a system that could only recognize them independently of each other. She used case studies to illustrate how this lack of 'fit' within existing legislation had negative consequences for black women litigants (discussed further in this chapter). Crenshaw argued that, rather than constructing identity through a single axis of discrimination, identities overlapped and multiple marginalizations intersected with one another in various ways, depending on the context and the situation. It is this 'intersection' of marginalized identities that is at the root of intersectionality. Drawing upon distinct experiences of black women, as different to both white women and black men, Crenshaw aptly demonstrated how their experiences of multiple and overlapping elements of identity and experiences of discrimination and subordination could not be compared.

While acknowledging Crenshaw's significant contribution to the introduction of intersectionality, its provenance lies in earlier works of black feminism, such as by hooks (1982) and the Combahee River Collective (1982). Black women activists consistently highlighted the differences in experiences of white and black women. The first- and second-wave feminist movements, founded by predominantly white feminists, focused on white women's experiences of inequality and failed to consider any need to also address simultaneous racial inequality. White women's experiences were prioritized, overlooking the differential experiences of other women of colour (hooks, 2000). Campaigning by mainstream feminism towards equality consequently further marginalized black women's experiences. Potter (2013) describes this as 'colourblind' feminism in failing to acknowledge or recognize racial inequality as a priority factor in women's experiences of discrimination and marginalization.

Almost one and a half centuries before Crenshaw's writings, Sojourner Truth, who was born into slavery to a Dutch slave owner in New York, campaigned for the abolition of slavery and the equal rights for women. Her 1851 speech at the Women's Rights Convention in Akron, Ohio, underlined the contribution of power to challenging the subordination and invisibility of black women. Although no formal record of her speech survived, different versions exist in publication, each of which emphasize her attempts to deconstruct conceptualizations of gender in a patriarchal enslaved environment. At this time, she drew upon the first women's anti-slavery society, which was founded in 1832 by black women in Massachusetts (Brah and Phoenix, 2004). Truth challenged listeners to consider how as an enslaved woman she was equally as strong as a man, but not recognized as distinct. At the same time, she was bearing children, just as white women did, but was not acknowledged as a mother. She highlights the othering of black women's experiences as she charts her contribution to both manual labour and to childbearing and asked 'ain't I a woman?' She dared to defy essentialist thinking around categories of womanhood by relating her experiences to 'white' women and to men.

Brah and Phoenix (2004) illustrate how since Truth's efforts many feminists have consistently campaigned for the application of intersectionality to later works. A key feature of this is what they describe as the 'decentring' (p 78) of the normative subject of feminism, driven by existing social movements in the 1960s and 1970s, including Civil Rights, Black Power, Workers movements, and others. For example, the Combahee River Collective, a black lesbian feminist organization actively committed to fighting against multiple forms of oppression, advocated for an 'integrated analysis' of experiences of oppression. Similarly, activists such as hooks (1982) spoke of simultaneous 'interlocking oppressions' (p 78) that were both local and global and formed around this concept of a decentred subject. All the while, activists impressed upon how an individual's subordination is a combination or multiplication of identity elements. As Audre Lorde (1983, p 9) reflects, 'Within the lesbian community I am Black, and within the Black community I am a lesbian ... There is no hierarchy of oppression ... I cannot afford the luxury of fighting one form of oppression only.'

Alexander-Floyd (2012) charts historic movements in black feminist works. Early signs of the principles of intersectionality in the literature include Anna Julia Cooper (1892), Ann duCille (1996), bell hooks (as mentioned previously) and Maria Stewart (Dill and Zambrana, 2009). The introduction of terms such as double jeopardy (Beale, 1970) and multiple jeopardy (King, 1988) attempted to conceptualize the experiences of multiple, overlapping forms of discrimination, and particularly the prioritization of race, gender and class in combination in relation to black women's experiences (Hill Collins, 2000). In the UK, Brah and Phoenix (2004) identified how similar campaigning was formed around African, Caribbean and South Asian women's activism. Black British feminism emerged through local women's organizations, on issues such as employment conditions, immigration legislation and domestic violence. A national Organisation of Women of Asian and African Descent (OWAAD) was established in 1978, which campaigned for political and intellectual debate and mobilization. Their work was focused on engaging with analysis of racism, class and gender, while adhering to cultural specificities. They described it as a principle of 'Afro-Asian unity' (Mirza, 1997, p 43) that recognizes cultural differences (see also Grewal et al, 1988; Brah, 1996). As such, many of these movements drew upon Crenshaw's work, which enunciated the label from which this early black feminist thought could be conceptualized.

Constructing intersectionality

> Intersectionality is a way of understanding and analysing the complexity in the world, in people, and in human experiences. The events and conditions of social and political life and the self can seldom be understood as shaped by one factor. They are generally shaped by many factors in diverse and mutually influencing ways. When it comes to social inequality, people's lives and the organisation of power in a given society are better understood as being shaped not by a single axis of social division, be it race or gender or class, but by many axes that work together and influence each other. Intersectionality as an analytic tool gives people better access to the complexity of the world and themselves (Hill Collins and Bilge, 2016, p 2).

Hill Collins and Bilge emphasize the contribution of intersectionality to the conceptualization of social experiences, and constructions of marginalization and subordination along multiple axes of discrimination. To intersect, therefore, is to overlap, cut across or combine social identities, acknowledging how they continually interact with and affect each other (Potter, 2013). Identities cannot be divided, but rather at 'different times, spaces, and places, not all facets of an individual's blended identity are visible to others attempting to categorize that person' (p 152).

As mentioned earlier, Crenshaw built upon black feminist works in two influential pieces. Firstly, in *Demarginalizing the Intersection of Race and Sex* (1989) Crenshaw coins the term intersectionality as a method of explicating the unique experiences of black women who experience racism and sexism. She demonstrates how black women's experiences do not 'fit' with the existing legislation that positions discrimination as either resulting from sex or race discrimination, but not both. This lack of legislative framework has wider negative outcomes for black women's lives and presents a top-down approach where black women are multiply challenged and disadvantaged. Quoting Hull et al (1982) to support this argument, she convincingly surmises that all women are assumed to be white, and all blacks are men, denying the experiences and specificity of black women.

In Crenshaw's subsequent work, *Mapping the Margins: Intersectionality, Identity Politics, and Violence Against Women of Color* (1991), she elaborates upon her theory of intersectionality to present three forms in which it can be manifested. Through analysis of the experiences of black women of rape and domestic violence, she delineates intersectionality along structural, political and representational lines. *Structural* intersectionality recognizes the position of women of colour in lower social strata that put them at greater risk for forms of violence compared with white women. For example, immigration laws that restrict women from leaving their husbands, or language barriers that prevent women from accessing services. *Political* intersectionality addresses the discourses embedded in the laws, policies and social services related to domestic violence and rape that effectively silence or erase the experiences of women of colour, either by invoking white women's experiences as the norm, or by focusing on racism exclusively, so as to fail to consider that women's experiences might be different when compared with men's. *Representational* intersectionality analyses the broader cultural discourses to show how contemporary critiques of race and sex representations marginalize women of colour. Here, she uses the example of black male rappers receiving harsher and more negative press than white rappers, while simultaneously displaying little concern for women of colour, but rather perpetuating the image of the violent black male predator as a threat to white women particularly. Here, Crenshaw shows how black women are again 'sidelined' as a pretext for focusing on white female experiences. Alexander-Floyd (2012) calls this a 'universalizing' strategy (p 8) that takes a particular issue beyond the experiences of women of colour and uses it to highlight the impact of it on 'all' women, which she proposes is rather a pretext for 'white' women.

From black women to all women

From the early foundations of intersectionality, rooted in black women's experiences, wider feminist movements were quick to adopt this concept within broader fields. Labelled recently as a fast-travelling concept (Knapp, 2005) or as a 'travelling theory', its movement across and between disciplines is not without criticism (discussed further in this chapter). Anthias (2014) suggests that its contribution could be in the construction of more 'hybrid' forms of social disadvantage, which historically were linked to the socio-legal framework of Crenshaw's early work, while moving beyond them. Similarly, Barmaki (2020) proposed that Crenshaw's intent for the term was to account for socioeconomic and political marginality, but that this was gradually extended to marginalized women of a variety of backgrounds. As will be discussed later, subsequent researchers have utilized an intersectional approach to explore oppression not simply on the basis of gender and race but also of other sources of discrimination and oppression, such as class, sexual orientation and ability. Its analytical approach to researching marginalized groups thus enables a broad range of research fields to examine the meaning and consequences of multiple and overlapping categories of identity, difference and disadvantage. Hence, there emerged a great deal of diversity towards applying and theorizing about intersectionality.

Long-standing interest in exploring the relationships between different forms of subordination and exploitation (Anthias, 2014), such as the work of feminism in relation to gender and class, and race theories looking at race and class, demonstrated how interconnections have existed long before they were labelled 'intersectionality'. However, the introduction of the term provided an opportunity to challenge traditional theories of stratification and essentialist understandings of social categories of difference and identity. What intersectionality offered was the construction of a new and more hybrid way of understanding various forms of social disadvantage. The emphasis was on the combination of two (or more) perceived minority traits that produce a distinct third minority entity, with his, hers or their own unique experience of disadvantage or position that cannot be produced by simply adding the first to the second. For researchers, this presented a formidable test in application, as demonstrated in many of the chapters of this collection.

More broadly, Anthias (2014) reflects on how intersectionality can assist in the framing of gendered violence, including domestic violence, rape and sexual assault, honour-based crimes and trafficking. Gender, sexuality and ethnicity are cultural forms that are determined by class 'forces' (p 153) and operate in different ways – as such, intersectionality demonstrates how people are not fixed within given hierarchical positions but occupy them at specific times in ways that are both contradictory and reinforcing. Elements such as class, gender and race cannot be essentialized as they are best understood when positioned interrelatedly. As demonstrated previously, before it was labelled 'intersectionality' these interconnections between social divisions existed, but the introduction of the term enabled its ability to challenge fixed and essentializing notions of the understanding of the operation of social categories of difference and identity.

Anthias (2014) suggests that intersectionality has left class relatively underexplored, however, in comparison to race and gender – by focusing on 'giving a voice to the voiceless' (p 158) – and encourages academic uptake in the fields of social class, as intersectionality offers a framework for understanding social hierarchy and stratification more broadly. An intersectional 'lens' has been able to make visible those categories of people who are particularly disadvantaged, and the differentiated nature of such disadvantage. She recognizes acutely the contribution of power in producing these social divisions. Indeed, Brah and Phoenix (2004) demonstrate how intersectionality enables a more complex understanding of the structural and subjective positioning of social class when combined with gender, 'race' and sexuality. Drawing on critical evaluations of historical feminisms, they chart the development of intersectionality through early anti-slavery and suffrage campaigns and expose the conflicts between racism, gender, sexuality and social class. Thus, they write extensively about the role of race, gender and social class in their work, charting the development of research in this area, and how privilege shapes advantage, particularly in relation to white middle-class communities. Their work demonstrates how intersectionality has enabled researchers to consider the complexity and multiplicity of power relations and that race, class and sexuality differentiated different women's experiences of womanhood, rejecting the notion of universality of experience.

In other fields, and as discussed in Chapter 11, intersectionality has contributed to hate crime research (Balderston, 2013; Liasidou, 2013; Healy, 2019). For example, Balderston contends that intersectionality helps to more accurately depict lived experiences by concurrently acknowledging the cumulative and compounding effects of intersecting oppressions of gender, disablism, poverty, racism and violence. These researchers thus fail to be convinced by the demands of some black feminists that intersectionality cannot function without black women at its centre (Alexander-Floyd, 2012; Bilge, 2020; and see criticisms section later in this chapter) and demonstrate the extent to which intersectionality has 'travelled'. Despite accusations that it is merely a 'buzzword' (Davis, 2008), intersectionality has been successfully embraced across broader feminist spheres. Indeed, to apply a 'buzzword' label is to fail to recognize the historical resonance of intersectionality to early black feminist and critical race theorists.

Consequentially, intersectionality effects all social interactions and institutions, including committing crime, being a victim of crime and the actions of the Criminal Justice System. Intersectionality offers a platform for new ways of recognizing and constructing the prevalent oppression and inequalities faced by social groups, such as violence against women, while simultaneously illuminating how the group is marginalized as a result of the intersection of different elements of social relations, such as violence against black women (Potter, 2013).

The next section considers the criticisms and challenges of using intersectionality.

Challenges of intersectionality

There have been a number of substantive and challenging appraisals of intersectionality, both as a concept and in terms of its application. One of the first criticisms of intersectionality has been in terms of its limited appeal. For example, Lim (2018) acknowledges that for some the theory of intersectionality narrowly focuses on marginalized groups in society, such as women of colour, and thus lacks universal appeal. Hill Collins and Bilge (2016) propose that this perspective overlooks the role of identity in examining the experiences of different groups. Intersectionality is concerned with the way things work rather than who they are, thus identities are the products of the intersection of multiple power dynamics. 'What makes an analysis intersectional – whatever terms it deploys, whatever its iteration, whatever its field or discipline – is its adoption of an intersectional way of thinking about the problem of sameness and difference and its relation to power' (Cho et al, 2013, p 795). Thus, there is a risk that researchers are unable to appreciate the impact and experiences of many marginalized groups if they fail to consider the elements of identity within them.

An additional challenge to this is determining how many groups or elements of identity should be taken into account within any research process. This could be a potentially infinite number of intersecting categories of identity, producing many more 'hybrid' groups (Anthias, 2014). The relevance of any category could be argued to be its social saliency but there can be other categories that have historically been overlooked or ignored in society; as such, the political salience of a category is not equivalent to a social salience, or the importance of such experiences.

Anthias (2014) also questions the concept of the 'intersection' as being the most important source of inequalities. Instead, she suggests we need to consider how it is not just the intersection of specific identity characteristics that collide but also how they interact within their environment – the political or legal frameworks that exclude or include minority groups. Power relations and dominant social structures that enable the reproduction of such discrimination must always be considered. What intersectionality offers, though, is a corrective to essentializing elements of identity that contribute to homogenizing social categories that fail to account for social differences. Intersectionality has been able to illuminate particularly disadvantaged categories and Anthias is keen to promote a 'translocational' positionality that she says constitutes the wider landscape in which power is produced and replicated, focusing on context, situation and process. Being translocal enables a recognition of experiences across multiple and interrelated social spaces. As such, domination and subordination can simultaneously be experienced by any one individual, in different times or spaces. An intersectional framework, therefore, is about not just looking at differences across race, gender, class and so on, but at wider discourses and practices as well as structures of dominance, locating it, in her view, not just on local and national axes but also globally.

There has also been a lack of theoretical engagement or clear conceptualization of the term in some research fields. As Naples (2009) rightly admonishes, to say your study uses 'intersectionality' is not enough; researchers must be clear about what aspects have been deployed, what have been left out, and why. Relatedly, many critics have questioned the 'etcetera' element, that intersectionality does not discern which identities need to be included in any particular analysis (for example, Yuval-Davis, 2006). As such, it risks becoming a somewhat ambiguous term, with Davis (2008) arguing that this ambiguity is the driving force behind its appeal and success, enabling space for critical enquiry and further debate.

Anthias' (2014) contention about the global appeal of intersectionality, beyond subordination and discrimination, is a controversial one. There is a divergence between those who define intersectionality within the limits of marginalized groups, and particularly women of colour (for example, Alexander-Floyd, 2012), and those who endorse intersectionality in any category of research study (McCall, 2005). Hill Collins (2015, p 2), one of the leading proponents of the conceptualization of intersectionality, contends that it can be utilized in research with both marginalized and privileged groups because 'the critical insight that race, class, gender, sexuality, ethnicity, nation, ability, and age operate not as unitary, mutually exclusive entities, but as reciprocally constructing phenomena that in turn shape social inequalities'.

Resultingly, insistence on a 'triple' oppression of race, class and gender could lead to unintended consequences of normalizing certain social categories as having fixed and essential characteristics and create hegemony of some categories over others. For example, Lim (2018) uses the study of migrant women holding both dominant and subordinate positions, depending on context and environment. In her example, Korean middle-class women can be subordinated in the labour market due to their minority ethnic and gendered position, but their middle-class standing ensures their dominance over other Korean women with fewer financial resources or support.

Much of the draw of intersectionality away from its roots in black feminist research has been in the direction of feminist studies generally. For many academics, this risks stripping intersectionality of its origins. Bilge's (2020) criticism goes further, describing intersectionality as 'an empty shell onto which scholars of all stripes can conveniently project their own concerns and feel completely legitimate to do so' (p 1), suggesting intersectionality has experienced a post-black feminist makeover, resulting in the removal of black women and black feminism from intersectionality itself. By commodifying intersectionality to feminist studies, she suggests its own black feminist roots are paid only lip service, resulting in the trivialization of its former black feminist centring. Instead, intersectionality has become the 'hottest feminist commodity' (p 2) celebrated by women and gender studies' academics who hail it as the most significant theoretical contribution of feminism. In juxtaposition, she contends that at the same time as intersectionality was put upon a pedestal it was simultaneously failed and devalued by others. For Bilge, intersectionality's success has arguably come at the cost of marginalizing black women's studies from within to the point of it being 'emptied and disfigured' (p 4) in current academe.

Correspondingly, Alexander-Floyd (2012) describes this process as a post-black feminist intersectionality, resulting in the marginalization of black women within contemporary intersectionality studies. She describes how black women have been 'disappeared' as knowledge producers through strategies she describes as a 'universalizing tendency' and 'bait-and-switch' (p 2). Charting two distinct strategies of misappropriation of intersectionality, as illustrated in the works of McCall (2005) and Hancock (2007a; 2007b), Alexander-Floyd presents a convincing argument for the misappropriation of black women's experiences as the foci of intersectionality. She suggests that both McCall and Hancock are among the most well known and most cited authors in regards to intersectionality studies. McCall's (2005) work frames intersectionality within 'complexity', offering three approaches to constructing intersectionality: an anti-categorical approach, which embraces post-structural feminist work by rejecting and deconstructing identity categories altogether; an intra-categorical approach, which focuses on black women's experiences as a central tenet, which she acknowledges as the origin of intersectionality; and an inter-categorical (or categorical) approach, which enables comparisons for different groups along different forms of identity. Alexander-Floyd (2012, p 2) accuses McCall of applying a 'bait-and-switch' approach here, which disappears black women and subverts the aims and objectives of intersectionality scholars. She decries this as post-black feminist politics that removes black women from the central focus on intersectionality to justify intersectionality analyses produced by those outside of work on black women. Though she acknowledges that McCall cites a range of women of colour scholars, she suggests this is insubstantive and lacks examination, saying that her work 'directly contradicts central tenets expressed in a variety of the theorists she cites' (p 12).

Similarly, in a critique of Hancock's (2007a; 2007b) work, Alexander-Floyd (2012) demonstrates how Hancock has displaced black women's subjectivity by broadening the appeal of intersectionality. Acknowledging the benefits of widening the influence of intersectionality within mainstream political science, Alexander-Floyd subsequently criticizes it for removing the experiences of black women and disappearing black women in many ways, accusing Hancock of silencing the work of early black scholars.

Alexander-Floyd's (2012) solution is to suggest that those scholars who would prefer to disarticulate intersectionality from its 'theoretical, political and methodological roots' (pp 18–19) would do better to develop new terms, concepts and approaches to conduct research. Research that does not include black women or women of colour can be 'informed' by intersectionality but the prerogative of any use of intersectionality must be to focus on black women. She calls this disrupting the 'colonization of intersectionality' (p 19). She positions intersectionality as part of a larger movement and body of work on theorizing black women's oppression and central to women of colour's experiences, though criticizes those scholars who reduce intersectionality to Crenshaw's original definition, without paying attention to wider structural inequality. She calls this the 'flattening' of intersectionality, stripping away intersectionality's ideographic dimension, which is crucial to its positioning beyond simplistic definitions to broader dimensions of social justice theorizing and black women's historical oppression. Broadening intersectionality's realms to disciplines beyond race and sex has resulted in an undermining of the ideational and ideographic dimensions of intersectionality. As such new approaches to intersectionality research in social sciences are an affront to 'intersectionality's central tenets' (p 9), resulting in the disappearing or re-marginalizing of black women's lives.

In a powerful rebuke to intersectionality's co-option within wider social science disciplines, Bilge (2020) describes how intersectionality's universality, or exchangeability, is a form of fungibility, as a function of the severing of ties with its ancestry ('natal alienation') and a reinforcer of the framing of black 'bodies' as liberated outside of time and space, as previously evidenced within Afropessimism. The travelling theory approach, as mentioned earlier, has left intersectionality's original forebearers behind, which Bilge describes as '*moving past* (rather than *moving with*) Black women' (p 20, italics in original). Bilge thus accuses the academy of utilizing intersectionality for both justifying a solution to a 'race problem' while at the same time promoting a post-black feminist intersectionality constructed through women's and gender studies instead.

By utilizing the concepts of black fungibility, natal alienation and slavery's 'afterlife', Bilge exposes intersectionality's post-black feminist guise. This adoption of intersectionality to other fields has resulted in an annexation of black feminism from intersectionality, resulting in a denial of the core value of intersectionality to black feminism. She confidently critiques those who claim that intersectionality is feminism first, decentring race and black women in particular. This is symptomatic of a history of fungibility and a co-optedness of intersectionality to white European feminism in particular.

Bilge notes that one of the premises of Afropessimism was the dehumanization of blackness, creating the 'Black non-human', the fungible object existing in slavery, one of interchangeability. For fungibility then, the ontological status of exchangeable commodities, via black bodies and intersectionality, are in a state of change and exchange. As she rightly argues, we must acknowledge and position intersectionality within a historical framework of black activism and black studies, rather than trying to whiten it by more recent academic research. Correspondingly, the creation of a new post-black feminist intersectionality that becomes a 'catch all' universality for feminist research leads to a devaluing of its contribution and the suggestion of it being more of an 'empty vessel' (Bilge, 2020, p 16) than a theoretically grounded commodity. This results in a repackaging of intersectionality for 'universal consumption' (Crenshaw, 2011, p 224), and an inherent marginalization of black women's experiences as a result. Bilge powerfully demonstrates how the removal of black feminism from intersectionality is a symbolic replication of the violence and severing of generations through natal alienation in slavery and its afterlife.

The challenge therefore remains to what extent can contemporary intersectionality do justice to the original tenets of its name, and its foundations in black feminism, while maintaining universal appeal? When researching this chapter, some of the authors list 'gender' before 'race' when they consider intersectionality; others fail to acknowledge its roots at all. Intersectionality has an unequivocal birthplace in black feminism, yet much of its success has been on illuminating multiple but distinct forms of inequalities, something that is particularly significant given the growing inequality in contemporary society (Verloo, 2006).

Intersectionality and criminology

As Potter (2013) notes, criminal legal systems do not operate in a vacuum; they are affected by the mechanisms of society, and its social interactions. Consequently, systems of power, hierarchies and interconnected identities traverse all lived experiences and as a result power and identity traverse experiences with crime and the Criminal Justice System, impacting offenders, victims, policy makers, law makers and members of the public. Potter acknowledges the role of the media in representing and contributing to perceptions of members of minority communities; they are not usually aware of the effects social pressure has on crime and may not recognize social reaction in action. Rather, they focus on the labelling of certain minority groups, particularly young black men (for example, Hall et al, 1978). However, as Messerschmidt (2013, p 124) contends, 'to better understand crime generally, we need to bring criminology 'out of the closet' by supporting extensive historical and contemporary research on the relationship among sexualities, gender, race, class and crime'.

Thus, there is ample opportunity to consider the differential effects minority groups experience in their criminality and experiences of criminal justice compared with those of other ethnic or racial backgrounds, yet historically there has been a tendency for criminologists to make participants inconspicuous at best. Potter's work is instrumental in challenging this, as to consider, for example, the experiences of white men engaged in criminal behaviour is to acknowledge that many others are not equally situated and that the privileges afforded to white men – even those behaving badly – put them in advantageous situations. For her, the challenge becomes how we identify those who are marginalized and represent them without marginalizing the experiences of others in the process. She quotes Du Bois (1899, p 241) in saying: 'There is a widespread feeling that something is wrong with a race that is responsible for so much crime, and that strong remedies are called for.' In this regard, we must therefore not just consider issues of race and gender, but also reflect on identity and power as influencing factors. For Potter, criminology needs to centre the experiences of research participants or subjects based on the impact of socially constructed identities on their experiences. Criminologists must ensure that we do not privilege white experiences and by default erase the distinct experiences of people of colour. Thus, despite the foundations of criminology being influenced by the relationship between crime and race, gender and class, we must continue to explore how other factors share or determine differences in offending, victimization and criminal justice processes and outcomes, and intersectionality offers a route into doing so authentically.

This remit is not purely the purview of feminist criminology either. Although Barmaki (2020) says intersectionality is a key theory in feminist criminology, and of particular importance to black feminist criminology (Potter, 2013) specifically, this chapter argues that intersectionality needs to be mainstreamed within criminology itself, rather than confined to feminist approaches. That said, the extent of criminological literature thus far that is concerned with utilizing intersectionality has tended to come from an inclusive feminist criminology (Burgess-Proctor, 2006). As with intersectionality gaining notoriety, feminist criminology also emerged during second-wave feminism in the 1960s and 1970s. Feminist scholars objected to the exclusion of gender from criminological analyses, citing that gender is the strongest predictor of offending. They also protested the exclusion of women's experiences in 'general' theories of crime being based as they were on male offending and male subjects (see also Potter's work). At the same time, feminism was also experiencing rebuttal as minority-group feminists reported a lack of voice in mainstream feminism, challenging the established hegemony of white, middle-class straight women that was dominant at the time. Claims of essentialism and reductionism were pointed at the broader feminist movement, as well as feminist criminology itself. The arrival of third-wave feminism in the 1980s and 1990s with a focus on multiplicities of genders, races and sexualities, and a concurrent dissatisfaction with the lack of engagement of race, class, sexuality and other elements of inequality in mainstream feminism, laid the groundwork for the adoption of intersectionality. Feminist criminologists recognized the value of it to criminology as its emphasis on power and privilege aligns with issues of inequality in the justice system. It challenged the 'dominance' approach to gender, informed by radical feminism, in that many third-wave feminists felt the dominance model essentialized women as speaking for 'all'. It assumes all women have shared experiences and thus is reductionist in assuming all women will have been oppressed in the same way. One can see clearly how attractive the lens of intersectionality would be to appreciating how intersecting systems of race, class, gender and so on are simultaneously experienced and multiplicative.

Feminist criminologists thus needed to acknowledge the diversity of women and that they do not all share the same experiences of oppression and sexism. An intersectional model, informed by multiracial feminism, considers gender through different forms of difference and acknowledges issues of power and dominance (Burgess-Proctor, 2006). The focus is on multiplicative rather than additive experiences as such, which also recognize the role of power and hierarchy on these intersecting systems. It avoids essentializing women's experiences but acknowledges relationality between different women in different ways, so that experiences are structurally linked, which results in women benefiting from the oppression of other women in lower social positions, often when they do not realize their own privilege. For Burgess-Proctor there is a strong contribution to be had from feminism and intersectionality to the development of feminist criminology, though she says that 'few feminist criminologists' have embraced an intersectional approach (p 38).

It is difficult, therefore, to identify why there is not greater operation of intersectionality within criminology. Early criminological intersectionality emerged in the works of Schwartz and Milavanovic (1996), according to Barmaki (2020), or Few (1999). Similarly, Daly (1993) and Daly and Stephens (1995) recognized the need for intersectionality within feminist criminology, suggesting that intersectionality in criminology has an opportunity to explore how race, class, gender and other areas of oppression are combined to create norms and deviants, and how legislation and the state challenge and reproduce those inequalities. Yet, uptake and application of intersectionality appears to have been more successful in US studies than within the UK. For example, Parker and Hefner (2015) cite a number of studies in criminology, all of which were US-based, that utilize intersectionality or an intersectional, or compound, approach to both male and female offending.

Parker and Hefner (2015) acknowledge how intersectional researchers offer valuable contributions to the 'social locations of women in relation to criminal involvement and victimization' (p 225), within both micro- and macro-structures that consider economic disadvantage and marginalization, in their focus on gender-specific homicides. However, very few researchers have 'theorized about the intersections of those factors and crime in substantive ways' (Paik, 2017, p 4).

Most intersectional criminology that does so has sought to understand the lived experiences of offenders and victims, and how these can be complicated by considering race, class, gender, place or sexuality. To do so authentically, and avoid stereotyping, is better suited to more qualitative measures and so the absence of a greater uptake of intersectional criminology may be because, for many practitioners in criminology, qualitative research is usurped by attempts to focus on mainstream 'administrative' approaches, such as the use of large scale, national data sets. This can make the utility of intersectionality more difficult, though it is not impossible. Qualitative research by contrast requires reflexivity and positionality as crucial elements in any understanding of participants' experiences. For example, Boggess et al (2018) look at the intersections of gender, ethnicity and class in young offending but do so using a quantitative approach and with no great elaboration on what intersectionality can offer or how it was applied to their study. Additionally, crime statistics drawn from large data sets may unintentionally or unwittingly reinforce images of crime based on broader patterns of discrimination, drawing the researcher away from more nuanced, informed examination of structural and political patterns of subordination. Indeed, Crenshaw (1991) proffers how social sciences reinforce politicized views on crime by emphasizing or reinforcing broader patterns of race, gender and class discrimination; in doing so, there is the potential for other criminal acts to go unnoticed and be absent from informed analysis.

Furthermore, how can we as criminology researchers achieve intersectionality in criminological research when, for example, people being interviewed or observed do not see their identities as relevant? How might our perceptions (as researchers) compromise or complicate how we define and measure the identities of our participants? These questions highlight the challenges to doing research intersectionally – how do we incorporate forms of discrimination into analysis based on data on individual cases where the various intersections affect the cases differently and at different points?

Potter (2015) offers us the opportunity to do this by saying that we must 'utilise intersectionality within criminology because of the salient existence and ferocity of socially structured and stratified identities' (p 160). We have been given the opportunity, through the use of intersectionality, to consider the structural inequality and power relations that shape crime and social harm in society. Intersectionality can contribute to knowledge beyond deterministic views of the relationship between social structures and crime 'by emphasizing that structures of gender, race, ethnicity, class, and sexuality weave together to create a complex tapestry of opportunities and motivations that shape variation in crime and violence across groups and situations' (de Coster and Heimer, 2017, p 11), and as such allows us to emphasize the interactive and multiplicative nature of structural inequalities.

How we apply this is for us to consider. For Potter, intersectional criminology can be, firstly, 'an epistemology for conducting research that better attempts to address the role and impact of identities and power dynamics regarding crime, criminality, and the criminal legal system' (2015, p 151). Secondly, it is 'a theory to understand the commission of crime and the responses to being criminally victimized' (p 151). For example, Crenshaw and Ritchie (2015) demonstrated how a focus on black men in common media representations of police brutality skew others' view of the scope of the problem, as there have also been a significant number of incidents of police brutality against black *women*. Thirdly, intersectionality offers us 'a theory to understand the formal responses to the commission of crime and to victims of crime' (Potter, 2015, p 152), in terms of how we make sense of criminal and victim actions and reactions, and how we label those involved. And finally, it is 'a perspective for informing communities and the polity about how better to prevent, control, and respond to acts designated as crimes' (Potter, 2015, p 152). Applying intersectionality enables us to see the whole person, not just one element.

Conclusion

Intersectionality regards power relations as based on multiple axes of dominance in our societies. How these axes interact and intersect varies according to environment, structure and policies. Intersectional criminology provides an opportunity for researchers to scrutinize crime-related policies to ensure they are non-racialized, non-sexist, non-sexualized and bias-free in all relevant ways. It supports raising attention to marginalized communities and individuals in a way that avoids sensationalizing or demonizing them. It can challenge neo-liberal mechanisms that are based on class inequalities that relegate some groups or others to lower classes, where they are unable to access opportunities afforded to those with greater social and cultural capital (Potter, 2013).

Rather than challenging those who pointedly chastise intersectionality researchers for failing to include the lived experiences of black women, I encourage criminology to embrace and embed intersectionality in its research process. I contend that we should be more focused on challenging those who use it only in weak or performative terms, who are more focused on the 'buzzword', particularly as seen in quantitative studies. Intersectionality offers criminologists the opportunity to fully acknowledge the experiential, lived experiences of research participants, in a respectful and meaningful way that recognizes its heritage, but endeavours to address all forms of marginalization and subordination.

References

Alexander-Floyd, N.G. (2012) 'Disappearing acts: reclaiming intersectionality in the social sciences in a post-black feminist era', *Feminist Formations*, 24(1): 1–25.

Anthias, F. (2014) 'The intersections of class, gender, sexuality and 'race': the political economy of gendered violence', *Int J Polit Cult Soc*, 27: 153–71.

Balderston, S. (2013) 'Victimized again? Intersectionality and injustice in disabled women's lives after hate crime and rape', *Gendered Perspectives on Conflict and Violence: Part A. Advances in Gender Research*, 18a: 17–51.

Barmaki, R. (2020) 'On the origin of concept of "intersectionality" in criminology: the civil rights movement and the rise of "scholarship of confrontation"', *Deviant Behavior*, 41(4): 483–496.

Beale, F. (1970) 'Double jeopardy: to be black and female', in T.C. Bambara (ed) *The Black Woman: An Anthology*, New York: New American Library, pp 90–100.

Bilge, S. (2020) 'The fungibility of intersectionality: an Afropessimist reading', *Ethnic and Racial Studies*, [online] DOI: 10.1080/01419870.2020.1740289.

Brah, A. (1996) *Cartographies of Diaspora, Contesting Identities*, London & New York: Routledge.

Brah, A. and Phoenix, A. (2004) 'Ain't I a woman?: Revisiting intersectionality', *Journal of International Women's Studies*, 5(3): 75–86.

Boggess, L. N., Powers, R. A. and Chamberlain, A. W. (2018) 'Sex, race, and place: taking an intersectional approach to understanding neighbourhood-level violent crime across race and sex', *Journal of Research in Crime and Delinquency*, 55(4): 493–537.

Burgess-Proctor, A. (2006) 'Intersections of race, class, gender, and crime: future directions for feminist criminology', *Feminist Criminology*, 1(1): 27–47.

Cho, S., Crenshaw, K.W. and McCall, L. (2013) 'Toward a field of intersectionality studies: theory, application, and praxis', *Signs: Journal of Women in Culture and Society*, 38(4): 785–810.

Combahee River Collective (1982) 'A black feminist statement: the Combahee River Collective', in G.T. Hull, P. Bell-Scott and B. Smith (eds) *All the Women are White, All the Blacks are Men, but Some of Us are Brave: Black Women's Studies*, New York: The Feminist Press at CUNY, pp 13–22.

Cooper, A.J. (1892) *A Voice from the South*, Ohio: The Aldine Printing Company.

Crenshaw, K. (1989) 'Demarginalizing the intersection of race and sex: a black feminist critique of antidiscrimination doctrine, feminist theory and antiracist politics', *University of Chicago Legal Forum*, 1(8): 139–67.

Crenshaw, K. (1991) 'Mapping the margins: intersectionality, identity politics, and violence against women of color', *Stanford Law Review*, 43(6): 1241–99.

Crenshaw, K. (2011) 'Postscript', in H. Lutz, M.T. Herrera-Vivar and L. Supik (eds) *Framing Intersectionality. Debates on a Multi-Faceted Concept in Gender Studies*, Farnham: Ashgate, pp 221–33.

Crenshaw, K.W. and Ritchie, A.J. (2015) '#Sayhername: Resisting Police Brutality Against Black Women', New York: Afr. Am. Policy Forum.

Daly, K. (1993) 'Class-race-gender: sloganeering in search of meaning', *Social Justice*, 20: 56–71.

Daly, K. and Stephens, D.J. (1995) 'The "dark figure" of criminology: towards a black and multi-ethnic feminist agenda for theory and research', in N. Hahn Rafter and F. Heidensohn (eds) *International Feminist Perspectives in Criminology: Engendering a Discipline*, Philadelphia: Open University Press, pp 189–215.

Davis, K. (2008) 'Intersectionality as buzzword: a sociology of science perspective on what makes a feminist theory successful', *Feminist Theory*, 9(1), 67–85.

De Coster, S. and Heimer, K. (2017) 'Choice within constraint: an explanation of crime at the intersections', *Theoretical Criminology*, 21(1), 11–22.

Dill, B.T. and Zambrana, R.E. (2009) 'Critical thinking about inequality: an emerging lens' in B.T. Dill and R.E. Zambrana (eds) *Emerging Intersections: Race, Class, and Gender in Theory, Policy, and Practice*, New Brunswich, NJ: Rutgers University Press, pp 1–21.

Du Bois, W.E.B. (1899) *The Philadelphia Negro: A Social Study*, Philadelphia, PA: University of Pennsylvania.

duCille, A. (1996) 'The occult of true black womanhood' in A. duCille (ed) *Skin Trade*, Cambridge, MA: Harvard University Press, pp 81–119.

Few, A.L. (1999) 'The (un)making of martyrs: black mothers, daughters, and intimate violence', *Journal for the Association of Research on Mothering*, 1: 68–75.

Grewal, S., Kay, J., Landor, L., Lewis, G. and Parmar, P. (eds) (1988) *Charting the Journey*, London: Sheba.

Hall, S., Critcher, C., Jefferson, T., Clarke, J. and Roberts, B. (1978) *Policing the Crisis: Mugging, the State, and Law and Order*, London: Macmillan.

Hancock, A. (2007a) 'Intersectionality as a normative and empirical paradigm', *Politics & Gender*, 3(2): 248–54.

Hancock, A. (2007b) 'When multiplication doesn't equal quick addition: examining intersectionality as a research paradigm', *Perspectives on Politics*, 5(1): 63–79.

Healy, J. (2019) 'Thinking outside the box: intersectionality as a hate crime research framework', *Papers from the British Criminology Conference*, 19: 60–83. [online] www.britsoccrim.org/pbcc2019/

Hill Collins, P. (2000) *Black Feminist Thought: Knowledge, Consciousness, and the Politics of Empowerment*, New York: Routledge.

Hill Collins, P. (2015) 'Intersectionality's definitional dilemmas', *Annual Review of Sociology*, 41: 1–20.

Hill Collins, P. and Bilge, S. (2016) *Intersectionality*, Cambridge: Polity Press.

hooks, b. (1982) *Ain't I a Woman: Black Women and Feminism*, London: Pluto Press.

hooks, b. (2000) *Feminist Theory: From Margin to Centre*, 2nd Ed., Cambridge, MA: South End Press.

King, D.K. (1988) 'Multiple jeopardy, multiple consciousness: the context of black feminist ideology', *Signs: Journal of Women in Culture and Society*, 14(1): 42–72.

Knapp, G.-A. (2005) 'Race, class, gender, reclaiming baggage in fast travelling theories', *European Journal of Women's Studies*, 12(3): 249–65.

Liasidou, A. (2013) 'Intersectional understandings of disability and implications for a social justice reform agenda in education policy and practice', *Disability & Society*, 28(3), 299–321.

Lim, H.-J. (2018) *East Asian Mothers in Britain. An Intersectional Exploration of Motherhood and Employment*, Cham: Palgrave Macmillan.

Lorde, A. (1983) 'There is no hierarchy of oppressions', *Bulletin: Homophobia and Education*, 14(3/4): 9.

McCall, L. (2005) 'The complexity of intersectionality', *Signs: Journal of Women in Culture and Society*, 30(3): 1771–800.

Messerschmidt, J.W. (2013) *Crime as Structured Action: On the Intersection of Masculinities, Race, Class, Sexuality, and Crime*, Lanham, MD: Rowman & Littlefield.

Mirza, H.S. (ed) (1997) *Black British Feminism*, London & New York: Routledge.

Naples, N.A. (2009) 'Teaching intersectionality intersectionally', *International Feminist Journal of Politics*, 11(4): 566–77.

Paik, L. (2017) 'Critical perspectives on intersectionality and criminology: introduction', *Theoretical Criminology*, 21(1): 4–10.

Parker, K. and Hefner, M.K. (2015) 'Intersections of race, gender, disadvantage, and violence: applying intersectionality to the macro-level study of female homicide', *Justice Quarterly*, 32: 223–54.

Parmer, A., Earl, R. and Phillips, C. (2020) 'Race matters in criminology: introduction to the special issue', *Theoretical Criminology*, 24(3): 421–6.

Potter, H. (2013) 'Intersectional criminology: interrogating identity and power in criminological research and theory', *Critical Criminology*, 21: 305–18.

Potter, H. (2015) *Intersectionality and Criminology: Disrupting and Revolutionizing Studies of Crime*, London: Routledge.

Salter, L. (2002) 'Challenging orthodoxy', in R. Mansell, R. Samarajiva and A. Mahan (eds) *Networking Knowledge for Information Societies*, Delft, Netherlands: Delft University Press, pp 60–7.

Schwartz, M.D. and Milavanovic, D. (1996) *Race, Gender and Class in Criminology. The Intersection*, New York: Garland Publishing.

Verloo, M. (2006) 'Multiple inequalities, intersectionality and the European Union', *European Journal of Women's Studies*, 13(3): 211–28.

Yuval-Davis, N. (2006) 'Intersectionality and feminist politics', *European Journal of Women's Studies*, 13(3): 193–209.

3

A Narrative Exposition of British Colonial Rule in the Americas

Melsia Tomlin-Kräftner

Black women produced, brown women served, and white women consumed.

Lucille Mathurin Mair

Introduction

When John Hawkins and eight of his associates received patents and ships from Queen Elizabeth to explore Africa for trading purposes in 1561–64, they did not know their foray into the transatlantic trade of enslaving Africans was an immoral legal act that would reverberate racial tensions across the world, to the present day. Britain, envious of the wealth the Europeans had amassed in their explorations, was keen to join them. John Hawkins took his first trip in 1562 with arms, materials, metals and alcohol to Africa, thus beginning the triangular trade of Africans to the Americas. The Americas include all the Caribbean islands, and North, Central and South America; however, this chapter will be focused on the Caribbean island of Jamaica, from where the largest immigration to the UK occurred during the Windrush period from 1948 to 1970. Although Barbados (colonized by Britain in 1627) was the most prosperous in the early colonial period, Jamaica later became the richest and most important, and 'the veritable jewel in the British Crown' (Padrón, 2003, p 31).

Enslaved Africans toiled and died in the tropics, lost their families, their homes, stability and ancestral belonging, while creating wealth for a patriarchal capitalist British society, where everyone, enslaved and enslaver, 'lost their souls' (Beckles and Shepherd, 2007, p 44). Enslavers from all walks of life capitalized on free labour to create and enrich their social, economic and political lives in their home societies. Rebellions by the enslaved freedom fighters in the colonies awakened the awareness of the planters to the seriousness of the demands for their freedom. British society, aware of the brutality of slavery in the colonies, joined the anti-slavery society in lobbying the government, and fought for the abolition of the slave trade in 1807, the abolition of slavery in 1834 and, finally, full emancipation for all British colonies on 1 August 1838.

Post-emancipation, the British colonies provided soldiers and assistance in both the First and Second World Wars, as the UK, by then with dire skills shortages, required assistance from their colonial territories. The descendants of the ex-enslaved answered the call of assistance from the British motherland, with the first arrivals on the Empire Windrush in 1948. They stayed, persevered and raised families despite the hardships and discrimination they experienced, and created an 'African-Caribbean' society, which we have today.

This chapter does not encompass a study on Britain's other colonies, and marginally mentions some Caribbean islands. There is significant scholarly literature on Britain's colonial past that provides solid discussions and debates, albeit not ones that contain a historiography of intersectionality and criminology of the colonial period. The purpose is to enable an understanding of Britain's relationship to the Americas, and why British society became a melting pot of people from the Americas. Using a constructivist epistemological position, with a narrative, interpretive approach, this chapter is a condensed journey of the British triangular slave trade in African people to the Americas, the combining of diasporic people from the influx of varied nations into the Americas and the exodus of families from the Caribbean to North America and Europe for economic reasons, especially those who returned to Britain during the Windrush era. The chapter will utilize an intersectional lens in its application, underlining the significance to criminology during the slavery and Windrush periods.

Intersectionality is applied to this period of study as a way of understanding and analysing the complex world of slavery and crime. Slave society was shaped by diverse intersecting factors, which influenced the macro environmental conditions of social, political and gender constructs that impacted the whole society, but especially enslaved men and women. Social equality was non-existent in slave society, as social power was held by the patriarchal order of men, built on a capitalist system where women were undermined at every axis of social division (Hill Collins and Bilge, 2016).

The human geography of people to the Americas, and their diasporic habitus (Bourdieu, 2010), created a multicultural British creole society through consensual and non-consensual (concubinage, rape, affinal and consanguineous) relationships. From the moment Columbus and his entourage arrived on the Americas, and John Hawkins set his sights on Africa, intersectional criminal injustices across gender, class, race and colour were enforced on black and mixed-heritage people and extended to the diasporic societies of present-day Great Britain.

The British triangular trade in Africans

John Hawkins (1532–95) began slave trading initially on his own accord, but subsequently with permission, and backing from the British monarchy. Hawkins lived in a period where it seems people had no souls; they lived in crude times, facing harsh realities, and poor people's lives were cheap. The 16th century highlighted a vast difference between the rich and the poor. Kelsey (2003) regarded Hawkins' hometown of Plymouth as 'a home to a rough breed of Englishmen, who were sometimes merchants, sometimes pirates, and often both at the same time' (Kelsey, 2003, p 3). People's attitudes, values, beliefs and religion changed, depending on the wind that blew the next financial gain, or their moral flexibility swayed by the missionary with a more enticing hope for their ill morals and weak faith, which they exhibited in often switching their religion. John Hawkins' father, William, switched his moral decisions so many times that he was considered a thief, a villain and a traitor, yet he was in a trusted position as the mayor of Plymouth, and had close allegiance to the monarchy (Kelsey, 2003). This life exposure to such an environment was John Hawkins' background and subsequent habitus, where he trained to be a ruffian, a pirate and a gentleman (Belvedere, 2013). Hawkins had three ships he used for his private slavery business from 1562 and had negotiated profitable business with the Spanish and Portuguese, bringing enslaved black people to the Spanish Caribbean. Queen Elizabeth, jealous of the amassed wealth of the experienced European competitors who had begun slavery in 1444, and revengeful of Spanish treachery, invested in Hawkins' voyage to enslave Africans in a triangular trade from Britain, to Africa, to the Americas and back to Britain, and allowed him to use the royal ship, Jesus of Lubeck, in 1564 (Bridges, 1826).

Enslaved Africans were transported to the Caribbean from the earliest days of the occupation of the Spanish and Portuguese, and began arriving in Jamaica from the Iberian Peninsula after 1513 (Wright, 1921; Cassidy, 1988). At this stage, society was intersected on white indentured male servants and black enslaved men, as women were not considered as important for the capitalist projects envisioned for slave society. In Barbados, it was initially noted that white indentured servants were not physically able to work the plantations in the production of sugar, as they were often ill in the tropical sun. African men befitted the environment with considerably more strength, agility, stamina and longevity, resulting in the transportation of more black men, followed by women from 1534, thus 'acquiring ever increasing importance as the cornerstone of the economy' (Padrón, 2003, pp 153–4). The nonchalant Spanish failed to realize the economic wealth of Jamaica, which they had captured in 1494, unsuccessfully protected the island from the British invaders in 1655 and ceded ownership in 1660 (Padrón, 2003). Although Britain struggled to attract white families to the islands, by 1690, it became the largest supplier of enslaved Africans to the New World (Heuman and Walvin, 2003). Between 1640 and 1807 Britain dominated slave trading, transporting 3.1 million Africans (of which only 2.7 million arrived) to the British colonies. Overall, it is estimated that, of the 12 million Africans who were transported by Europeans, five million were taken to the Caribbean (Eltis, 2005).

Early European emigrants to the Americas

With a lack of rewarding economic opportunities in Britain, religious persecutions, less social mobility and the opening of the New World, people were finding the lure to warmer territories appealing. While many young people were willing to serve as indentured servants for seven years or more from the 1680s, not all were willing participants. British laws were harsh, as 17-year-old Molly Walsh realized when the cow she was hired to milk as a dairy maid kicked over her pail of milk. She was charged, imprisoned and sentenced to death for stealing the milk. Her saving grace was the fact that she could read, and her sentence was commuted to transportation to a Maryland plantation in 1684 for seven years (McGill, 1999). Molly is an example of the thousands of indentured servants who chose this life of temporary servitude, bonded to landowners in the Americas for up to nine years. Many had hope of completing their apprenticeships, and although towards the end they would have no money, stock or land, being free to live as normal skilled white people was a great advantage. Their experience was in stark contrast to the enslaved people, who were subjected to permanent forced and unpaid labour that was perpetual throughout their generations, as the children of enslaved women were born enslaved (Jordan and Walsh, 2008). This level of multigenerational enslavement was not practised elsewhere in history, except for the enslavement of the Israelites by the ancient Egyptians. At this point, society was intersected on class (rich and poor), as there was no social mobility, and gender, representing patriarchal order.

When Britain captured Jamaica in 1655, their sparse army had to oversee the island while awaiting colonial administration from Britain. They formed a Privy Council, tried to maintain order among themselves and the remaining settlers, miserably planted crops and raised cattle for food, while fighting ailments and diseases. They soon failed in their efforts, as those officers left behind to settle in Jamaica had no experience of colonial settlements or planting. With the army stretched to their limits, and no women as nurses to assist in the daily care of the sick and dying, the Privy Council petitioned the Crown via Oliver Cromwell in 1655. They requested provisions, people with ability to farm, such as servants from Scotland to help with planting, well-disciplined veterans, nurses and companions to the British soldiers, including a list of 'urgent needs' (Gardner, 1971). The requests made for reinforcements, which seemed quite reasonable, were slow to materialize. Oliver Cromwell had an affinity with the Protestants in Ireland, and with permission from the Crown, ordered the kidnapping and removal of one thousand Catholic Irish girls to the island of Jamaica, and many more girls and boys across the Caribbean (Bennett, 2006). This dire act resulted in the start of an unlawful procurement trade in kidnapping white children and teenagers from the streets of Ireland and Scotland, to colonize Jamaica and the British Caribbean. There followed 27 years of kidnappings to the Americas before it was curbed. Irish history relates this episode, and many other stories of random kidnappings or 'spiriting' of children, teenagers, men and women, as advertisements appeared in many formats to find lost relatives and friends. This intersectional crime, on defenceless Irish and Scottish children, highlighted a criminal period of British history when the Irish and Scottish people were discriminated against on the grounds of nationality, ethnicity and religion (Barnes, 2008).

If we consider the criminal actions of Oliver Cromwell's men spiriting away boys and girls between 1655 and 1656, and multiply this action by more than three thousand, we have a small community of rebellious, dejected, dispirited children and teenagers on the small island of Jamaica. Transported with differing standards of values, diasporic habitus of childhood, beliefs, cultures, religious persuasion and only what they had been taught by parents up to the point of capture, they were introduced to the realities of colonial life (Besson, 2003). Having been tutored in the evils of colonialism and slavery, they developed desensitized attributes and behaviour patterns, having been introduced to immoral behaviour and debauchery at such young ages. Some married girls were having babies as young as 12 years old (Long, 1970). Those white people who survived the diseases of the island and their harsh lives grew up to be wives, husbands and workers within the development of slave society as a mixed-heritage creole society, on either cotton or tobacco estates in America, or on sugar plantations in the Caribbean. This scandal from the regular 'spiriting' away of children caused an uproar from the Caribbean to Ireland, Scotland and England, and the Jamaican merchants, beleaguered with a bad reputation of accepting kidnapped children, requested new procedures be formalized and implemented to stop those falsely claiming they were kidnapped, and to curb the kidnappers. On 13 December 1682, new procedures came into force to formally maintain records of indenture for people to work in the colonies, thus resolving those two problems (Wareing, 1976).

The British government proceeded with the targeted transportation of many more white people to the Caribbean, a prevalent practice from 1654, when convicts were sent to America to work (National Archives, nd). Convicts, vagrants and political prisoners, both men and women, were intersected on grounds of poverty, class, ethnicity, gender and nationality, under the guise of them having questionable backgrounds, and being undesirable for British society. Cromwell had ordered the council of Scotland to apprehend 'all known idle, master-less robbers and vagabonds, male and female, and transport them to the islands' (Williams, 1964, p 244). Political prisoners comprised of rich and poor people, such as the defeated army from the failed 1685 'Pitchfork or Monmouth Rebellion', fared the same fate. Over 890 people in that battle were transported to Barbados and Jamaica for treason and rebellion, and further political and civil disturbances in England between 1640 and 1740 helped to ensure a constant supply of white people as servants to the Caribbean, especially the Irish and the Scottish (Bridges, 1826; Macaulay, 1979). On arrival to the colonies, those kidnapped were treated similarly to transported Africans, being selected by local planters from a public line-up (Gardner, 1971).

Other settlers to Jamaica included British planters, their families and enslaved people from Surinam, who were evacuated after the exchange of Surinam for New Amsterdam (Dutch New York) in 1675, under the Treaty of Westminster in 1673 (Dunn, 1972). Much later, in 1776, the American War of Independence saw over 10,000 loyalists to the British Crown decide that Jamaica or Barbados was their next home (Jasanoff, 2012; Tomlin-Kräftner, 2020). The Jews, as an ethnic group, arrived in Spanish Jamaica as early as the 1600s; many spoke fluent Spanish and instructed the colonists in business, enterprise and negotiated business deals (Schorsch, 2004).

Most settlers, unmarried apprentices and indentured servants, took the opportunity of seeking their fortune to acquire riches in Jamaica by responding to advertisements and preferring Caribbean opportunities over Britain's lack of social movability. Advertisements promised resettlement incentives such as land, stock and money, and professional people such as doctors and rectors joined the throng. Although white people arrived in large numbers to replenish the population, just as many died from prevalent tropical diseases, and they failed to sustain their own population numbers to regard the island as a settler society, as the North American colonies did (Burnard, 1994).

British Caribbean slave society

The trade in Africans was brutal, heartless and cold. The traders had lost any essence of humanity as they collected payment for men, women and children, in the form of trinkets and goods, and drank sweet tea to seal their deals. Soulful hearts would have felt the agonizing pain of reality from the captured, seen them weeping, heard their groaning and experienced humanity's life ebb away. While with their feet, the traders walked the slave caravans back to their ships with the souls of their human cargo pondering their fate, leaving behind desolation, despair and death in the African homes and communities. Each step of the way, chains dragging with a human attached, it brought no feeling of heart to humans who were like themselves. Reflecting on the trade in humans highlights a much deeper multifaceted intersectional axis of race, colour, gender and systemic class violence. Enslaved people were estranged from their country of origin, language, culture and families, with diasporic habitus transferred into a new space. Noted sociologist Orlando Patterson (1982) described slavery as 'the permanent, violent domination of natally alienated and generally dishonoured persons' (p 13). The slave trade as a crime against humanity involved everything 'evil under the sun' that humans could perform, with no moral compass to gauge when to have stopped the atrocities that took place during this period.

Slave society involved the whole infrastructure of slavery. Higman (2001, pp 57–73) suggests that the framework of a 'slave society', originally coined by Elsa Goveia, was a society that encompassed everyone: enslaved and free, masters and mistresses in the production of goods, services and processes, managing those processes the political and legal establishment, transport, general infrastructure and the system. The colonial islands were treated like factories for the British, with people who lived and died there, where enslaved people were the tools, replaced when broken and discarded when old.

At this point in the slave trade, the intersections of gender and class were prominent in society. Although the women and children were needed, they played a back role in the plantation economy, as the men were more important, and were more expensive. Women's work and the birth of children were undermined; however, attitude and shift in gendered norms changed after the trade in African people was abolished in 1807, placing a greater emphasis on women reproducing strong children to replace older men in the fields. The intersectional chasm between enslaved men and women highlighted the macro level of social, political and economic divide between the sexes, and micro-level gender constructs during slavery. Those plantations with no strategic thought in the process fell at the first hurdle as women could not reproduce children if they were ill-treated, mutilated or kicked in the stomach (Lewis, 2005, p 181). Cruel behaviour towards enslaved people had a detrimental effect on the decline of plantation economies, their stirred anger aided rebellion by the freedom fighters and the anti-slavery society rhetoric on the emancipation of the enslaved brought into question the treatment of enslaved people on individual plantations. Most planters had believed there was a never-ending supply of fresh enslaved men on the African coasts, and as Higman stated, 'slaves were imported in the ratio of three males to every two females, creating an insufficiency of mates for the male slaves' (1995, p 119). Absentee owners (especially those who inherited the properties) left overseers to manage their plantations and remained in Britain, relying on natural replenishment through births, which did not materialize. This may have been due to enslaved women's resistance through infanticide, a high mortality rate caused by harsh treatment and the fact that children being born would take longer to become productive field workers than imported adults. Additionally, anti-rape laws, introduced in 1823, reduced the ability for overseers and masters to personally contribute to the replenishment of future new labour forces (Bush-Slimani, 1996; Hine, 1974).

Diasporic habitus among the Africans and the creole Caribbean people were not disparate, however. Africans were not simply a homogenous crowd of people transported into the islands from distant lands with the common factor of being enslaved. They represented different tribes, cultures, languages and social status. As Mintz has argued, 'millions of people were literally drawn together from different societies … and were obliged to create wholly remodelled cultural systems by which to live' (1974, p 297). The compulsion to optimize profits and wealth, and export bounteous goods, exacerbated the demand for enslaved people, which the British needed to develop the plantation system, and encourage growth and industry on the island, as Africans were considered as working capital and equipment. This demand intensified African supply of not only their war criminals, but also kidnapped Africans sold within Africa. The criminal act and cruelties of sale and transfer of enslaved Africans to plantations owned by the British, and other colonial powers, across the Atlantic Ocean continued for over four hundred years (Walvin, 2007).

Everyone in the slave society experiences intersections of role, function, colour, class, race and gender. More broadly, slave society further impacted upon these categories, with intersections of ethnicity, laws, codes and rules that shaped slave society. All were markers of identity, which could be used at any time to demarcate lines of discrimination and/or enslave or re-enslave a person of colour. Everyone played their part in creating and maintaining a capitalist patriarchal community, where women were second-class citizens. Women served the men in a slave society that was unequal, cruel, labour-intensive and diseased, whether they were free, enslaved, white, mixed heritage or black, married or single, young or old (Bush, 1990; Ferguson, 1992; Jones, 2003; Shepherd, 2011). White men held the power, as they ruled in a pure patriarchal capitalist society, described as a monstrous distortion of human society (Patterson, 1967). A phrase that has now come to epitomize the intersection or hierarchy of women in a slave society was Lucille Mathurin Mair's quote 'black women produced, brown women served and white women consumed' (Bush, 1990, p xii; Beckles, 1993).

The political establishment had not planned that the new people, those of mixed heritage, would arise between them and the enslaved people, with the potential power to usurp their plans, share in their profits and outnumber them (Tomlin-Kräftner, 2020). Sio (1987) posited the government's annoyance as 'the ideal of the masters that the two were to remain totally separate was never realized … a free coloured person was a third party in a system built for two' (1987, p 1). Mixed-heritage people initially resulted from consensual or non-consensual relations between enslaved black women and white men, and children born on the islands were regarded as 'Creole'. The application of the colour continuum of the Spanish lineal descent from the African woman segregated the level of whiteness for each racial miscegenation into 'sambo', 'mulatto', 'quadroon', 'octoroon', 'mustee' or 'legally white' (Brathwaite, 1978, p 167). Those with the mental capacity and opportunity would attempt to use their human survival instinct to escape slavery and therefore aim for the next colour elevation away from being 'black', the distinction between being black and considered property and a free white person with privileges. Thus, the racial taxonomies of Jamaican slave society allowed some liminal people of colour to determine advantageously their racial category based on their complexion. As more mixed-heritage people were enslaved across the islands, many received love, support and huge bequests from their white fathers, and those bequests included enslaved people, thus making them unwitting enslavers themselves (Tomlin-Kräftner, 2020).

Family life for the enslaved was largely non-existent in a slave society. However, on properties where the treatment was somewhat humane, any sense of a family life existed with trepidation, as life could change on a whim. Death of an owner and a will with bequests could change lives, and disrupt and break up family structures. The enslaved women cared for the children in a matrifocal community, while the enslaved black men were emasculated, stripped of all decency, pride and family life as they were dissuaded from getting married (Henriques, 1953; Patterson, 1967). They had children with the enslaved black women, but those children and their women belonged to the owner as his property. A black man could not protect, invest his love or build a life for them, as she may have had two children for him, but four other children for the various white men that chose her for their cruel pleasure, or to undermine him as a form of subjection. Her body, strength and time belonged to the white master, who she had to obey at all times (Cooper, 1824). Altink posited that 'the system of production in Jamaican slave society depended upon the successful subjugation of the slave body' (2002, p 1). Planter and writer Thomas Thistlewood, author of a salacious diary written between 1750 and 1786, was the most prolific sexual predator during slavery that we are aware of. He had sexual intercourse with any enslaved woman, anytime, anywhere and in whatever condition he found her across his plantation, and he wrote about it. Thistlewood's experience with white dominance in Jamaica taught him how to maintain authority, apportion punishment and control enslaved people through fear, sadistic violence and rape (Hall, 1999; Burnard, 2004).

Running away was a common method of resistance in slave society, with varying cruel consequences, and even some indentured servants as soon as they docked in Jamaica ran away rather than being confined to their indentureships (Anon, 1754). Slave revolts were few, rebellions were often, ambushes and skirmishes were commonplace throughout the Caribbean. The white planters' biggest fears were rebellions, which would destabilize the economy, and even worse, loss of lives of both enslavers, especially their families, and the enslaved. This was a volatile society, as enslaved people were resilient and ready to fight for their freedom, while the numbers of white people were falling daily. The Maroons, the runaway ex-enslaved Spanish Africans who lived high in the interiors, won the first Maroon war under the leadership of Nanny, the first woman general of the Windward Maroons, though the second Maroon war ended with executions and the transportation of over 600 Maroons to Canada in 1796. A truce was called with government officials and planters, who worked with the Maroons to stabilize the island and develop alliances (Sheridan, 1976). The largest slave revolt in Jamaica was on Christmas Day 1831, on the eve of emancipation, involving 60,000 enslaved people. This revolt resulted in hundreds of deaths and executions, and transportation of enslaved people (Craton, 1979). For the British, this was not the incitement they needed to add to the anti-slavery rhetoric, as this last rebellion resulted in the abolition of slavery. Terry Eagleton (1990) summarized power and resistance well:

> If there is not enough gratification for individuals, then they will demonstrate their freedom dramatically by rebellion. It is quite as certain that people will rebel in the long run against forms of oppressive power which allow them too few fulfilments … Individuals are in this sense as naturally revolutionary as they are naturally conservative. (p 37)

Under these extreme measures, enslaved people learnt how to conform to rules of subordination or risk their and their families' extreme harm or death. They had fun and enjoyed spiritual experiences, shared their heritage and engaged with Moravian, Baptist and Wesleyan Methodist churches to maintain a sense of calm in their troubled world.

Abolition of slavery and the apprenticeship period

Members of the London 'Clapham Sect', and those who sympathized with the anti-slavery cause, challenged the British government to abolish slavery. British middle-class women, in one of the first political campaigns, lobbied the government and encouraged other women to join them, boycotting sugar in their homes (Midgley, 1996). In the Caribbean, the enslaved people resisted slavery, while Wesleyan, Baptists and Moravian church missionaries preached of their impending freedom, increasing their hope and empowering their determination. The economy suffered, and fear among the whites grew (Drescher, 2010).

The Slavery Compensation Claims administration was a complicated system. By 1832, 54 per cent of enslaved people lived on properties owned by absentee landowners, as many white planters retired to Britain still holding financial interest in Jamaican planter life (Higman, 2005, p 18). As anti-slavery rhetoric increased, many lobbied Parliament for compensation for the loss of their investment in enslaved people, and Parliament met their arguments by a grant of less than half the estimated value of the enslaved people, raised through a government loan with the Rothschild's merchant bank (Green, 1996). British taxpayers finally completed payments on that 1834 loan in 2015.

Following the abolition of slavery on 1 August 1834, slave owners in the British colonies were awarded a combined total of £20 million compensation, plus interest accrued from the end of slavery until actual payments made for the loss of their enslaved people (Draper, 2007; Tomlin-Kräftner, 2020). Enslaved people received no payments, no lands, no infrastructure, nothing to start their lives of freedom. The decision in 1833 to abolish slavery was a compromise between the anti-slavery establishment, the pro-slavery body and deep fear from the growing numbers of enslaved black people, resulting in many whites deserting the island. At the time of emancipation all those enslaved who were over six years old were formally 'apprenticed' to their former owners for a period of up to six years, with no change in their treatment. The free mixed-heritage society as the real settlers, although much larger in number than the white population, were no match for the dissenting angry 'apprentices', who could see little difference between slavery and the new apprenticeship system. Eventually, Britain had no choice but to impose full emancipation as the apprenticeship system was no longer sustainable. By 1 August 1838, the apprenticeship system was abolished, and the poorer whites, and mixed-heritage and black people developed sustained peasant societies in the parishes after the abolition of slavery (Hall, 1953; Heuman, 2018).

Post-emancipation to the World Wars

The ex-enslaved people were jubilant with a new identity post-emancipation, whether they were of mixed-heritage Creole or African-born. Those born on the island, with many years of knowing their family only in the Caribbean, had no prior knowledge of their genealogy from Africa, and for them, that was a total natal alienation from Africa. Despite the joy of freedom, they lived in dire poverty, struggled to own land and created peasant societies, which lacked basic infrastructure. These peasant societies, studied by Mintz (1983) and Obrębski (2006a), consisted of small farmers who depended on their family members to farm for wages, but may also have farmed elsewhere to supplement their income. In addition, they had close kin family groups, with high levels of illegitimacy. This was the common development of family relationships across the Caribbean, with illegitimacy, unstable unions and many children born into poor families, though some families with stability, careers and finance followed the British church system in language, education, marriage and moral codes (Mintz et al, 1979; Mintz, 1983; Obrębski, 2006a; 2006b). Although the majority of the world by the 1840s was regarded as a peasant society, none were more depleted, impoverished and lacking basic amenities than the British colonies (Hobsbawm, 1962). To replace the ex-enslaved people, the British recruited Germans, Indians and Chinese as indentured servants to work on plantations that were still in operation after emancipation.

The Baptist, Moravian and Wesleyan Methodist missionaries knew the planters would plan to usurp any plans the freed ex-enslaved people made for their future, or any efforts made to improve their lives, by recreating pre-emancipation conditions, such as withholding wages, increasing rents, and firing and hiring cheaper employees, thus enhancing hunger and frustration over what they had in slavery. Missionaries pooled together, purchased lands and established new villages, which they initially sold to over 100,000 individual trusted freedmen who were their church members (Patterson, 1982; Mintz, 1985; Hall, 1995). The Caribbean islands became a multicultural melting pot of people of various cultures, intermixed with the freed people. Those of mixed heritage with established lives, property and financial stability developed kin groups as consanguineous (marrying cousins) and affinal families, while many emigrated to the United States and the UK, where they either passed as white or assimilated into white society.

The British had not created an infrastructure to assist the transition, leading to arguments that are still ongoing today in the calls for reparations. The British Caribbean islands became colonial outposts, largely ignored, quickly losing significance within the British Empire during the second half of the 19th and early 20th centuries, with the focus moving to Australia, South

Africa, South Asia and the Middle East. In 1926, the British Commonwealth of Nations was established as a result of agreements on equality across the colonies. Despite the long-held racial stereotypes and discrimination of people of colour, when Britain needed support from the British Empire, nearly 16,000 Caribbean men volunteered for the First World War as the British West Indies Regiment (BWIR). Although the British War Office resisted the formation of a Caribbean regiment for the Second World War, nearly 10,000 British Caribbean men and women travelled to Britain to join the army (Healy, 2000; Smith, 2004; Jenkinson, 2012).

The Windrush era

After the First and Second World Wars, Britain called on her colonies again for assistance, this time to rebuild the nation, to address labour shortages on the docks, ports, construction, hospitals, trains and transport due to retirements at the end of the war, and emigration of younger people to Australia, New Zealand and Canada. Under the 1948 Nationality Act, Caribbean men and women responded in large numbers to the 'motherland', with the first migrants arriving in Tilbury on the Empire Windrush, which docked on 22 June 1948; this was the first of many during 1948–70, which came to be named the 'Windrush era' (Selvon, 1956; Brinkhurst-Cuff, 2018). In Britain, all of the Caribbean migrants were treated as a single black entity and, inspired by the press, they were called 'Jamaicans', even though they came from different islands and areas of the Americas, and had different traditions, accents, cultures, complexions, musical language and experiences. This was a culture shock for many, because the mixed-heritage people of fair complexions who enjoyed privileges in their Caribbean homeland were now considered 'black' in Britain, receiving the same discriminatory treatment as others. Braithwaite (1959) tells of how he felt when he realized the colour of his skin prevented him from getting jobs for which he was qualified.

Many Caribbean migrants intended to return to their islands after five years. However, some got married and started families, while some Caribbean nurses, teachers and teenagers grasped the opportunity to gain more qualifications, thus improving their prospects. Many migrants chose to work and send money home to assist their parents and educate younger siblings. Other parents arrived in the UK first to settle down and then sent for their 'barrel children' later (those who were left behind) (Crawford-Brown, 1997; Jokhan, 2017). Other migrants who had gained employment and acquired mortgages went on to purchase a few houses to let to their incoming migrant family members to combat the racism they received from white home owners, epitomized in the adverts in windows of 'no Irish, no Blacks, no dogs' (Tomlin-Kräftner, 2020). During this period within British society there existed a different intersectional divide. Caribbean and African immigrants lived within white communities who had an insular knowledge of their predicament of disadvantage and discrimination, unless they were the perpetrators. The immigrant women as matriarchs of their families developed resilience and ways of overcoming obstacles, even though they had their own inner cultural challenges, such as division of domestic responsibilities, financial challenges, inadequate housing, unfaithful husbands, domestic violence and 'barrel children' remaining in their homelands. Nigerian writer and sociologist Buchi Emecheta (1944–2017) prolifically explored the unequal role of immigrant women of colour both with their homeland traditions and the issues experienced when those deep-rooted inequalities were transferred to the British society, which had ingrained discriminations.

Soon after arrival in the UK, with anticipated temporary residence, these migrants were met with hostility, and faced discrimination, hatred and racism that their enslaved ancestors experienced all those years prior when stolen from their homelands. After the 1958 Notting Hill riots between white British working-class and Caribbean migrants, multiculturalism became more entrenched in post-war London. There were many skirmishes around Britain's urban cities and especially London, with unwarranted arrests of black men and brewing trouble leading to Powell's racist provocative rhetoric (Modern Records Centre, 2020). These increasing arrests grew more year on year, into today's society, where black people remain disadvantaged and harassed. For example, between April 2019 and March 2020, there were six stop-and-searches for every 1,000 white people, compared with 54 stop-and-searches for every 1,000 black people (HM Government, 2021). The majority of those Caribbean migrants from the Windrush era never returned to the Caribbean (Hall and Schwarz, 2018). They had arrived believing they were equal citizens of the British Empire, but not only did they encounter discrimination in their daily lives, but hundreds of them, mostly those arriving as children who had never acquired a passport of their own, were cruelly treated by British government officials due to their inability to prove their immigration statuses. The barbarity of the cases was not public knowledge until 2018 when the UK press broke a story that became known as the 'Windrush scandal': that many Windrush migrants had been wrongly detained, deported and denied legal rights for many years. As David Lammy (2018) bemoaned, 'The Windrush generation had given so much, and asked for so little in return, and seventy years on the government thanked them for their service to this country by deporting so many and throwing others into illegal detention … [as] … they did not belong' (p xviii). This intersection of ethnicity, origin, race and poverty resulted in the marginalization and discrimination of a group of people who had done nothing wrong, but were caught up in the government's policy of hostility to immigrants and treated like criminals. Many writers of the Caribbean have explored the real stories of the Windrush generation, some of which makes harrowing reading, while also addressing how black people stoically raised their heads above the torment, abuse and oppression they experienced. Their stories were entrenched in slavery, and nearly 200 years after the abolition of slavery, the descendants of enslaved people are still suffering the long-term consequences of the cruellest government-sponsored atrocity in human history.

Conclusion

The Bank of England, Barclays Bank, Lloyds Insurance, universities and hospitals are some of the establishments who profited from slavery, as well as thousands of wealthy individuals, with the City of London the financial hub of slavery business. Present-day nostalgia for the British Empire is based on the idea that British imperialism was fundamentally commercial, on a natural right to rule and a unique national genius, completely ignoring evidence that the Empire was built on slave labour (Scanlan, 2020). The ill treatment of people of African origin by the British over many centuries was justified by an ideology of white superiority and supremacy. Imperialistic policies were essentially based on exploiting the assets of these colonies, draining the lifeblood of the lands, without investing in the infrastructure of the islands. In addition, ownership of privately owned inaccessible quality lands of the pre-colonial era, which black people could access for their own farming to raise their economic prospects, remains unobtainable. All the wealth and investment continue to be directed to the UK and other colonizing countries, leaving those colonies without meaningful industries, thus resulting in a struggle to build the local economy, unable and unallowed to be self-sustaining and dependent on imports. Left economically dependent on World Bank funding and International Monetary Fund (IMF) loans, these repayments lasted for years at high interest rates. This in turn created a vicious cycle that encouraged emigration, like the Windrush immigrants who gravitated to the motherland decades before expecting to be treated like citizens, 'real children' of the empire. Emigration to the US and other countries continues, as does increased crime on the islands due to intersectional poverty. Despite their ill treatment, immigrants still aim to reach the UK, where black men make up a disproportionally high percentage of the prison population, thus shifting and creating an alternative gendered intersectional axis.

Bringing the intersections of race, gender, age and class from the slavery period into contemporary British society, while there has been some progress in attitudes towards race over the decades, as in the support for the Black Lives Matter movement, there is also evidence of decline and insufficient progress, with retrograde ideologies coming to the fore, such as the recently published Sewell (2021) report. Where there were once individuals suffering in silence, as in the Windrush scandal, media intervention has highlighted the political forces of strategy and policy that have markedly, and painfully, disadvantaged people that migrated from the Caribbean as British citizens. Sewell's report on racism in the UK, commissioned by the current government, acknowledged that racism was still prevalent, but that it was no longer institutional (Sewell et al, 2021). The counterargument to the official finding of the report is that as long as there is racial bias in people, there will always be a form of institutional racism in organizations and public services, as these are managed and operated by the same people who, the report admits, can still have racial bias. Because discrimination on the grounds of race is officially illegal does not mean, for example, that lay juries who decide on guilt in trials, judges who sentence people, police who have the power to stop, search and arrest are completely devoid of any form of racial prejudice. This, therefore, must affect the decisions made by the institutions they serve, as evidenced by the disproportionate numbers of black people in prison – 25 per cent compared with 14 per cent of the wider population in England and Wales (Lammy, 2018).

The intersections of historical slavery, contemporary prejudice and ongoing marginalization of populations from former colonies is clearly evidenced today. Britain lags behind in the number of black professors in universities, where fewer than 1 per cent are black, and in many areas of society such as education and health, there exist disproportionate challenges that African, Caribbean and other ethnicities experience. Black women in management experience a glass ceiling more than white women and other ethnicities and are overrepresented in the care home industry as carers, on temporary contracts, receiving very low wages for long hours of work caring for mainly white people (Women's Budget Group, 2020). The average wealth black people have accumulated over the past decade in property ownership is zero, while in contrast, white British families have amassed a net of £115,000 through property ownership over the same period (Konotey-Ahulu, 2021). From slavery, through to the Windrush generation into today's society, injustice, discrimination and intersectional prejudices against black British people still prevail and are perpetuated in various ways. Resistance against inequality continues in modern society, although in different forms, and less overtly than in slave society. Despite this, black people continue to resist, and let their voices be heard in prominent places to realize change.

References

Altink, H. (2002) '"An outrage on all decency": abolitionist reactions to flogging Jamaican slave women, 1780–1834', *Slavery & Abolition*, 23(2): 107–22.

Anon. (1754) Runaways. *The Jamaica Courant: Saturday June 22 to Saturday June 29, 1754* [online] www.jamaicanfamilysearch.com/Members/c/Courant1754.htm, William Daniel, p 295.

Barnes, R.W. (2008) Missing Relatives and Lost Friends, Maryland: Genealogical Publishing Company.

Beckles, H.M. (1993) 'White women and slavery in the Caribbean', *History Workshop*, 36(1): 66–82.

Beckles, H.M. and Shepherd, V. (2007) *Saving Souls. The Struggle to End the Transatlantic Trade in Africans*, Kingston: Ian Randle Publishers Ltd.

Belvedere, C. (2013) 'The habitus made me do it: Bourdieu's key concept as a substruction of the monad', *Philosophy Study*, 3(12): 1094–108.

Bennett, M. (2006) *Oliver Cromwell*. London & New York: Routledge.

Besson, J. (2003) 'Euro-Creole, Afro-Creole, Meso-Creole: Creolization and ethnic identity in West Central Jamaica', in G. Collier and U. Fleischmann (eds), *Aspects of Creolization in the Caribbean*, Amsterdam and New York, Matatu, pp 169–88.

Bourdieu, P. (2010) 'The habitus and the space of life-styles', *Distinction: A Social Critique of the Judgement of Taste*, Oxon, Routledge, pp 165–222.

Braithwaite, E.R. (1959) *To Sir With Love*, London: Vintage.

Brathwaite, E. (1978) *The Development of Creole Society in Jamaica 1770–1820*, Oxford: Oxford University Press.

Bridges, R.G.W. (1826) *The Annals of Jamaica*, London: John Murray, Albermarle-Street.

Brinkhurst-Cuff, C. (2018) *Mother Country: Real Stories of the Windrush Children*, London: Headline Publishing Group.

Burnard, T. (1994) 'A failed settler society: marriage and demographic failure in early Jamaica', *Journal of Social History*, 28(1): 63–82.

Burnard, T. (2004) *Mastery, Tyranny and Desire: Thomas Thistlewood and His Slaves in the Anglo-Jamaican World*, Chapel Hill: The University of North Carolina Press.

Bush-Slimani, B. (1996) 'Hard labour: women, childbirth and resistance in British Caribbean slave societies', in D.B. Gaspar and D. Clark Hine (eds), *More Than Chattel: Black Women and Slavery in the Americas*, Bloomington and Indianapolis: Indiana University Press, pp 193–217.

Bush, B. (1990) *Slave Women in Caribbean Society: 1650–1838*, London: James Carey Ltd.

Cassidy, F.G. (1988) 'The earliest placenames in Jamaica', *A Journal of Onomastics*, 36(3 & 4): 151–62.

Cooper, T. (1824) *Facts Illustrative of the Condition of the Negro Slaves in Jamaica*, London: Smallfield, G., p 27.

Craton, M. (1979) 'Proto-peasant revolts? The late slave rebellions in the British West Indies 1816–1832', *Past & Present*, 85(1): 99–125.

Crawford-Brown, C. (1997) *Who Will Save Our Children?: The Plight of the Jamaican Child in the Nineties*, Kingston: The University of the West Indies Press.

Draper, N. (2007) '"Possessing slaves": ownership, compensation and metropolitan society in Britain at the time of emancipation 1834–40', *History Workshop Journal*, 64(1): 74–102.

Drescher, S. (2010) *Econocide: British Slavery in the Era of Abolition*: Chapel Hill, NC: University of North Carolina Press.

Dunn, R.S. (1972) *Sugar & Slaves, The Rise of the Planter Class in the English West Indies, 1624–1713*: Chapel Hill, NC: University of North Carolina Press.

Eagleton, T. (1990) *The Significance of Theory*, Oxford: Basil Blackwell Ltd.

Eltis, D. (2005) 'Slave voyages: explore the dispersal of enslaved Africans across the Atlantic world', *The Trans-Atlantic Slave Trade Database* [online] www.slavevoyages.org/, Emory Libraries and Information Technology: Emory Centre for Digital Scholarship.

Ferguson, M. (1992) *Subject to Others: British Women Writers and Colonial Slavery, 1670–1834*, New York and London: Routledge.

Gardner, R.W.J. (1971) *A History of Jamaica from its Discovery by Christopher Columbus to the Year 1872*, London: Psychology Press.

Green, W.A. (1996) 'Review: [untitled] the economics of emancipation: Jamaica and Barbados, 1823–1843 by Kathleen Mary Butler', *The American Historical Review*, 101(5): 1655–6.

HM Government (2021) *Stop and search.* [online] www.ethnicity-facts-figures.service.gov.uk/crime-justice-and-the-law/policing/stop-and-search/latest

Hall, D.G. (1953) 'The apprenticeship period in Jamaica, 1834–1838', *Caribbean Quarterly*, 3(3): 142–66.

Hall, C. (1995) *White, Male and Middle Class. Explorations in Feminism and History*, Cambridge: Polity Press.

Hall, D. (1999) *In Miserable Slavery: Thomas Thistlewood in Jamaica 1750–86*, Kingston: The University of the West Indies Press.

Hall, S. and Schwarz, B. (2018) *Familiar Stranger: A Life Between Two Islands*, UK: Penguin Books.

Healy, M.S. (2000) 'Colour, climate, and combat: the Caribbean regiment in the Second World War', *The International History Review*, 22(1): 65–85.

Henriques, F. (1953) *Family and Colour in Jamaica*, London: Eyre & Spottiswoode.

Heuman, G. (2018) 'Apprenticeship and emancipation in the Caribbean: the seeds of citizenship', in W.N. Stewart and J.G. Marks (eds), *Race and Nation in the Age of Emancipations*, Georgia: University of Georgia Press.

Heuman, G. and Walvin, J. (2003) *The Slavery Reader.* London and New York: Routledge Taylor & Francis Group, p. 800.

Higman, B.W. (1995) *Slave Population and Economy in Jamaica 1807–1834*. Kingston: The University of The West Indies Press.

Higman, B.W. (2001) 'The invention of slave society', in B.W. Higman, B.L. Moore, C. Campbell and P. Bryan (eds), *Slavery, Freedom and Gender: The Dynamic of Caribbean Society*, Kingston: University of the West Indies Press.

Higman, B.W. (2005) *Plantation Jamaica 1750–1850: Capital and Control in a Colonial Economy*, Kingston: University of The West Indies Press.

Hill Collins, P. and Bilge, S. (2016) *Intersectionality*, Cambridge: Polity Press.

Hine, D.C. (1974) *Hine Sight: Black Women and the Re-construction of American History*, Bloomington & Indianapolis: Indiana University Press.

Hobsbawm, E. (1962) *The Age of Revolution 1789–1848*, London: Weidenfeld & Nicholson Ltd.

Jasanoff, M. (2012) *Liberty's Exiles: American Loyalists in the Revolutionary World*, New York: Vintage Books.

Jenkinson, J. (2012) '"All in the same uniform?" The participation of black colonial residents in the British armed forces in the First World War', *The Journal of Imperial and Commonwealth History*, 40(2): 207–30.

Jokhan, M. (2017) 'Exploring the "barrel Children" cycle: parent–child separation due to migration', in: C.E. International (ed), *Childhood Explorer* [online] www.childhoodexplorer.org/exploring-the-barrel-children-cycle-parentchild-separation-due-to-migration, Trinidad & Tobago: The University of the West Indies.

Jones, C. (2003) 'Contesting the boundaries of gender, race and sexuality in Barbadian plantation society', *Women's History Review*, 12(2): 195–232.

Jordan, D. and Walsh, M. (2008) *White Cargo: The Forgotten History of Britain's White Slaves in America*, Edinburgh: Mainstream Publishing Company Ltd.

Kelsey, H. (2003) *Sir John Hawkins: Queen Elizabeth's Slave Trader*, New Haven & London: Yale University Press.

Konotey-Ahulu, O. (2021) *How London's property boom left black Britons with nothing*, [online] www.bloomberg.com/news/features/2021-05-18/uk-property-wealth-data-2021-show-big-gap-between-black-and-white-homeowners

Lammy, D. (2018) 'Foreward', in C. Brinkhurst-Cuff (ed), *Mother Country: Real Stories of the Windrush Children*, Great Britain: Headline Publishing Group, p. 290.

Lewis, M. (2005) *Journal of a Residence Among the Negroes in the West Indies*, Gloucestershire: Nonsuch Publishing Ltd.

Long, E. (1970) *The History of Jamaica, or General Survey of the Antient and Modern State of That Island with Reflections on its Situation, Settlements, Inhabitants, Climate, Products, Commerce, Laws and Government*, London: Frank Cass & Co. Ltd.

Macaulay, T.B. (1979) *History of England*, London: Penguin.

McGill, A. (1999) *Molly Bannaky*, New York: The Houghton Mifflin Co.

Midgley, C. (1996) 'Slave sugar boycotts, female activism and the domestic base of British antislavery culture', *Slavery & Abolition*, 17(3): 137–62.

Mintz, S.W. (1974) *Caribbean Transformations*. London: Aldine Publishing Company.

Mintz, S.W. (1983) 'Reflections on Caribbean peasantries', *Nieuwe West-Indische Gids / New West Indian Guide*, 57(1/2): 17.

Mintz, S.W. (1985) *Sweetness and Power*, New York: Penguin Books.

Mintz, S.W., Marshall, W.K., Karasch, M. and Frucht, R. (1979) 'Slavery and the rise of peasantries [with commentary]', *Historical Reflections / Réflexions Historiques*, 6(1): 213–53.

Modern Records Centre (2020) 'The Notting Hill riots of 1958'. Racism and Xenophobia, https://warwick.ac.uk/services/library/mrc/studying/docs/racism/riots, United Kingdom: University Library, University of Warwick.

Obrębski, J. (2006a) 'Legitimacy and illegitimacy in Jamaica: A non-deviant case', *Sprawy NarodowościoweNationalities Affairs*, 29: 296–304.

Obrębski, J. (2006b) 'Peasant family and national society in Jamaica', *Sprawy Narodowościowe Nationalities Affairs*, 29: 305–11.

Padrón, F.M. (2003) *Spanish Jamaica*, Kingston: Ian Randle Publishers.

Patterson, O. (1967) *The Sociology of Slavery: An Analysis of the Origins, Development and Structure of Negro Slave Society in Jamaica*, London: MacGibbon & Kee.

Patterson, O. (1982) *Slavery and Social Death: A Comparative Study*, Cambridge & London: Harvard University Press.

Scanlan, P. (2020) *Slave Empire: How Slavery Built Modern Britain*, London: Robinson: An Inprint of Little Brown Book Group.

Schorsch, J. (2004) *Jews and Blacks in the Early Modern World*, New York: Cambridge University Press.

Selvon, S. (1956) *The Lonely Londoners*, London: Alan Wingate.

Sewell, T., Aderin-Pocock, M., Chughtai, A., Fraser, K., Khalid, N. and Moyo, D. (2021) *Commission on Race and Ethnic Disparities: The Report*, London: Commission on Race and Ethnic Disparities.

Shepherd, V. (2011) *Engendering Caribbean History: Cross-Cultural Perspectives*, Kingston: Ian Randle Publishers, p 942.

Sheridan, R.B. (1976) 'The Jamaican slave insurrection scare of 1776 and the American revolution', *The Journal of Negro History*, 61(3): 290–308.

Sio, A.A. (1987) 'Marginality and free coloured identity in Caribbean slave society', *Slavery & Abolition*, 8(2): 166–82.

Smith, R. (2004) *Jamaican Volunteers in the First World War: Race, Masculinity and the Development of National Consciousness*, Manchester: Manchester University Press.

Tomlin-Kräftner, M. (2014) 'Up from slavery: exploring economic positions & strategies of mixed heritage women in St. Elizabeth Jamaica, up to the slavery compensation awards 1800–1845', *History*, Coventry, Warwick: MPhil., p 245.

Tomlin-Kräftner, M. (2020) 'Colonial matriarchs in the British slavery economy: exploring the socioeconomic landscape of mixed-heritage women in Jamaica from 1750–1850', *Faculty of Health and Social Sciences, Sociology & Anthropology*, United Kingdom: Bournemouth University, p 410.

Walvin, J. (2007) *The Trader, The Owner, The Slave*, London: Jonathan Cape.

Wareing, J. (1976) 'Some early emigrants to America, 1683–4: a supplementary list', *Genealogists' Magazine*, 18: 239–46.

Williams, E. (1964) *Capitalism and Slavery*, London: Andre Deutsch.

Women's Budget Group (2020) *Inequalities in Academia: Impact on Early Career Researchers* [online] https://wbg.org.uk/blog/it-is-women-especia lly-low-paid-bame-migrant-women-putting-their-lives-on-the-line-to-deliver-vital-care/, London: Women's Budget Group.

Wright, I.A. (1921) 'The early history of Jamaica (1511–1536)', *The English Historical Review*, 36(141): 70–95.

4

Healing from Identity-Based Violence: An Intersectional Discussion

James Pickles

Introduction

Violence is a social phenomenon that occurs in all known human societies and manifests in a variety of complex ways. Due to the multifaceted and multi-layered contexts in which violence operates, it is extremely difficult to define and quantify. Violent acts can be broadly categorized in several ways (Ray, 2018): collective violence (such as social, political and economic violence), self-directed violence (suicide, self-injury and self-abuse), interpersonal violence (familial, intimate partner and community violence) and structural violence (systems in which society organizes its sociality, such as race, class, gender and sexual norms that establish conflict between groups through marginalization and oppression). The World Health Organization (Krug et al, 2002) recognizes that violence can manifest across the typologies as physical, sexual and psychological, or violence that involves deprivation or neglect. While these typologies are imperfect, lack precision and may not be universally accepted, what seems to be shared in all types of violence is its role, through an exploitation and abuse of power, in causing pain and suffering. Unfortunately, it is so entwined within the social world that it appears to be part of the human condition. This chapter will focus exclusively on violence that is aggravated by and directed towards identity in its many forms by utilizing intersectional analytical frameworks to understand the harms that manifest across multiple and interlocking power systems. By exploring identity-based violence intersectionally, the lived experiences of victims are able to be understood more fully and the potential to heal is much greater.

There is a plethora of empirical criminological evidence to suggest that violence aggravated by personal characteristics and identities, such as hate crimes, violence against women, violent extremism and genocides – of which the term identity-based violence is used as an umbrella term (Desrosiers, 2015) – can leave indelible physical, emotional, spiritual and psychological harms on those who are victimized. Victimologists have found that identity-based violence brutalizes and degrades the very essence of a person, becoming an injury to the spirit (Spalek, 2006). Such spirit injuries are 'the product of the psychological, spiritual, and cultural effects of multiple types of racism, sexism and discrimination ... it can lead to the slow death of a person's spirit' (Chakraborti and Zempi, 2013, p 69), becoming an immensely traumatic experience. Further, Iganski and Lagou (2015) argue that crimes aggravated by identity often 'hurt' more, psychologically, emotionally and spiritually, than crimes not aggravated by identity, due to the personal modalities in which this violence occurs. Thus, there is compelling evidence to suggest that those who are victimized through identity-based violence experience greater post-victimization stress than other victims.

While the specific harms caused by identity-based violence are well documented, there has been little acknowledgement within criminological inquiry on how those who are victimized may heal or recover from their experiences – individually, collectively and spiritually – marking a significant gap in our epistemological understanding over how criminologists and victimologists can assist a victim's healing process, post-victimization. According to Bryant-David (2019, p 400) 'trauma recovery care must attend to the multiple layers of identity within each person, considering race, ethnicity, culture, gender, age, migration status, disability, sexual orientation, and religion and/or spirituality'. This is particularly important as marginalized groups experience identity-based violence due to their identities being subject to wider societal oppression. Drawing on criminological data, black feminist thought, intersectional analysis and liberation theory, this conceptual chapter uses a victimological lens and focuses on the potential for healing from the trauma brought on by identity-based violence. I outline different forms of violence enacted upon identity by exploring the individual, collective and structural violence that marginalized groups experience. I then move to explore the intersectional dynamics that must be accounted for in order for healing to take place.

Identity-based violence

Identity-based violence has a long history within the evolution of human societies. Many wars and conflicts throughout history have been fought on the basis of differing identities trying to cement themselves over others. Countless nations have seen their indigenous populations pillaged, with their ancestral roots, identities and cultures ruthlessly suppressed and destroyed to pave the way for competing identities and cultures. In modern history, many native populations were forcibly Christianized and colonized by European powers (Gone et al, 2019; Russell, 2020), resulting in their identities, politics and cultural and religious beliefs becoming marginalized to this day. In addition, generations of religious groups have fought wars with one another to stake claims over the 'true' version of religious identity. Identity-based violence has therefore long been associated with violence enacted by members of a certain group to those outside of a specific racial, religious and national group. Violence against groups who are deemed the antithesis to the 'norm' group is a mechanism of power to dehumanize and reinforce who 'belongs' ('in-group' members) and who does not belong ('out-group' members) (Perry, 2001; Jenkins, 2014). Indeed, as seen by the Jewish Holocaust, extreme violence was committed against many groups – Jewish, gay and disabled – who were considered to deviate away from the constructed normal or desired identity as espoused by Nazi ideology.

In the post-Cold-War era, international efforts and activism have focused on reducing identity-based violence in order to maintain harmony and co-existence between differing groups with the aim of promoting equity among those that are socially and economically marginalized. Discussions on how violence is committed against specific groups have grown to include a number of marginalized identities, such as sexuality, disability, age, gender and so forth. Despite efforts to promote harmony and inclusion, Hardy and Chakraborti (2020) argue that violence against identity in the form of hate crimes is one of the biggest global challenges in modern times, affecting the lives of many millions.

In England and Wales, individuals are protected through a variety of legislation from both the *enactment* and *incitement* of violence being directed towards their identities. Criminal acts aggravated by identity are consequently categorized as hate crimes. The Crown Prosecution Service (2012, p 8) defines hate crimes as targeted crimes 'motivated by a hostility or prejudice based on race or perceived race; religion or perceived religion; sexual orientation or perceived sexual orientation; disability or perceived disability [...] or a person who is transgender or perceived to be transgender.' The debate over the phraseology of categorizing such violence as 'hate crimes' has been extensive within criminological discourse, with some scholars preferring the term bias crimes (Perry, 2003) and advocating for additional groups beyond the five strands to be included (Chakraborti and Garland, 2012). These debates promote a hate crime framework based on difference and vulnerability over siloed approaches to identity. Perry (2009), for instance, argues that intersectional approaches to hate violence refrain us from making singular assumptions about one identity over another and enable us to understand a victim's experience and risk of violence across multiple identities and contexts. It is not in the scope of this chapter to rehash these debates; thus, the concept of identity-based violence is used as an inclusive term to denote the structural and social violence that is enacted upon identity as well as targeted acts of violence that are criminalized.

Statistics for England and Wales show a year-on-year increase in overall hate crimes, with 103,379 instances recorded in 2019 (Home Office, 2019) and 105,090 recorded in 2020 (Home Office, 2020). These increases are often accounted for by better reporting mechanisms rather than a genuine increase in perpetration. However, trigger events such as the Brexit EU referendum result can spark a proliferation of hate towards minority groups (Awan and Zempi, 2017). Recorded instances of hate crimes, while helpful in determining the nature of many incidents, present an unclear picture over their true prevalence, as the lasting impact of violence against one's identity often extends far beyond the original act. For example, Bryant-Davis and Ocampo (2005) demonstrate that racist incidents are experienced as traumatic events that can lead to post-traumatic stress. Thus, there is a recognition that violence against structurally oppressed identities is not contained within a single act but is a manifestation and reinforcement of structurally embedded marginalization of minoritized groups, which contribute to the overall trauma experienced by victims. Importantly, this trauma of identity-based violence can be inherited by future generations through a process of intergenerational transmission of trauma. For instance, first-, second- and third-generation descendants of Holocaust survivors are known to exhibit personal trauma, fear and pain over collective memories of the genocidal violence perpetrated towards Jewish populations (Lev-Wiesel, 2007). Therefore, identity-based violence is shown to be situated within historical, cultural and social power structures that maintain the legacies of oppression directed towards specific social groups.

While identity-based violence is often committed to advance a particular social agenda, such as spreading racist sentiment, homophobic rhetoric or sexist attitudes, it is also a mechanism to uphold the very hegemonic power structures within society that allow it to occur. After being shot in the face by a man in Sweden, during a xenophobic and racist anti-refugee demonstration, refugee and academic Shahram Khosravi visited his perpetrator in prison. The shooter of this crime told Shahram not to take it personally, as the attack was not about him as an individual, but about anti-refugee sentiment generally. Reflecting on this encounter and on the violence enacted towards his identity(ies), he writes:

> I did not take the bullet personally for the same simple reason that
> I had been shot for the same reason the young black man had been
> killed in that Mississippi town in the 1960s. It was the same reason that
> sent millions of Jews to the death chambers, that triggered the Tutsi

massacre in Rwanda in 1994, the killing of thousands of Bosnians in 1995 in the Srebrenica region, or the hundreds of Palestinian minors in Gaza in January 2009. My history is only a fragment of a longer history of racism and hatred. I am one detail in the continuum of racial othering, of dehumanizing those who are of another colour, belief or culture. So how could I take it personally? (Khosravi, 2010, pp 83–4)

Shahram exemplifies in his reflection that violence perpetrated towards his (perceived) identity was rooted in the historical, global, structural and systemic oppression of those identities. In other words, it was not him specifically who the perpetrator hated, but the identity group(s) that he belonged to or represented. Perry (2001, p 125) argues that violence in this form 'is about the assertion of the offender's own identity and belongingness over and above others; in short it is about power'. Thus, acts of oppression and 'hate' that are homophobic reinforce systems of heteronormativity and position heterosexuality as the normative expression of sexuality. The same is true for acts of nationalism, racism, disablism, sexism, transphobia and other manifestations of oppression. These oppressive structures can cause individuals to experience internalized shame, self-hate, self-debasement and soul death, in what Neisen (1993) refers to as cultural victimization. Consequently, individuals who are victimized through targeted acts of violence towards their identity navigate this within the context of the structures of oppression that have enabled it to occur.

Although descriptions of identity-based violence evoke strong images of extreme physical violence – such as the Jewish Holocaust, the enforced enslavement of Africans and people of African ancestry, and the many genocides of indigenous populations such as the Queensland Massacre in what is now Australia – there are a multiplicity of ways in which it manifests. Enacting violence on the aggravation of one's identity is part of a wide spectrum of behaviours designed to 'other' and marginalize (Jensen, 2011), and can range from extreme forms of terrorism, murder, rape and genocide to everyday 'indignities' of hate that carry subtle messages of invalidation. In other words, while there are extreme acts of violence, there are also everyday perpetrations of what Sue et al (2007) call microaggressions, which act as small invalidations towards people occupying marginalized identities and reinforce systems of othering.

Microaggressions, according to Sue et al (2007), are small acts that carry hidden messages intended to demean those who experience them. These acts are often perpetrated unconsciously and stem from our unconscious biases about groups who hold certain identities. For example, in relation to racial microaggressions, 'A white man or woman clutches her purse or his wallet as a black or Latino man approaches or passes them. (Hidden message: You and your group are criminals)' or, in relation to sexual orientation microaggressions, 'Two gay men are holding hands in public and are told not to flaunt their sexuality. (Hidden message: Homosexual displays of affection are abnormal or offensive. Keep it to private and to yourselves.)' (Sue, 2010, p 5). These acts of othering are often a recurring and constant feature of one's everyday life (Hall, 2013; Hardy and Chakraborti, 2020). Women, for instance, are documented as frequently experiencing daily microaggressions and sexual harassment such as catcalling, unnecessary touching and wolf-whistling (Kearl, 2010; Osmond, 2013) that go unreported. The consistent vigilance and fear of violence manifests in the form of self-policing and self-coping behaviours – for example, risk aversion strategies – which are often employed as 'technologies of the soul' to avoid such harassment (Stanko, 1990; 1997). Thus, acts of violence, predicated by identity, shape the daily navigational patterns of individuals who experience them and contribute to high levels of stress and vigilance. These are not extreme acts of *physical* violence. However, as the beginning quote from Shahram Khosravi exemplifies, these are part of a rich tapestry of *social* violence and discrimination that can contribute to the brutalization of the self and spirit (Spalek, 2006).

This tapestry of social violence means that one does not have to be a direct victim to experience the harms associated with this violence. Arguably, when one person is targeted because of their identity, those who share in that identity also share the potential to be victimized. Iganski (2001) demonstrates this using a 'waves of harm' model, arguing that identity-based violence has an extended impact on other group members when one person is targeted. As shown by Figure 4.1, acts of violence towards identity have a ripple effect, which carries messages to all those who share in the victimized identity beyond the initial victim that they are also the target. This moves through to neighbourhoods and communities, and eventually becomes a mechanism to reinforce society's core structures of marginality. Examples of this can be seen in identity-aggravated terror attacks, such as the 2016 Pulse shooting in Orlando, where international lesbian, gay, bisexual, trans and queer (LGBTQ) communities were indirectly impacted by the homophobic attack on LGBTQ Floridians (Schweppe and Walters, 2016).

Intersectionality and identity-based violence

As identity-based violence upholds and reinforces systems of power and marginality, the manifestation, and the emotional and social harms of this, are experienced intersectionally. Intersectionality is a useful analytical framework that perceives multiple systems of power as interlocking, in which a social experience, brought about by one identity or characteristic, intersects with others (Carastathis, 2014). Women of colour[1], for example, experience discrimination on the basis of both their gendered and racialized

Figure 4.1: Waves of harm generated by hate crimes (adapted from Iganski, 2001, p 629).

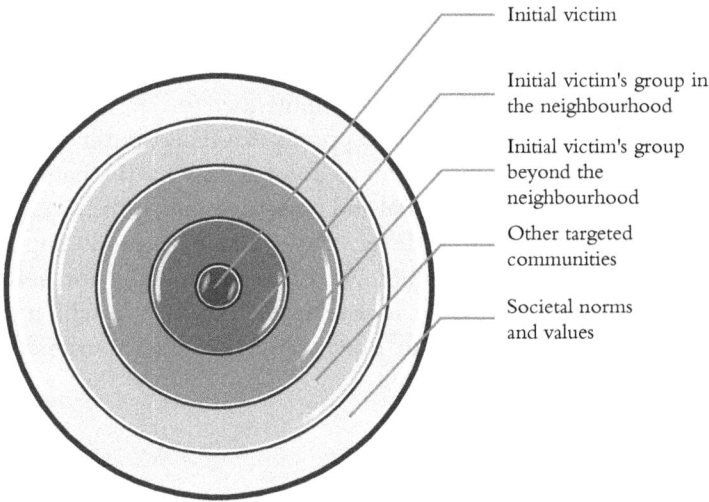

Initial victim

Initial victim's group in the neighbourhood

Initial victim's group beyond the neighbourhood

Other targeted communities

Societal norms and values

identities (Crenshaw, 1991), thus experiencing oppression at the intersection of these converging systems as a form of gendered racism where they are (as one example) reduced to daily stereotypes about their race *and* gender; for example, black women specifically can be stereotyped as being angry, aggressive or 'sassy' (Lewis et al, 2013), whereas white women do not experience these same stereotypes. Examining violence and victimization through a siloed lens minimizes the differential experiences that individuals navigate and risks essentializing specific social groups as homogenous, that is, rendering all disabled/black and brown/queer/working-class people as having exactly the same experience of violence and trauma. Without examining identity-based violence intersectionally, individual standpointisms are overlooked and scrutinized outside of their social, cultural and relational contexts. For example, across intersections of sexuality, gender and race, gay men of colour feel higher levels of shame in relation to their gender by feeling that they are weaker men for identifying as gay, while also feeling that they negatively represent their racial communities (Meyer, 2012). At the same time, gay men of colour judge their experiences as less severe than their middle-class white counterparts (Meyer, 2010). Without acknowledging and exploring these intersections, gay men in the above example – or any community – are rendered a monolithic social group, which risks overlooking (a) the specific and interconnected harms that manifest due to identity-based violence and (b) the specific healing pathways that are available to overcome identity-based trauma. Individuals who inhabit and navigate these intersections of violence experience these injuries to the psyche across multiple layers of their personhood. This is compounded when those who belong to 'marginalised communities are more likely to experience interpersonal trauma, to develop severe PTSD, and to face barriers to safety, justice, and mental health services' (Bryant-Davis, 2019, p 401). Therefore, it is essential, when responding to identity-based violence, to consider intersectional factors so that unintended further harm is prevented when developing mechanisms that respond to violence. For instance, higher levels of police surveillance that aim to combat anti-LGBT hate crime can negatively affect black, gay, bisexual and trans men due to the racialized ways in which policing manifests (Meyer, 2010) and by reproducing systemic racism towards black communities. Accordingly, in order for healing and justice to take place, the specific intersectional contexts in which this issue manifests must be prioritized to understand the full experience of pain caused by identity-based violence.

Intersectional healing

As this chapter has so far demonstrated, the harms and traumas caused by identity-based violence exist within individual, collective, social, historical and intersectional contexts. Although many acts of identity-based violence are criminalized, many do not meet a criminal threshold within the legislative framework of England and Wales. The true extent of systematic othering and the harm caused by non-criminal identity-based violence is therefore difficult to ascertain. Specifically, generational, collective and individual harms and pains go unrecognized due to the subtle ways in which they manifest. In order to combat the higher levels of post-victimization trauma that victims of identity-based violence experience, criminologists must be attuned to the intersectional needs and contexts – historical, political, social, cultural and spiritual – that individuals experience violence within. Indeed, Zehr (2008) argues that trauma is rooted in this social and economic injustice and, as such, peacebuilding cannot take place without examining the individual and social dimensions of trauma and pain.

Identity-based trauma affects both individuals and communities on an emotional, physical, psychological and spiritual level, so much so that cognitive patterns of the brain are shaped and altered. Experiences of racism, for example, can manifest as daily mini-traumas and require exhaustive emotional and psychic energy to be expended that can result in psychological detriments, which mirror those of sexual and intimate partner violence (see Bryant-Davis and Ocampo, 2005). Similarly, when remarking on the harm of daily normativities, Yep articulates, in relation to LGBTQ people, that

in addition to deeply affecting an individual and group cognitively (for example, how sexual minority people think of themselves), behaviourally (for example, how sexual minority people act to avoid psychological and physical danger), and structurally (for example, how sexual minority people negotiate a social system that tacitly and overtly discriminates against them), normativities also leave indelible emotional and psychic wounds. (2017, p 118)

Criminologists and victimologists therefore have a very delicate and sensitive task if their overall aim is to reduce the harm and suffering caused by structural marginalization and violence.

In line with French et al (2020), who advocate for a radical healing that is aimed at achieving social justice – by being grounded in (a) collectivism, (b) critical consciousness, (c) radical hope, (d) strength and resistance, and (e) cultural authenticity and self-knowledge – the healing that is discussed in this chapter is based on a social model of recovery, whereby individual agency and collectivism provide the means to healing rather than medical interventions. The medicalization of healing involves pathologizing the individual and their pain as a 'sickness' with the overall aim of reducing 'symptoms' (Whitley and Drake, 2010), whereas social models view suffering as a response to social injustices with a view to providing agency in changing oppressive social structures. In this view, ongoing self-love, self-liberation and a transcendence beyond hegemonic social norms is, for Yep (2017), the key to moving in the direction of transformative healing and collective freedom.

It must be emphasized that no amount of therapeutic work, counselling or community action can undo past injustices or rewrite the pains of an individual's history. Indeed, we cannot change the past, only the future. The literature on healing emphasizes self-acceptance of the past with the goal to retain agency that shapes the future. Haglili's (2020) work on social activism proposes that altruistic action aimed to help others who experience similar forms of social trauma enhances the likelihood of post-traumatic growth. Her view is that recovery can only take place in the context of relationships, such as within loving friendships, community and support networks who can bear witness to the pain caused by violence – specifically, bearing witness to one's own pain, bearing witness as a community and forming links of activism as a witness to one's oppression. Making sense of identity-based trauma, by establishing collective meaning and thus active resistance, contributes to a sense of coherence, empowerment and ultimately completeness when one is systemically and interactionally victimized. This cannot occur without first fostering a sense of agency among those who are victimized so that meanings of self-love and growth can be made from trauma.

Criminological enterprise has had a strong tradition for bearing witness to the individual and community impact of crime and theorizing how the social mechanics and ordering of society influence victimization and violence. In the pursuit of an intersectional criminology, we must bear witness to the historical, cultural and social structures that carry the impacts of victimization in order to promote healing within the communities that we research and aim to support. A key component of the criminological imagination is the ability to imagine better worlds and better futures (Seal and O'Neill, 2019), where individuals have achieved economic and social justice. The task for criminology is to reimagine ways of liberating individuals from the violence and marginality that they experience due to their identity. However, individualizing trauma can be counterproductive, as, according to French et al (2020), healing involves identifying the source of trauma and engaging in collective resistance against that source through community-oriented psychological liberation.

Early work on psychological liberation emphasized it as a dialectic and relational process in which individuals change internally while their relationships and interactions with others concurrently change (Luque-Ribelles et al, 2009). Further developments have emphasized the relationship between critical consciousness[2], spirituality[3] and social action[4] in achieving liberation and healing. As already highlighted, identity-based violence carries trauma across collectives and generations that is specific to the violence enacted on certain identity groups. Native American tribes carry ancestral trauma of colonization while still experiencing contemporary persecution and racism (Gone et al, 2019). Descendants of Holocaust survivors carry with them the trauma of the genocide against their ancestors while still navigating modern anti-Semitism (Lev-Wiesel, 2007). Healing from inherited and contemporary trauma requires a great deal of emotional and psychological effort to work through this pain as many individuals are still navigating the contemporaneous legacies of historical and structural violence. By understanding the collective histories of trauma that have been passed through generations of oppressive actions against minoritized identity groups, collective critical consciousness can be raised to allow marginalized groups to reconcile their histories (French et al, 2020). This critical consciousness must be intersectional if criminology is to fully encompass the spectrum of emotional pain caused by identity-based violence.

Within the criminological imagination, liberation cannot be achieved without accounting for the multiple layers of oppressions that marginalized groups experience intersectionally. In this instance, black liberation must involve the liberation of queer individuals and vice versa. The same is true for disabled communities and religious communities, and so on, as articulated by Audre Lorde:

Within the lesbian community I am Black, and within the Black community I am a lesbian. Any attack against Black people is a lesbian and gay issue, because I and thousands of other Black women are part of the lesbian community. Any attack against lesbians and gays is a Black issue, because thousands of lesbians and gay men are Black. There is no hierarchy of oppression. (Lorde, 1983, np)

One example in achieving intersectional black liberation and healing is the deconstruction of Eurocentric assumptions and standards that prioritize whiteness as beautiful, good or pure, and blackness as dirty, ugly or exotic (Robinson-Moore, 2008). While black individuals are constrained by Eurocentric beauty and body standards that deem black bodies as either exotic or deviant, these still operate within a gender-based, patriarchal, heteronormative, ableist matrix (Loja et al, 2013). Thus, queer, disabled, black lives experience Eurocentric assumptions differently. Healing, therefore, must involve raising collective critical consciousness to an awareness of the interlocking web of oppressive forces (Carastathis, 2014), which impact individuals across race, gender, class, education, age and sexual lines. In other words, learning that one's trauma is rooted in ableist, heteronormative, classed, patriarchal and racialized structures rather than the individual or collective 'self', and actively working towards radical self-love of the identities that are victimized, allows for liberationist-focused psychological healing.

While raising critical consciousness is shown to promote psychological healing, Carmen et al (2015) argue that there is a risk of reproducing individualistic and cognitive processes to healing. To prevent this, the ontological and intersectional dimensions of marginality need to be made visible for sociopolitical development to occur. In other words, 'the complicated, messy work of making sense of one's existence and identity in the face of widespread, systemic, institutional racial, ethnic, linguistic, epistemic, and spiritual 'Othering' that can constrain subjectivity and agency' (Carmen et al, 2015, p 828). Thus, they advocate that ontological healing – healing the pains and traumas that have occurred through existing as a marginalized individual within oppressive social realities that limit one's existence as an agentic being – is key to transforming how individuals positively navigate their social landscape. Importantly, this is not to minimize the agency that has been denied to marginalized groups, nor to ignore the trauma caused by the violence directed towards identity. Rather, it is to alleviate the spirit injuries (Spalek, 2006) caused by identity-based violence by reconnecting the individual with their community, foster a sense of agency that has been historically denied and provide space for individuals to develop autonomous ways of expressing their identity. Lewis et al (2015), for instance, have found that politically driven identity-based spaces act as environments of civic engagement, personhood and freedom. Specifically, feminist women-only spaces allow women the safety to be cognitively, intellectually and emotionally expressive, whereby they are able to engage in their womanhood freely and explore different and deeper meanings of what it is to be a woman within society.

Importantly, healing in this context is distinct to notions of coping. Many individuals normalize the identity-based violence that they experience in order to navigate through society and cope with the daily oppressions faced across class, gendered, racial, religious and sexual lines (Chakraborti and Garland, 2015). 'Coping' frameworks emphasize a passivity and reduce agentic steps towards individual and collective justice. Healing, on the other hand, is a process by which one moves beyond *surviving* in an oppressive society to *thriving*, by centring resistance at the heart of their recovery process to find individual peace and justice (Watts, 2004).

Such ontological healing is a continuous process of growth that reconciles experiences of identity-based violence with the social environment, structures and histories that shape individual and collective positionalities and subjectivities. These are non-linear processes that must engage with social, collective, communal, generational and embodied experiences of pain caused by identity-based violence, so that one can process these experiential paradigms and engage in radical healing. For criminology, such healing is an inherently political act in that it actively seeks to resist oppression and violence brought about by poverty, racism, sexism, homophobia and class oppression. Therefore, it moves from a deficit model of victimization in which one self-blames or remains in a victim mindset by fostering a sense of agency that empowers collectives (Carmen et al, 2015) to challenge oppressive conditions and reach an identity-centric practice of love and self-worth (Nash, 2011), where blackness is celebrated, queerness is embraced, disability is normalized and rejoiced, and gender is emboldened.

Finally, individualizing healing from identity-based violence places the onus on socially oppressed groups and victims to achieve healing. The onus of responsibility for community and sociopolitical development work, access to healthcare and therapy, reducing poverty, prioritizing economic justice and removing social barriers also belongs to groups with social privilege in society through critical allyship to marginalized groups (Curtin, Kende and Kende, 2016; Nixon, 2019). Criminology must therefore remain actively opposed to social injustice and promote radical self-love among marginalized communities. By engaging in criminological research and inquiry, the onus is also on criminologists to bear witness to the intersectional trauma that individuals and communities experience, to align ourselves with the social justice aims of specific marginalized groups and to raise our critical consciousness to achieve psychological liberation across intersectional realities.

Conclusion

'Freedom and love may be the most revolutionary ideas available to us, and yet as intellectuals, we have failed miserably to grapple with their political and analytical importance' (Kelley, 2003, pp 11–12). This chapter has highlighted the specific emotional, psychological and spiritual trauma that have been inflicted, across generations, on many individuals on the premise of their identity. Utilizing concepts from black feminist thought, theories of intersectionality and paradigms of psychological liberation, it has advocated for criminology to acknowledge the intersectional trauma of identity-based violence and to promote radical healing within its theoretical scope. Criminological enterprise has a responsibility to raise the critical consciousness of marginalized groups, facilitate community connection, foster active resistance to the structural oppression that individuals navigate and promote active agency to resist and heal from the impact of identity-based violence. Navigating a society and culture in which systems of power exist to marginalize, exclude and sow seeds of hatred towards many identity groups within society causes members of these communities to internalize this marginality, resulting in hatred, debasement, fear and brutalization of the self. Liberation must therefore come in the form of collective self-love. This love should be actively political and intersectional in order to avoid reproducing heteronormative, patriarchal, ableist, white-centric 'love'. Radical healing takes the form of affirmatively and unconditionally loving blackness, queerness, disability and womanhood across all of these intersecting lines. By bearing witness to and working against systemic trauma inflicted by identity-based violence, the criminological 'imagination' can become a reality through the intersectional and ontological healing of pain and injustice.

Notes

[1] The term women of colour/person of colour is used to discuss racism against all people who are not white. Black, brown, mixed race, Asian, Jewish, traveller and so on experience different forms, types and systems of racism. When identifying particular forms of racism, such as anti-black stereotypes, black is used for more specificity.

[2] Critical consciousness allows for a sociopolitical version of thinking that enables individuals to situate and contextualize their experiences as existing within broader social structures.

[3] Spirituality in this context involves healing the internal state of a person by overcoming internalized oppression – for example, internalized misogyny, homophobia, racism and so on – and achieving a state where oppressive structures no longer inhibit personal freedom.

[4] Social action is the individual and collective action one undertakes to fight against social injustices (see Watts, Diemer and Voight, 2011).

References

Awan, I. and Zempi, I. (2017) '"I will blow your face off"; virtual and physical world anti-Muslim hate crime, *British Journal of Criminology*, 57(2), 362–80.

Bryant-Davis, T. (2019) 'The cultural context of trauma recovery: considering the post-traumatic stress disorder practice guideline and intersectionality', *Psychotherapy*, 56(3), 400–08.

Bryant-Davis, T. and Ocampo, C. (2005) 'The trauma of racism: implications for counseling, research, and education', *The Counseling Psychologist*, 33(4), 574–8.

Carastathis, A. (2014) 'The concept of intersectionality in feminist theory', *Philosophy Compass*, 9(5): 304–14.

Carmen, S.A., Dominguez, M., Greene, A.C., Mendoza, E., Fine, M., Neville, H.A. and Gutierrez, K.D. (2015) 'Revisiting the collective in critical consciousness: diverse sociopolitical wisdoms and ontological healing in sociopolitical development', *The Urban Review*, 47: 824–46.

Chakraborti, N. and Garland, J. (2012) 'Reconceptualizing hate crime victimization through the lens of vulnerability and "difference"', *Theoretical Criminology*, 16(4): 499–514.

Chakraborti, N. and Garland, J. (2015) *Hate Crime: Impact, Causes & Responses*, 2nd Ed., London: Sage.

Chakraborti, N. and Zempi, I. (2013) 'Criminalising oppression or reinforcing oppression? The implications of veil ban laws for Muslim women in the West', *Northern Ireland Legal Quarterly*, 64(1): 63–74.

Crenshaw, K. (1991) 'Mapping the margins: intersectionality, identity politics, and violence against women of color', *Stanford Law Review*, 43(6): 1241–99.

Christie, N. (1986) 'The ideal victim', in E.A. Fattah (ed.), *From Crime Policy to Victim Policy*, Basingstoke: Macmillan, pp 17–30.

Crown Prosecution Service (2012) *Hate Crime and Crimes Against Older People Report*, London: Crown Prosecution Service.

Curtin, N., Kende, A. and Kende, J. (2016) 'Navigating multiple identities: I simultaneous influence of advantaged and disadvantaged identities on politicization and activism', *Journal of Social Issues*, 72(2): 264–85.

De La Rue, L. and Ortega, L. (2019) 'Intersectional trauma-responsive care: a framework for humanizing care for justice involved girls and women of color', *Journal of Aggression, Maltreatment & Trauma*, 28(4): 502–17, DOI: 10.1080/10926771.2019.1572403.

Desrosiers, M.-E. (2015) 'Tackling puzzles of identity-based conflict: I promise of framing theory', *Civil Wars*, 17(2): 120–40.

French, B.H., Lewis, J.A., Mosley, D.V., Adames, H.Y., Chavez-Dueñas, N.Y., Chen, G.A. and Neville, H.A. (2020) 'Toward a psychological framework of radical healing in communities of color', *The Counselling Psychologist*, 48(1): 14–46.

Gone, J.P., Hartmann, W.E., Pomerville, A., Wendt, D.C., Klem, S.C. and Burrage, R.L. (2019) 'The impact of historical trauma on health outcomes for indigenous populations in the USA and Canada: a systematic review', *American Psychologist*, 74(1): 20–35.

Haglili, R.M. (2020) 'The intersectionality of trauma and activism: narratives constructed ore a qualitative study', *Journal of Humanistic Psychology*, 60(4): 514–24.

Hall, N. (2013) *Hate Crime*, 2nd Ed., Abingdon: Routledge.

Hardy, S.-J. and Chakraborti, N. (2020) *Blood, Threats and Fears: The Hidden Worlds of Hate Crime Victims*, eBook: Palgrave Macmillan.

Home Office (2019) *Hate Crime, England and Wales, 2018/19*, London: Home Office.

Home Office (2020) *Hate Crime, England and Wales, 2019/20*, London: Home Office.

Iganski, P. (2001) 'Hate crimes hurt ore', *American Behavioral Scientist*, 45(4): 626–38.

Iganski, P. and Lagou, S. (2015) 'Hate crimes hurt some more than others: implications for the just sentencing of offenders', *Journal of Interpersonal Violence*, 30(10): 1696–718.

Jenkins, R. (2014) *Social Identity*, London: Routledge.

Jensen, S.Q. (2011) 'Othering, identity formation and agency', *Qualitative Studies*, 2(2): 63–78.

Kearl, H. (2010) *Stop Street Harassment*, Oxford: Praeger.

Kelley, R.D. (2003) *Freedom Dreams: The Black Radical Imagination*, Boston: Beacon Press.

Khosravi, S. (2010) *'Illegal' Traveller: An Auto-Ethnography of Borders*, New York: Palgrave Macmillan.

Krug, E.G., Dahlberg, L.L., Mercy, J.A., Zwi, A.B. and Lozano, R. (2002) *World Report on Violence and Health*, Geneva: World Health Organization.

Lev-Wiesel, R. (2007) 'Intergenerational transmission of trauma across three generations', *Qualitative Social Work*, 6(1): 75–94.

Lewis, J.A., Mendenhall, R., Harwood, S.A. and Huntt, M.B. (2013) 'Coping with gendered racial microaggressions among black women college students', *Journal of African American Studies*, 17: 51–73.

Lewis, R., Sharp, E., Remnant, J. and Redpath, R. (2015) '"Safe spaces": experiences of feminist women-only space', *Sociological Research Online*, 20(4): 105–18.

Loja, E., Costa, M.E., Hughes, B. and Menezes, I. (2013) 'Disability, embodiment and ableism: stories of resistance', *Disability & Society*, 28(2): 190–203.

Lorde, A. (1983) *From Homophobia and Education*, New York: Council on Interracial Books for Children.

Luque-Ribelles, V., Garcia-Ramirez, M. and Portillo, N. (2009) *Gendering Peace and Liberation: A Participatory-Action Approach to Critical Consciousness Acquisition among Women in a Marginalized Neighborhood*, New York: Springer.

Meyer, D. (2010) 'Evaluating the severity of hate-motivated violence: intersectional differences among LGBT hate victims', *Sociology*, 44(5): 980–95.

Meyer, D. (2012) 'An intersectional analysis of lesbian, gay, bisexual, and transgender (LGBT) people's evaluations of anti-queer violence', *Gender & Society*, 26(6): 849–73.

Nash, J.C. (2011) 'Practicing love: black feminism, love-politics, and post-intersectionality', *Meridians*, 2(1–21): 11.

Neisen, J.H. (1993) 'Healing from cultural victimization: recovery from shame due to heterosexism', *Journal of Gay & Lesbian Psychotherapy*, 2(1), 49–63.

Nixon, S.A. (2019) 'The coin model of privilege and critical allyship: implications for health', *BMC Public Health*, 19(1637): 1–13.

Osmond, J. (2013) *Public Spaces and Gender: An Everyday Occurrence: Women and Sexual Harassment*, Coventry: Coventry University.

Perry, B. (2001) *In the Name of Hate: Understanding Hate Crimes*, Abingdon: Routledge.

Perry, B. (2003) *Hate and Bias Crime: A Reader*, Abingdon: Routledge.

Perry, J. (2009) 'At the intersection: hate crime policy and practice in England and Wales', *Safer Communities*, 8(4): 9–18.

Ray, L. (2018) *Violence & Society*, 2nd Ed., London: Sage.

Robinson-Moore, C.L. (2008) 'Beauty standards reflect Eurocentric paradigms—so what? Skin color, identity, and black female beauty', *Journal of Race & Policy*, 4(1): 66–85.

Russell, E.K. (2020) *Queer Histories and the Politics of Policing*, London: Routledge.

Schweppe, J. and Walters, M. (2016) '*Thinking about Orlando*' [online] https://internationalhatestudies.com/thinking-about-orlando/

Seal, L. and O'Neill, M. (2019) *Imaginative Criminology of Spaces Past, Present and Future*, Bristol: Bristol University Press.

Spalek, B. (2006) *Crime Victims: Theory, Policy and Practice*, Basingstoke: Palgrave Macmillan.

Stanko, E. (1990) *Everyday Violence: How Women and Men Experience Sexual and Physical Danger*, Toledo, OH: HarperCollins.

Stanko, E. (1997) 'Safety talk: conceptualizing women's risk assessment as a "technology of the soul"', *Theoretical Criminology*, 1(4): 479–99.

Sue, D.W., Capodilupo, C.M., Torino, G.C., Bucceri, J.M., Holder, A.M.B., Nadal, K.L. and Esquilin, M. (2007) 'Racial microaggressions in everyday life: implications for clinical practice', *American Psychologist*, 62(4): 271–84.

Sue, D.W. (2010) Microaggressions, marginality, and oppression, in D.W. Sue (ed) *Microaggressions and Marginality: Manifestation, Dynamics, and Impact*, Hoboken, New Jersey: Wiley, pp 3–22.

Watts, R.J. (2004) 'Integrating social justice and psychology', *The Counseling Psychologist*, 32: 855–65.

Watts, R.J., Diemer, M.A. and Voight, A.M. (2011) 'Critical consciousness: current status and future directions', *New Directions for Child and Adolescent Development* (Special Issue 134: Youth Civic Development: Work at the Cutting Edge): 43–57.

Whitley, R. and Drake, R. (2010) 'Recovery: a dimensional approach', *Psychiatric Services*, 61(12): 1248–50.

Yep, G. (2017) 'Further notes on healing from "the violence of heteronormativity in communication studies"', *QED: A Journal in GLBTQ Worldmaking*, 4(2): 115–22.

Zehr, H. (2008) 'Doing justice, healing trauma – the role of restorative justice in peacebuilding', *South Asian Journal of Peace Building*, 1(1): 1–16.

PART II

Crime, Harm and Criminal Justice Systems: Intersectionality's Engagement with Crime and Deviance

5

Navigating Probation and Managing Substance Use: The Roles of Gender and Class

Melindy Duffus

Introduction

The Criminal Justice System (CJS) in the UK has been criticized for disproportionately impacting specific groups of people more than others (Lammy, 2017). When discussions of this topic arise, the focus tends to sway towards experiences in prison, rather than the probation service (Phelps, 2013; Robinson, 2016), but while experiences in prison will be reflective of certain aspects of the CJS, they cannot reflect experiences of the entire CJS as a whole. People's experiences of the probation service are often overshadowed by this focus on prison experiences. It is therefore important to explore the experiences of oppression within the probation service specifically. This chapter considers the experiences of women within the probation service, utilizing an intersectional framework of analysis that considers gender, social class, drug use and experiences of domestic violence and abuse intersectionally.

The probation service

There have been a number of changes that have occurred within the probation service regarding support for those who have committed offences in England and Wales. The changes were not only on the basis of trying to reduce reoffending, but also in response to substance misuse. Substance misuse is understood as the consumption of legal and illegal psychoactive and intoxicant substances at a rate that can risk being harmful or problematic to the individual (DrugScope, nd). In 2002, a national delivery plan was developed by the National Offender Management Service, which laid out plans to improve support for those who misused substances (Home Office, 2004). One of the implications of this was the introduction of the 'Transforming Rehabilitation' reform programme (Ministry of Justice, 2013). This programme has since been found to be ineffective (HM Inspectorate of Probation, 2019b), but nevertheless, has had a lasting impact on the probation service. One of the key ways this has occurred has been through Community Rehabilitation Companies (CRCs) being granted responsibility to manage those service users who have committed low- to medium-risk offences (HM Inspectorate of Probation, 2016). These CRCs, which are run by private organizations, work alongside the voluntary and social sectors with the overall aim of reducing reoffending. However, it is worth noting that although reducing reoffending is the aim, they are doing so within the pressures of a private organization, whereby profit is essential. A central factor of privatization within the probation service has been Payment by Results, with a focus on incentivizing performance (Bean, 2018). CRCs are paid for the types of activities they provide, putting the onus on effectiveness rather than the volume of people that are being supervised (House of Commons, 2018). With this in mind, private organizations can respond to this through practices such as 'cherry picking', whereby those individuals who are considered the most likely to succeed or easiest to support are focused upon (Webster, 2016).

Two of the reasons that the 'Transforming Rehabilitation' programme was not successful included lack of resources and high caseloads (HM Inspectorate of Probation, 2019a). As such, these pressures have impacted how and where the probation service as a whole (National Probation Service and CRCs) directs their resources. Furthermore, lack of resources can make it more difficult for service users to engage with or access support while on probation.

Gender and class in service provision

Women are a group who have been discussed throughout criminological literature regarding barriers to desistance, with the environment to which they are re-entering post-release from prison often being a key factor. Baldry (2010) recognized that women are often returning to areas of disadvantage such as victimization during childhood, lower levels of education and socioeconomic status, and poor family ties and accommodation. Childhood abuse has been found to impact women throughout their lives, from their schooling and employment experiences to their choices of spouse. As such, this may increase the necessity of relying on individuals who engage in criminal activity, domestic violence or substance use, as their partners and friends (DeHart, 2008; Fuentes, 2014). Furthermore, lack of supportive family ties and financial issues prior to entering prison enhances the chances of women being subject to poverty and homelessness upon release. In turn, it can also heighten a woman's chances of staying with an abusive partner (Zust, 2009). Further to this, substance use plays a key role in many women's criminal justice involvement, and as such their transition out of it. Studies have noted that around half of women entering prison reported that they required support for a drug problem and nearly 60 per cent of women who had drank alcohol in the four weeks prior to entering prison reported having an alcohol problem (Light et al, 2013). This suggests that these factors, either in combination or separate to one another, can impact the ability of women to successfully engage in support provided by the probation service.

Being from a lower socioeconomic background has been highlighted as an aspect that affects women and men, albeit gendered differences can occur. The definition of social class in itself is one of great debate. Definitions have ranged from discussions of status, income, power and wealth, to relying on others' understanding of an individual's class (Argyle, 1994). One viewpoint that is clear is that social class stereotypes can feed into inequality, particularly of individuals who have lower levels of economic income (Durante and Fiske, 2017). The criminalization of those considered homeless or socially economically deprived has been a long-standing discussion within criminology. For example, Irwin (2013/1985) discussed how the police and the courts have been used as ways of managing and rehabilitating those who are considered to be from lower socioeconomic backgrounds, particularly when misusing substances. The laws of the land are known to be dependent on the values of the ruling class (Marx and Engels, 1970). As such, those individuals who fit in to the same class system as those ruling them are potentially more likely to be subject to positive class bias (Cavadino and Dignan, 2007). Consequently, those from lower socioeconomic backgrounds, perceived as working class or lower class, may be perceived as disrespectful due to class and cultural norms (Cavadino and Dignan, 2007).

In addition to the impact of social class and gender separately, further challenges can be faced when they intersect. Socioeconomic status has been noted to play a key role in influencing women's quality of life (Lee et al, 2020). This in turn can likely impact their families, and in particular, their children. The level of wealth and quality of life for women has been noted as being at an imbalance when compared with men (Lee et al, 2020). Many factors exacerbate inequalities between men and women, from pay gaps (Marmot et al, 2008), to increased levels of responsibility for childcare (Clawson and Gerstel, 2014), to higher rates of poverty (Entmacher et al, 2013). When looking at women within the CJS, they continue to be affected by some of the challenges that may come from being from a lower socioeconomic background. One of the common reasons that has been noted as to why women turn to crime is out of financial necessity (Elonheimo et al, 2014), potentially driving them to engage in property and drug crimes at a higher rate than that of men (Huebner et al, 2010).

The probation service continues to have its own challenges in terms of staff ability to maximize support for all. However, there are certain individuals who face these downfalls at higher rates. This chapter uses an intersectional lens to add to existing knowledge of the experiences faced by women and those who consider themselves to be from a lower social class.

Methodology

This study was philosophically underpinned by phenomenology. Phenomenology is considered a discipline that concentrates on the lived experience, by considering how an individual perceives or understands a phenomenon and looks to their individual experience to understand how those perceptions were derived (Langdridge, 2007). With this in mind, this research project sought to determine the effectiveness of the probation service through comparing the individual experiences of staff and service users at a CRC in England and Wales.

The main aim of the study was to establish the most effective support for desistance and rehabilitation, for service users who had, or were, misusing substances. A particularly important aspect of the research was to recognize the intersectional differences of service users and how that has impacted their lived experiences within the CJS. Intersectionality, as defined in previous chapters in this edition, considers the multiple, overlapping and intersecting elements of marginalized identities when conducting analysis (see Chapter 2). Its contribution is centred around the conceptualization of social experiences, as constructed through individual participants' various intertwined identity characteristics (Hill Collins and Bilge, 2016). As such, the perspectives and voices of the participants were key, and therefore the study focused on gaining qualitative data through a series of semi-structured interviews with service users, probation officers and drug/alcohol workers who all engage with the CRC. Semi-structured interviews allowed participants to share their lived experiences while also enabling further probing and discussion to occur when needed (Adams, 2015). Standard interview schedules were devised, one suited for service users and one for staff. The questions were structured around factors that are commonly noted to either contribute to, or be a barrier for, desistance. The open-ended nature of these questions provided a clear space for discussions regarding participant experiences.

Given the importance of staff and service user views, ensuring that due measures took place when recruiting participants was imperative. The area manager of the relevant CRC supported in the recruitment of participants by distributing the relevant information sheets to teams supporting service users who have misused, or are currently misusing, substances. These teams were then able to provide this information to service users who fit the criteria for the research project. Taking this approach enabled only those staff members and service users who had actively familiarized themselves with the nature of the project, and having done so, been interested in the project, to take part. Six female and four male staff members participated in this study. Of those, seven worked directly for the CRC as probation officers, and three were drug and alcohol workers that work for an organization outsourced to provide rehabilitation support. All service user participants were receiving support from the same CRC, and were either on a Rehabilitation Activity Requirement, Alcohol Treatment Requirement or Drug Rehabilitation Requirement.

One of the key factors of this research was to determine whether experiences within probation differ based on their individual or combined characteristics. The service user sample encompassed three females and five males, ranged between the ages of 31 and 54 years old. In terms of social class, this has been centred on how the participants refer to themselves from an economic perspective. As the researcher, I did not define class myself, as I felt that class in this case was more important from a subjective perceived perspective, rather than a phenomenon that participants were objectively aware of. As such the analysis draws more upon the impact of perceived class rather than objectively defined class. Six of the service users referred to themselves as working/lower class, and often considered their housing and employment status to reflect this. For example, some participants described themselves as living in a council estate or temporary accommodation in relation to being working/lower class. Two of the service users described themselves as middle class, often discussing their employment status and job titles as justification. It was important for this research to not see participants as one homogenous group, and rather to take an intersectional approach that allows an appreciation to be given to the overlapping structures of oppression of participants and how these can impact people's lived experiences.

The research had full ethical approval and participant information was anonymized. Given the application of intersectionality within this study, it is important to discuss the positionality of myself as the researcher. In the interest of ethical research, it is necessary to critically reflect on how my identity impacts the study in terms of my interactions with participants and the subject matter as a whole. I am an academic and do not have a criminal record, meaning that in one way I can be seen as an outsider by being neither a practitioner nor a service user. However, for the practitioners, it provided them with a space to open up about their experiences, without the fear of it impacting their employment. There was a feeling of empowerment that came through in the interviews with many of the practitioners. It was seen as their opportunity to provide insight and real-life knowledge to policy change, in a way that they are often not considered.

A similar response was received by the service users with a number of participants describing the interview process in a positive light, such as rewarding, calming and helpful. Service users of the probation service are often a forgotten group, within society and the CJS, with the focus within research mainly being on individuals who are currently incarcerated.

Findings and discussion

The interviews demonstrated how intersectional oppressions impact how individuals navigate through the probation service. This study helps explain how such oppressions can impact experiences of receiving support for reducing reoffending and substance use. The geographical structure of the CRC, from which the participants in these interviews are connected to, helps provide an awareness of how individuals receiving support within urban and rural areas experience probation. This section will highlight through an intersectional lens the way that women and those from lower class backgrounds are subject to various challenges throughout their probation experience.

Gender and domestic violence

Participants shared experiences that centred on a few specific issues. Gender, particularly discussions of female experiences, were raised by both service users and staff. Females service users' experiences of domestic violence and issues of control were raised by numerous participants. Diane, a service user, explains how over the years she has struggled with the unsupportive aspects of being with a controlling partner during substance use recovery:

> 'No what I did was, when I did my methadone a few years ago, I did a home detox because my partner at the time wouldn't come home to have the children so I could go to rehab, so I had to do it at home by myself with the kids and I, erm, I did a two-week Subutex detox at home by myself, with three kids [sign of sadness in voice]. Then I was clean for 16 years, until I met that idiot out there.'

Similarly, Sharon, also a service user who has experienced domestic violence herself, describes that she "used to talk to my probation officer about my partner, but I did explain to her that he's changed, he's not domestic violence anymore, he's in recovery himself from drugs". Previous literature suggests that some women believe that their partners will desist from being domestically violent towards them after having received support for their substance use; however, there is limited evidence to suggest that reducing substance use will cause a definitive stop (Wilson et al, 2017).

Staff were able to provide insights into how supporting women who experience domestic violence led to challenges in terms of them receiving support from probation. One staff member explained an experience in which she was providing support:

'I had a lady who I supported, she was experiencing DV and she never had a prescription and she came in and she said, I really need a prescription, and I then got the services, that probation use, and they said that she needs to be clean for a certain amount of time to get it, but my problem is, is that, that's likely going to lead to her reoffending to get her drug, because she can't get her prescription.' (Charlotte, probation officer)

A further probation officer explains how issues of control by partners are present with his female clients. He says that "For the female clients I have, their male partners can be controlling, it's not always the physical violence, but they can be controlling about their drug use, their appointments" (Nolan, probation officer). This experience of providing support is not in isolation. Concerns have been raised regarding provision for women in these situations as there have been many recent funding cuts in the UK within the domestic abuse and substance use treatment sectors (Women's Aid, 2015; Advisory Council on the Misuse of Drugs, 2017).

The increased likelihood of domestic violence and sex work for women on probation is clear by the pathways to desistance that probation officers are required to provide support for, on the basis of gender. Sarah, a probation officer, describes how "for males, we have seven pathways, and for females we have nine, so we have accommodation, education, training and employment, finance, relationships, thinking and behaviour, attitudes, and health and wellbeing, and then for females its sex working and DV is the last one".

These additional pathways for female service users show the additional challenges that can be faced by women within the CJS, and how the probation service has been adapted to respond to them. This is reflective of guidelines presented to support individuals working with former sex workers and those who have experienced domestic abuse; the guidance is directed at supporting women (National Offender Management Service, 2015). It has been noted that involvement in sex work can have links to substance misuse, mental and physical health problems, and trauma (Nuttbrock et al, 2004). Within this research, no women who referred to themselves as middle class had reported engaging in sex work. This may mean that for financial reasons, working-class women are more likely to be involved in sex work than middle-class women. In turn, this may mean that working-class women face additional barriers to desistance that middle-class women do not. Here, the intersection of gender and social class is important in the way participants understand their experience. As domestic violence may be considered a gender-based issue, it is likely that women experience the probation service differently to men, and involvement in sex work may result in a higher likelihood of experiencing abuse (Corteen, 2018). Failing to adopt an intersectional approach would result in these structural relationships being overlooked, therefore leaving an oversimplistic account of how people understand their probation experience.

While having additional pathways that recognize gender-based concerns is positive, it is important to consider the role substance use plays, as although traditionally women will be supported by the women's team within probation, this is not always the case for those with substance use concerns. Women who have been identified as requiring support for their substance use are required by the court to receive this support. However, this means that they are then allocated to substance use support teams, rather than within the women's team in the probation service. This 'single-issue' approach to probation support services can create significant, and detrimental, difficulties for women being able to receive and access adequate levels of support for all their needs, highlighting how structural assumptions around substance use needs marginalizes female substance users and potentially disadvantages them in terms of meeting their specific needs.

Additionally, the increased likelihood of women engaging in sex work has been highlighted as a factor that causes them to be at a higher risk of continued substance use. Charlotte, a probation officer, says that "they often utilize substances to cope with the sex work that they've been through, or that they go through and deal with". Literature has also identified that struggling to treat trauma-related symptoms can cause women who are recovering from substance use and previously engaged in sex work to turn back to substance use (National Offender Management Service, 2015). This clearly identifies a need for a radical change within the probation service, to ensure that women are supported, *as women recovering from substance use*, in relation to any issues they may be experiencing.

Those on probation and the staff providing support to service users clearly draw a connection between domestic violence and women's experiences on probation. Overall, women are more likely to experience higher levels of domestic violence, and with this, it is more difficult for them to seek support for their substance use or to remain abstinent. If a woman is unable to receive support such as medication, because of the level of control that is exerted over them, they are more likely to continue misusing, and in turn revert to criminal activity to support their substance use. Furthermore, when women are in prison, they are more likely to feel an extra layer of pressure due to others relying on them. The support that they may need from partners is commonly not present when they are released. As such, this can cause a continued pressure and added difficulty when going through the process of recovery. It is important to note that these are problems that are not typically experienced by men, and therefore when discussing experiences of probation, it needs to be done so through a gendered lens. This research has shown domestic violence and sex work to be more centred on the experiences of women. Moreover, many of these discussions are centred on the experiences of females who consider themselves lower or working class. As such, social class is another element that needs to be considered in more depth, in interaction with these other individual factors.

Social class

Social class is a further factor that was present within the research in terms of highlighting areas of oppression. The experiences of those participants who considered themselves working/lower class were different to those who described themselves as middle class. Sharon, a service user who considered herself lower class, drew upon some of the various factors that she felt had impacted her, and to which may not have been as present if she was not lower class. She says that "there [are] so many issues, so many separate parts of like, there's homelessness, there's drug misuse, there's alcoholism, there's like abuse from family, trauma, that brings people to offending or reoffending, erm, poverty, like, these are outside forces that are creating the problem" (Sharon, service user).

As can be evidenced from this quote, it is the intersections of multiple factors *in combination* that put these women at higher risk of reoffending. One of the factors drawn upon by Sharon, which has been highlighted by other service users who describe themselves as lower class, is interaction with close relationships. The types of support offered from within relationships differed for those who considered themselves lower or working class to those who did not. In comparison to female experiences, however, William discussed how issues in his relationship, in connection with lack of money, led to his criminal activity:

> 'Erm, yeah possibly, so, I was in a bad relationship, quite toxic, like both big drinkers, cocaine users, that was quite bad. Never had no money, so there were lots of arguments about that, no money coming into the house, so yeah, the relationship was like the main factor behind my offence.' (William, service user)

This could be perceived to relate to gendered pressures around men being the 'provider' and this pressure potentially influencing his offending. Therefore, we see how classed expectations of masculinity may impact an individual's experiences with crime and criminal justice. Simon further supports the family connection by explaining the impact that substance use has had on his family. He explains how he has "lost [himself]", and that substance use has been at the centre of both his and his family's life since he was young:

'my family, my brothers already died, one brother to addiction, and my other brother, is a "snowballo" as well, crack–heroin mixed, my sister's the same, and my other brother ... smokes religiously ... he smokes a bit of crack ... there's just no family relationship there, my mum and dad admitted to me the other day that she's an addict, but it's controlled ... but they used to do speed when we was younger.' (Simon, service user)

The importance of having supportive people around you has been highlighted by other participants. One probation officer draws upon some of the aspects that have been highlighted above as issues for those who consider themselves lower or working class:

'I think you've got to have circles of support; you've got to have enough to say, it is not worth reoffending, what I've got is not worth losing. So, if you're moving around, you're on benefits, you're cold, you're homeless, you've got no relationships. No money, no opportunity, losing hope, losing belief, then what have you got to lose?' (Mitchell, probation officer)

Thus, for those of lower-/working-class backgrounds, networks of support appear to be less robust as a consequence of their environment, again reinforcing the impact of multiple social, structural and environmental factors intersecting. Jardine (2014) supports this perspective, recognizing that close family ties can provide individuals with support that promotes inclusivity within society, such as emotional support, financial provision and offering accommodation. All these factors, and other aspects that support an investment in one's social capital, can help promote desistance, showing how relationships play a key role (Farrall, 2004; Jardine, 2014).

A factor that tends to closely align with close relations and social class is accommodation. This study highlighted that, for the participants, a lack of stable accommodation had a strong impact on how service users are able to respond to support. If a service user is homeless at the time where they would be due to start receiving support by probation, then they will not be eligible for that support without a fixed address. This reinforces social power hierarchies and further oppresses those who are already marginalized within society. For the service users in this study, it has been clear that homelessness plays a factor in many of those who consider themselves lower or working class. Nina explains the complexity that can come with supporting a client who is homeless:

'if they are rough sleeping, they are going to be using drugs to be out in the cold, so to fund the drugs, they are having to commit crime, so it's just a vicious circle all the time. Then their physical health is deteriorating, then their mental health, then they are not attending appointments, then they can't register with a doctor because they've got no address, can't get benefits because they've got no address.' (Nina, drug and alcohol worker)

A further factor to consider in regard to social class oppression relates to finances and employment. One probation officer draws upon three key factors that link these two points together. To start, Nolan explains what can happen if someone who is in shared accommodation was to gain employment:

'if we are talking about employment, as soon as these people have got a paid job, housing benefits stop, so the shared accommodation are usually sort of immediately begin charging them sort of anywhere between £2–300 a week, so the incentive for them to actually get a job is like well nonexistent'. (Nolan, probation officer)

He recognizes that this in itself puts service users at a disadvantage to those who are living in stable households and have the financial support of others. Nolan further discusses the financial impact that being on probation and engaging with activities that are required as part of an order can have for some service users. For example, with regards to the commute to the probation office:

'It makes it harder obviously, getting to Birmingham City centre is hard for some people ... to get here on a bus and to get home its £5. If we want them to come in twice a week, that's £10 and if they are on benefits and they are also spending the money on their habits, it's extremely hard.' (Nolan, probation officer)

Probation offices within CRCs have taken a centralized approach, meaning that there is one main probation office to attend. As highlighted by Nolan, this has been a particular issue for service users. Literature has supported the move towards decentralization, arguing that the focus should be on probation offices being a community resource, that are accessible and local, while providing several services that will support the move towards desistance (Smith and Stewart, 1997).

A financial issue that is not discussed in as much depth is the access to technology in a primarily technical world. With recent events, such as COVID-19, technology is having to be used more than before. As such, this has had even more of an impact on service users, as not all have the financial means to access technology or are subject to restrictions due to social distancing measures or isolation. Furthermore, access to financial support, primarily Universal Credit, is heavily reliant on access to a phone or the internet to discuss any issues. Nolan explains the issue with this:

'Universal Credit, a real pain ... it's all geared towards accessing it online ... a lot of our service users either don't have access or they are not very good with computers. Erm, again if they miss their job centre appointments ... these are alcohol, drug users, they're chaotic, they've got other problems, then they get sanctioned, they've not got any money, so what are they going to do? ... they're going to reoffend aren't they.' (Nolan, probation officer)

These experiences are contradictory to those who consider themselves middle class. For example, Leanne highlights that her offence and substance use have not impacted her employment. She says "my employment is fine, because that was never under any threat. I was full-time employed before the crime and I remained full-time employed in the same employment after it." Additionally, Max recognizes that although he is not in his previous employment, he is in a position whereby he can make a choice to not take what he considers a 'normal' job. Max, a service user, says "I can't face getting a normal job, it is making me physically ill thinking about it. Stacking shelves in Tesco, or pulling trolleys in, or whatever, delivering parcels, I've done that, and its mind draining."

These findings highlight how the challenges and barriers faced by those who consider themselves as lower or working class impact their chances of being in situations whereby they remain within the CJS for longer, and face higher levels of issues with finances and accommodation. As such, this research has underlined and emphasized the intersections of gender, class, poverty, employment and opportunity for these individuals.

Conclusion

Exploring the experiences of service users and staff working within probation has highlighted that both receiving and giving support for substance use and desistance can be particularly difficult for those who are considered to be lower class or women, and even more difficult for those who are *lower-class women*. This study adds to literature that recognizes that service users on probation can be oppressed because of a combination of social class and gender, both separately and in intersection with one another. This oppression, however, is often worsened by additional personal pressures, whether that be parental responsibility or financial shortfalls, that impact their ability to engage in the support offered by probation services. These concerns are heightened when looking at lower-class women, who had to deal with the intersectional challenges of their gender and social class within the probation service and indeed the structural barriers some of these women faced, as discussed above.

The study showed that women are more likely to be with an abusive partner, which can reduce their ability to attend appointments with probation and to be able to get into a mindset where they can look into rehabilitation for their substance use. In addition to providing support for domestic abuse, probation staff are also expected to support women on probation for sex work, as these are the two factors that have been noted to impact women more than men. Sex work has been noted to have links to trauma and substance use, making it more difficult for service users to receive support from the probation service. Additionally, when discussing the challenges faced by women, the discussions were often based around the experiences of women who would classify themselves as lower or working class, whereas women who classed themselves as middle class did not report experiences of sex work or domestic abuse. The research highlighted the intersectional nature between socioeconomic status and gender, and how that interplays with what support is required by probation.

When looking at social class independently, it was found that those who considered themselves to be from a lower-class background faced numerous challenges that other service users did not. A number of those considered lower class did not have the level of support from family members they needed. There tended to be a trend of other family members either misusing substances themselves or not providing support for the service user to seek out the resources provided by probation. Literature highlights the importance of strong family ties and support in the journey to desistance (Farrall, 2004; Jardine, 2014), and therefore this has been a key point. Unsuitable or lack of accommodation is a further aspect that has been identified. This is particularly important when discussing probation, as if an individual does not have an address to provide to probation, they are unable to receive any initial support. If they become homeless post entering probation, this causes further challenges in regard to a reliance on technology to communicate and in terms of finances and employment, in turn impacting their ability to engage in the support available.

In summary, this chapter has highlighted that service users who are considered low to medium risk in England and Wales and receiving support from the probation service have faced many challenges on the basis of gender and social class over the last few years. With this in mind, it is evident that when an individual living in England and Wales enters into the CJS, their histories and identities are likely to shape their overall experience. These oppressions must be recognized and reflected upon when considering not only how the public can be kept safe, but also in how we can avoid further excluding marginalized groups when attempting to provide them support for reducing reoffending and substance misuse. It is imperative that this is explored utilizing an intersectional framework; otherwise, it is likely that these needs will be responded too with reductive, oversimplistic initiatives that do not appreciate interlocking structural pressures and oppressions.

References

Adams, W.C. (2015) 'Conducting semi-structured interviews', in J.S. Wholey, H.P. Harty and K.E. Newcomer (eds) *Handbook of Practical Program Evaluation*, San Francisco: Jossey-Bass, pp 492–505.

Advisory Council on the Misuse of Drugs (2017) *Commissioning Impact on Drug Treatment*, London: Home Office.

Argyle, M. (1994) *The Psychology of Social Class*, London: Routledge.

Baldry, E. (2010) 'Women in transition: from prison to ...', *Current Issues in Criminal Justice*, 22: 253–67.

Bean, P. (2018) *Probation and Privatisation*, London: Routledge.

Cavadino, M. and Dignan, J. (2007) *The Penal System: An Introduction* (4th Ed.), London: Sage.

Clawson, D. and Gerstel, N. (2014) *Unequal Time: Gender, Class, and Family in Employment Schedules*, New York: Russell Sage Foundation.

Corteen, K. (2018) New victimisations: female sex worker hate crime and the 'ideal victim', in M. Duggan (ed.) *Revisiting the Ideal Victim*, Bristol: Policy Press, pp 103–22.

DeHart, D.D. (2008) 'Pathways to prison: impact of victimization in the lives of incarcerated women', *Violence Against Women*, 14: 1362–81.

DrugScope (nd) *Mental health and substance misuse: summary*. [online] www.drugwise.org.uk/wp-content/uploads/Mental-health-and-substance-use-summary-report.pdf

Durante, F. and Fiske, S.T. (2017) 'How social-class stereotypes maintain inequality', *Current Opinion in Psychology*, 18: 43–8.

Elonheimo, H., Gyllenberg, D., Huttunen, J., Ristkari, T., Sillanmaki, L. and Sourander, A. (2014) 'Criminal offending among males and females between ages 15 and 30 in a population-based nationwide 1981 birth cohort: results from the FinnCrime Study', *Journal of Adolescence*, 37(8): 1269–79.

Farrall, S. (2004) 'Social capital and offender reintegration: making probation desistance focused', in S. Maruna and R. Immarigeon (eds) *After Crime and Punishment: Pathways to Offender Reintegration*, Devon: Willan Publishing, pp 57–84.

Entmacher, J., Robbins, K.G., Vogtman, J. and Frohlich, L. (2013) *Insecure and Unequal: Poverty and Income among Women and Families 2000–2012*, Washington, DC: National Women's Law Center.

Fuentes, C.M. (2014) 'Nobody's child: the role of trauma and interpersonal violence in women's pathways to incarceration and resultant service needs', *Medical Anthropology Quarterly*, 28: 85–104.

HM Inspectorate of Probation (2016) *Transforming Rehabilitation Early Implementation 4: An Independent Inspection of the Arrangements for Offender Supervision*, Manchester: Her Majesty's Inspectorate of Probation.

HM Inspectorate of Probation (2019a) *Report of the chief inspector of probation March 2019.* [online] www.justiceinspectorates.gov.uk/hmiprobation/wp-content/uploads/sites/5/2019/03/HMI-Probation-Chief-Inspectors-Report.pdf

HM Inspectorate of Probation (2019b) *The transforming rehabilitation model for probation service is irredeemably flawed.* [online] www.justiceinspectorates.gov.uk/hmiprobation/media/press-releases/2019/03/reportofthechiefinspectorofprobation/

Hill Collins, P. and Bilge, S. (2016) *Intersectionality*, Cambridge: Polity Press.

House of Commons (2018) *Government Contracts for Community Rehabilitation Companies: Twenty-Seventh Report of Session 2017–19*, London: House of Commons.

Home Office (2004) *Reducing Reoffending: National Action Plan*, London: Home Office.

Huebner, B.M., DeJong, C. and Cobbina, J. (2010) 'Women coming home: long-term patterns of recidivism', *Justice Quarterly*, 27(2): 225–54.

Irwin, J. (2013/1985) *The Jail: Managing the Under-Class in American Society*, Berkeley, CA: University of California Press.

Jardine, C. (2014) *The role of family ties in desistance from crime.* [online] www.familiesoutside.org.uk/content/uploads/2017/11/families-outside-in-brief-9.pdf

Lammy, D. (2017*) The Lammy review: an independent review into the treatment of, and outcomes for, black, Asian and minority ethnic individuals in the Criminal Justice System* [online] https://assets.publishing.service.gov.uk/government/uploads/system/uploads/attachment_data/file/643001/lammy-review-final-report.pdf

Langdridge, D. (2007) *Phenomenological Psychology: Theory, Research and Methods*, London: Pearson.

Lee, K.H., Xu, H. and Wu, B. (2020) 'Gender differences in quality of life among community-dwelling older adults in low- and middle-income countries: results from the study on global AGEing and adult health', *BMC Public Health*, 20: 114.

Light, M., Grant, E., Hopkins, K. and Ministry of Justice Analytical Services (2013) *Gender Differences in Substance Misuse and Mental Health among Prisoners*, London: Ministry of Justice.

Marmot, M., Friel, S., Bell, R., Houweling, T.A., Taylor, S. and Commission on Social Determinants of Health (2008) 'Closing the gap in a generation: health equity through action on the social determinants of health', *Lancet*, 372(9650): 1661–9.

Marx, K. and Engels, F. (1970) 'Ruling class and ruling ideas' in J. Storey (ed) *Cultural Theory and Popular Culture: A Reader* (4th Ed), Essex: Pearson.

Ministry of Justice (2013) *Transforming Rehabilitation: A Strategy for Reform*, London: The Stationery Office.

Nuttbrock, N.A., Rosenblum, A., Magura, S., Villano, C. and Wallace, J. (2004) 'Linking female sex workers with substance abuse treatment', *Journal of Substance Abuse Treatment*, 27: 233–9.

National Offender Management Service (2015) *Better outcomes: a guide to working with former sex workers and victims of domestic abuse.* [online] https://assets.publishing.service.gov.uk/government/uploads/system/uploads/attachment_data/file/462140/Better_Outcomes_A_guide_to_working_with_Former_Sex_Workers_and_Victims_of_Domestic_Abuse.pdf

Phelps, M. (2013) 'The paradox of probation: community supervision in the age of mass incarceration', *Law Policy*, 35(1–2): 51–80.

Robinson, G. (2016) 'The Cinderella complex: punishment, society and community sanctions', *Punishment & Society*, 18(1): 95–112.

Rubin, J. and Rubin, I. (1995) *Qualitative Interviewing: The Art of Hearing Data*, Thousand Oaks, CA: Sage Publications.

Smith, D. and Stewart, J. (1997) 'Probation and social exclusion', *Social Policy & Administration*, 31(5): 96–115.

Webster, R. (2016) *Payment by results: lessons from the literature.* [online] http://russellwebster.com/PbRlitreview.pdf

Wilson, I., Graham, K. and Taft, A. (2017) 'Living the cycle of drinking and violence: a qualitative study of women's experience of alcohol related intimate partner violence', *Drug and Alcohol Review*, 36: 115–24.

Women's Aid (2015) *SOS: save refuges, save lives: why we need to save our services* [online] www.womensaid.org.uk/wp-content/uploads/2015/11/SOS_Data_Report.pdf

Zust, B.L. (2009) 'Partner violence, depression, and recidivism: the case of incarcerated women and why we need programs designed for them', *Issues in Mental Health Nursing*, 30: 246–51.

6

Young Men's Perspectives on Child Criminal Exploitation and Their Involvement in County Lines Drug Dealing: An Intersectional Analysis

Hannah Marshall

Introduction

Since 2010, the UK has seen a significant expansion of research, policy and media attention regarding the exploitation of young people within 'county lines' drug distribution networks, in which illicit substances, most commonly heroin and crack cocaine (National Crime Agency, 2019, p 2), are transported from urban hubs to rural, market and coastal towns where the drugs are then supplied (National Crime Agency, 2017). Yet, as highlighted by Moyle (2019) and Spicer (2020), for too long now, a decontextualized one-dimensional narrative of young people's involvement in county lines drug markets has persisted, depicting county lines solely as an issue of interpersonal violence in which the passive and the powerless, devoid of agency, are preyed upon, groomed and exploited by violent predators. This narrative erases the possibility of recognizing young people's involvement in exploitative work as a response to multifaceted and complex experiences of socioeconomic marginalization (Ford, 2018; Hudek, 2018; The Children's Society, 2019) and, in doing do, it severely limits our ability to respond effectively to young people's needs (Phoenix, 2002). While Spicer (2020, p 4) reminds us that it is 'convenient for those in power to promote an understanding of young people's involvement in drug markets solely as a result of grooming and exploitation, rather than responses to the conditions that their social policies have engendered', we can only develop effective support for young people involved in county lines when we recognize that their experiences are shaped by their relative positions in social hierarchies of marginalization and oppression.

Accordingly, it is imperative that researchers working with young people involved in county lines engage with analytical approaches that enable us to recognize the ways in which young people's involvement in, and perceptions of, county lines are shaped by many intersecting aspects of their lived realities. The application of an intersectional lens to the study of young people's experiences of county lines enables us to do just this. As Hill Collins and Bilge (2016, p 1) emphasize, 'intersectionality is a way of understanding and analysing the complexity in the world, in people, and in human experiences', one which recognizes that 'the events and conditions of social and political life ... are generally shaped by many factors in diverse and mutually influencing ways'. Engaging with intersectional scholarship opens up the possibility of recognizing the ways in which young people's 'social locations within intersecting power relations' (Hill Collins, 2019, p 44) shape their experiences of and perspectives on county lines. Applying an intersectional lens enables us to challenge one-dimensional narratives of young people's county lines involvement and work towards representing their experiences with nuance and complexity.

This chapter uses an intersectional approach to provide insight into the experiences of a group of young men based in one English county, who were involved in county lines drug distribution, and who had been identified by the professionals in their lives as potential victims of criminal exploitation. It will begin by providing a brief overview of existing research literature on county lines and exploitation, and the use of intersectionality in this chapter, before providing an outline of the methodology of the research on which this chapter is based. The findings section focuses specifically on two ways in which these young men's intersecting experiences of gender and class shape their experiences of involvement in county lines. Firstly, it considers how these young men's decisions to become involved in county lines were shaped by intersecting pressures of economic hardship and their expectations of their familial roles. It then considers how young people's conceptualizations of their involvement, specifically, their identification with the idea of involvement as a 'constrained choice' (Scott and Harper, 2006; Moyle, 2019) and their rejection of the term 'victim of exploitation', were further shaped by the intersections of masculinity, socioeconomic marginalization and working-class identity. In doing so, it further demonstrates the significance of intersectionality as a lens that enables greater insight into the perspectives and experiences of young men involved in county lines.

County lines and child criminal exploitation

As previously discussed, 'county lines' refers to the practice of travelling or commuting from urban centres in order to sell drugs in provincial markets (National Crime Agency, 2019). This model of drug distribution has developed in the UK as a response to a variety of factors including the saturation of urban drug markets (Hales and Hobbs, 2010) and the possibility of making larger profits and encountering less competition and police surveillance in rural, market and coastal towns (Windle and Briggs, 2015; McLean et al, 2019; Harding, 2020). It is widely accepted that the use of children and vulnerable adults to transport and sell drugs is an integral part of the county lines model (National Crime Agency, 2019; Robinson et al, 2019), leading to widespread concern regarding the prevalence of 'child criminal exploitation' (CCE) within county lines networks (The Children's Society, 2019).

Currently, there is no statutory definition of CCE (The Children's Society, 2019, p 4). A number of useful definitions are in circulation including from the 'Not in Our Community' campaign against exploitation, which draws on the words of 'D', a young person affected by CCE, to define criminal exploitation as: 'When someone you trusted makes you commit crimes for their benefit' (Not in Our Community, 2017), and the Home Office's definition, which describes CCE as a situation in which

> an individual or group takes advantage of an imbalance of power to coerce, control, manipulate or deceive a child or young person under the age of 18 into any criminal activity in exchange for something that the victim needs or wants, and/or for the financial or other advantage of the perpetrator or facilitator, and/or through violence or the threat of violence. (Home Office UK, 2018, p 48)

As both definitions emphasize, CCE can occur in relation to any form of criminal activity, but this research focuses specifically on CCE in the context of county lines drug distribution and will use the term 'county lines exploitation' as a shorthand.

As indicated in the introduction to this chapter, the term 'exploitation' is far from unproblematic. Research into related issues including child sexual exploitation and child labour has highlighted that young people themselves often reject the term 'exploitation' and its connotations of passivity, instead describing decisions to enter into exploitative situations as survival strategies, acts that represent both 'constrained choices' (Scott and Harper, 2006; Moyle, 2019) 'not in conditions of their own choosing' (Phoenix, 2002, p 362) and expressions of agency, however 'thin' (Klocker, 2007). In relation to county lines, Moyle's (2019) research with adults emphasizes that county lines labourers exhibit 'practical rationality' (Grundetjern and Sandberg, 2012), creatively evaluating their options for income generation (Fleetwood, 2014) in light of their restricted socioeconomic capital and structural vulnerabilities. However, while a small number of studies with young people involved in county lines exist (McLean et al, 2019; Harding, 2020), we are yet to fully engage with young people's own perspectives and experiences of county lines and the concept of exploitation. This is a gap that this chapter will address. Engaging with young people's intersecting social positionalities facilitates a crucial insight into their perspectives on involvement in county lines, and on the label 'exploitation'.

Applying an intersectional lens

In relation to young people's participation in county lines drug markets, the application of an intersectional lens is extremely valuable because it enables us to better contextualize young people's involvement and to capture its complexities (Hill Collins, 2019). Intersectionality is an analytical tool that recognizes our lives as being shaped 'by many axes that work together and influence each other' (Hill Collins and Bilge, 2016, p 1). Broadly, intersectional approaches consider how our experiences are shaped by the ways in which our various hierarchized social identities are 'interwoven, and continually interact with and affect each other' (Potter, 2015, p 152). This chapter focuses specifically on the impact of intersections of gender and class, exploring the ways in which the intersections of masculinity, socioeconomic marginalization and working-class identity shape young people's experiences of county lines involvement, as these identities were those that young people taking part in this research described as most salient. In exploring these intersections, this chapter departs from intersectional scholarship's foundational focus on 'interlocking structures of oppression' (Collins, 1995, p 492), as masculinities are sites of privilege, and from intersectionality's foundational focus on the experiences of black women (Truth, 1851; Combahee River Collective, 1974; Shakur and Chesimard, 1978; Crenshaw, 1991). This approach follows Potter (2015) and Hill Collins (2019) in emphasizing that we should encourage intersectionality's expanded use in considering 'all lived experiences, regardless of the identities individuals hold' (Potter, 2015, p 79) while also recognizing that intersectionality is rooted in black feminist activism and scholarship.

In recognizing the nuances of young people's narratives of their involvement in county lines, this chapter will also explore the ways in which young people conceptualize themselves, specifically focusing on young people's assertion of 'constrained choice' and their rejection of the term 'victim of exploitation'. Intersectionality-informed scholarship and activism again helps to further the analysis here, having long advocated that the extent to which an individual's victimization is foregrounded is influenced by one's social location (Potter, 2015), particularly through research into institutional failures to recognize the ways in which black women's experiences of victimization can create pathways into offending (Richie, 2012). While this existing research has explored how those with the power to do so attribute the victim label in ways informed by social positionalities, this chapter uses an intersectional approach to explore some of the ways in which young people claim or reject the victim label for themselves in ways that are informed by their particular intersecting social locations.

Methodology

This chapter draws on semi-structured interviews with 14 young men who were completing orders with the Youth Offending Service (YOS) as a result of county lines–related offences and who had been identified by YOS staff as potential victims of criminal exploitation. They were aged between 14 and 18 at the time of the research and were currently living in the same English county. Seven of the young men identified as white and were either first- or second-generation immigrants from Eastern Europe[1], six identified as white British and one young person identified as black British. These interviews were completed as part of a wider study into the issue of criminal exploitation involving over 75 young people and youth justice professionals. All participants were recruited through the YOS and young people were interviewed either in person or over the phone. Interviews lasted between 45 minutes and two hours and some interviews were conducted over multiple sessions. The research received ethical approval from both the University of Cambridge and the local authority. Interviews were transcribed by the author and thematic coding was conducted in NVivo using a grounded theory approach (Charmaz, 2014).

Seeking to involve young people affected by CCE in the context of county lines drug distribution networks in qualitative research presented a number of methodological hurdles. Based on their own research experiences, Bosworth, Hoyle and Dempsey (2011), Windle and Briggs (2015) and Moyle (2019) emphasize that recruiting research participants who have experienced exploitation, or who are involved in drug dealing, is extremely challenging. Building trust with potential participants was a gradual and critical element of this research, greatly assisted by staff working within the YOS. There were potential participants who decided not to take part because, despite assurances of confidentiality and anonymity, they were concerned about the ramifications of speaking about their experiences. The resulting sample of 14 young people is comparable with existing qualitative research with young people involved in county lines drug distribution (for example, Robinson et al, 2019 and Harding, 2020) and provides an exploratory initial insight into young people's experiences and perceptions of county lines exploitation.

Qualitative research is, by its very nature, an interactional process (England, 1994; Holstein and Gubrium, 2011) inescapably shaped by the multiple intersecting identities of researcher and participant, which must therefore by analysed and considered. My positionalities as a white British and middle-class researcher working with young men, all of whom had experienced significant socioeconomic marginalization, undoubtedly created a gradient of power and privilege in the research interaction. In designing and carrying out the research my approach was to render this dynamic visible, disrupting it where possible, while acknowledging the impossibility of its complete erasure (Ahmed, 2004).

I focused on disrupting the power gradient between researcher and participant in three main ways: by enhancing opportunities for participant involvement in decisions about the research; by engaging in self-disclosure and reciprocal sharing; and by taking a reflexive approach, examining the influence of my own positionalities in relation to participants on the research process. In terms of the impact of my positionalities as a white British middle-class woman on the research, I found that this was neither static nor fixed. Spaces of difference between myself and participants expanded and contracted as contexts and conversations shifted. There were points at which I could see that expansively different experiences of class and xeno-racialized privilege created a vast gap between myself and young people. Yet there were other moments of exchange in which shared experience brought us closer together. At times it was possible to lean into differences and find ways of using this to position young people as experts and teachers. At other times it felt more appropriate to listen, and to recognize and validate the frustration and anger that young people expressed towards the white British and middle-class privileges from which I have benefited. The differences in positionality between myself and young people sometimes meant that young people felt that I would not understand their perspectives. My hope was that the approach that I took worked to acknowledge the areas where I lacked shared experience, and to create a welcoming and safe space for young people to explore this if they wished.

Findings

"For me, it's to help my mum"

The young people taking part in this research described their involvement in county lines drug markets as rooted in the interrelation between their perspectives on their familial roles as young men and their experiences of financial hardship, specifically, in conceptualizations of the ability to provide for and look after one's family as an important marker of masculinity

(Coston and Kimmel, 2012, p 109). Participants saw themselves as becoming involved in county lines out of a sense of responsibility to fulfil the role of the 'provider' or 'breadwinner' as their families navigated financial hardship that was often further exacerbated by the marginalization they experienced as first- or second-generation migrants to the UK.

At the time of the research, Jakub was aged 16 and living with his mum and sister. Jakub had spent time growing up in both the UK and in Eastern Europe and had set his sights on working in the construction industry. Jakub was completing a referral order with the Youth Offending Service after being convicted of possession with intent to supply but was also receiving support from the YOS' specialist CCE team. In the following interview extract, Jakub describes some of his reasons for becoming involved in county lines drug distribution:

> 'Yeah cos obviously we didn't really have like much [in Eastern Europe], you know what I'm saying, so we came here to have a better life and I just feel like they failed my, like the government in general, failed my whole family innit ... My house doesn't have enough money to fucking feed us all, you get me? So for me, it's to help my mum, to get her out of that debt, that she's put herself into, or got put into ... I haven't taken money off my mum in like seven months.' (Jakub)

Jakub's assertion that "for me, it's to help my mum" and his emphasis that "I haven't taken money off my mum in like seven months" highlights the intersecting roles played by the socioeconomic marginalization experienced by working-class migrants to the UK and the gendered expectations that associate masculinity with 'breadwinning' and the ability to provide for oneself and one's family (Coston and Kimmel, 2012, p 109; Fiałkowska, 2019; Wojnicka, 2019) in his involvement in county lines drug distribution.

Similarly, Matis, who had just turned 18 at the time of the research and was living in supported accommodation, describes becoming involved in county lines drug distribution:

> 'Mum works two jobs and that and not enough pay. Obviously, you're still in school so you can't get benefits. So this is why like I say to people like it's hard for youths like to I dunno innit ... if their family is struggling for money and they're still in school, they're not 18 yet, what else are they like supposed to do? ... Myself yeah like my mum ... even now she's struggling with money cos my stepdad obviously broke his leg. And my stepdad, yeah, he couldn't work for like eight months. So they had to apply for Universal Credit. Cos they never received benefits before. And obviously my mum and my stepdad

they're not from the UK, but they're UK residents, I think it's, they're UK residents, I think it took some time.' (Matis)

Matis locates his involvement as a result of a lack of other options to support his mum financially, particularly after an incident in which an accident left his stepdad unable to work. In Matis' case this incident was further exacerbated by the challenges that foreign nationals experience when attempting to access state welfare support in the UK (Harris, 2016; Dwyer et al, 2019). What is evident in this extract is Matis' sense of duty in supporting his mum: "what else are [young people] supposed to do?" This sense of responsibility is also evident in the matter-of-fact tone of Lukas' description of why he became involved in county lines drug distribution:

'We needed some money for rent, I didn't have any money, because that friend has been my source of money and he's been locked up, so I thought would make money quickly to pay mum's rent. I thought I'd sell it quickly and we'd be happy, food on the table.' (Lukas)

In these examples, the young men present their involvement in county lines drug distribution as a decision informed by the intersections of socioeconomic pressure, often exacerbated by experiences of migration, and the expectations of 'breadwinning' associated with masculinity. Clearly then, we cannot simply understand these young people's experiences in terms of the narrative of violence at the hands of an individual exploiter. An intersectional approach calls us to recognize the ways in which individuals' experiences of exploitative work are shaped by their positions within intersecting dynamics of power, marginalization and oppression, which yet in turn engender responses infused with anger, frustration, struggle and resistance, as well as care, love and hope (Sanchez, 2017).

"Wanting to make it, having to make it or just being forced to make it"

In addition to helping us to understand why young people become involved in county lines drug markets, an intersectional lens can also help to shed light on how young people conceptualize and understand these experiences – particularly regarding young people's descriptions of their involvement as a 'constrained choice', and their rejection of the term 'victim of exploitation'. Much has been written about the extent to which processes of grooming may produce false consciousness and negatively impact individuals' capacities to recognize their own exploitation (see Melrose and Pearce, 2013 and Temple, 2020 for a critical look at this issue), but these debates are not the focus of this chapter. This analysis proceeds on the basis that it is valuable to understand the ways in which young people think and talk about being involved in county lines in the midst of these experiences, even when these views do not concur with those of professionals and may also change for young people if and when they transition out of involvement in county lines.

In our discussions, I asked the young people whether anyone had ever described them as 'a victim of exploitation' and what they thought of the term. While the majority of young people said that they had heard the term applied to them, most often by a social worker or professional from the Youth Offending Service, the vast majority of the young people rejected the relevance of the term 'victim of exploitation' to their experiences. One reason for this was that young men viewed being labelled as exploited as highly emasculating. Participants asserted that they associated being exploited with being a "pussy", and with being mentally and physically "weak", "easy to break", "forced" to do something against their will and easy to "violate". These responses resonate with the explanation of young people's rejection of the term 'victim of exploitation' as 'an attempt to uphold their masculine status' (Robinson et al 2019, p 706). The conceptualizations of exploitation offered by young people clearly conflict with qualities classically associated with hegemonic masculinity: strength, independence and control over one's own life (Kimmel, 2005).

Yet the application of an intersectional lens highlights that the rejection of the term 'victim of exploitation' as emasculating is only one part of the story. An intersectional approach draws attention to the fact that the ways in which young people sought to claim the qualities of control and autonomy by rejecting the label 'victim of exploitation' were also influenced and shaped by their experiences of navigating poverty and deprivation. In the following interview extract, Jakub explains his rejection of the term 'exploitation':

'If you choose to work then it's not exploitation because it's your own choice and you need that money innit … It's like there's a difference between wanting to make money and needing to make money you get me? Or being trapped in it, and you ain't got a choice to do it. So it's like three things, it's not even two things, it's like three different things: wanting to make it, having to make it or just being forced to make it.' (Jakub)

Lukas, who was aged 17 at the time of the research, had just been released from a custodial sentence and was also receiving support from both the YOS and a CCE support worker, expressed similar views. Lukas claimed that "drug dealing is the easiest way to make money – because there aren't other opportunities … Money made me drive for it, nobody can really make me do things they want me to do for them."

Lukas and Jakub both find ways of expressing their involvement in county lines as a 'constrained choice' (Scott and Harper, 2006; Moyle, 2019). Jakub describes a spectrum with "wanting" to make money at one end and "being forced" to make money at the other, carving out a space in the middle of "having" to make money in which he can exist as both a young person struggling in the face of socioeconomic marginalization and as a young man who is able to exert control and make choices in ways that conforms to expectations around masculine agency and control. Similarly, Lukas acknowledges the role of economic pressure in his involvement, stating that "money made me drive for it", but in the same moment is keen to reject the idea that anyone else can "make" him do anything – thereby asserting a sense of agency and control. These descriptions of constrained choice fit with Lukas' and Jakub's interrelating expectations of masculine identity and experiences of socioeconomic marginalization.

"They don't know how to handle themselves"

Furthermore, young people rejected the label 'victim of exploitation' because it jarred with their conceptualizations of working-class masculine identity. Specifically, multiple young people expressed the view that 'exploitation' was something that happened to 'high-class' young men, who they saw as failing to possess the same levels of resilience, capability and control that they had attained as working-class young men. The following extract comes from an interview with Vanya, who was aged 15 at the time of the research:

> 'These other boys, they're not living poor. They've got decent pocket money, like £10 a week pocket money, they're living at home, they've got their own room – and the guys in charge think they don't know how to handle themselves, so they can take advantage of them. So they get exploited. They're vulnerable. Kids that are doing it for their families … they're gonna be smarter, they've got their heads screwed on, they know what they're doing and they're more in control of the situation.' (Vanya)

Strikingly, Vanya subverts normative expectations around the use of the term 'vulnerable', applying it to children whose privilege, he argues, makes them more vulnerable to exploitation than young people dealing as a survival strategy. These standpoints were echoed by Dan, aged 18 at the time of our interview. Dan explained that he felt that, in entering into county lines drug distribution, as he put it, "high-class kids" were getting involved in something that they "didn't understand" in the same way that "us lower-class kids" do and that they would therefore be unable to navigate situations as effectively, and be more at risk of exploitation.

The inclusion of these comments is not to suggest that any of the young people who took part in this research were not vulnerable, had not experienced exploitation or could navigate experiences of drug distribution more successfully than anyone else because of their gender and class. The violence and trauma experienced by many young people who become involved in county lines drug distribution is well documented (The Children's Society, 2019), and the young people whose insights are included in this chapter all also relayed experiences of serious violence; found that money that they did accrue from dealing was often either confiscated by the police, robbed or was subsumed in the payment of spurious debts; and were aware that their criminal records would ultimately limit their prospects of earning a living in the long run. Yet despite this, Vanya's and Dan's perspectives remain important because they demonstrate the ways in which young people's experiences at the intersections of class and gender contribute to a reluctance to engage with the 'victim of exploitation' label.

It is also worth noting that while young people taking part in this research characterized themselves as smarter, more capable and in control than young men who had greater class privilege, they did not romanticize their involvement in county lines. For example, in the following extract, Jakub expresses palpable frustration and anger with white English middle- and upper-class young men involved in dealing:

'Some people just do it to look bad innit, like they got money from their parents but they choose to be a drug dealer for some fucking reason. And I will never understand why … I think those people are little fucking idiots, and they don't know what they're doing. Cos they've got so much chances in life that they could take. And they're wasting their whole life… . If you're a white English man, like kid yeah, and you've got money because of your parents are rich, you should never bother to do drugs, it's not worth it. It's not worth it for what you're doing, and it's just fucking shit innit. Just go do your own thing, get a legal job, live off your parents' money while you can.' (Jakub)

Like Vanya and Dan, Jakub expresses the view that middle- and upper-class children who become involved in county lines "don't know what they're doing", but his words also demonstrate clear frustration and anger at not having the same privileges around familial financial security, and (as discussed previously) "having to deal" as a survival strategy. Even though Jakub rejected the term 'exploitation' as a description of his experiences, he still emphasized the significant hardship he had experienced through his involvement in county lines: "It's not worth it … it's just fucking shit."

Conclusion

As Parmar (2017) emphasizes, British criminology has been somewhat slow to adopt intersectional framing in research. However, as this chapter has demonstrated, an intersectional approach can allow criminologists to recognize how young people's multiple and intersecting social positionalities can influence their perceptions and attitudes towards their involvement in an important area of criminological research: county lines exploitation. In particular, our understanding of why young people might reject the term 'victim of exploitation' is enriched by an understanding of these individuals' intersecting experiences and expectations in relation to masculinity, socioeconomic marginalization and working-class identity. Future research into county lines exploitation could benefit from a continued engagement with intersectional scholarship, in order to offer further critical reflection on the ways in which 'race', gender, class, nationality, disability status and other identities intersect to shape young people's experiences of county lines drug markets.

Intersectionality's core constructs have long included a focus on working to solve social problems (Hill Collins, 2019), and the intersectional approach in this chapter also opens up potential implications for the ways in which we might work to support young people affected by county lines. Phoenix (2002, p 363) emphasizes that failing to consider the fact that young people may enter into an exploitative situation as 'a rational response to very limited material or social opportunities and circumstances' will ultimately lead to approaches in policy and practice that are weakened because their 'needs for adequate employment, education, housing, social networks and so on are eclipsed' (Phoenix, 2002, p 366). Indeed, the insights offered by young people in this chapter remind us of the importance of a holistic response to county lines exploitation, one that does more than target perpetrators, but which works collaboratively with young people to address the interrelating contexts and pressures of lived realities of socioeconomic status, gender, nationality and beyond that influence their experiences of involvement.

Note

[1] To protect the anonymity of the young people taking part I refer to Eastern Europe throughout the chapter, rather than to the specific countries of the young people's origin or heritage.

References

Ahmed, S. (2004) 'Declarations of whiteness: The non-performativity of anti-racism', *Borderlands*, 3(2): 1–15.

Bosworth, M., Hoyle, C. and Dempsey, M.M. (2011) 'Researching trafficked women: on institutional resistance and the limits to feminist reflexivity', *Qualitative Inquiry*, 17(9): 769–79. DOI: 10.1177/1077800411423192.

Charmaz, K. (2014) *Constructing Grounded Theory*, 2nd Ed., London: Sage.

Collins, P.H. (1995) 'Symposium: on West and Fenstermaker's "Doing difference"', *Gender & Society*, 9: 491–513.

Combahee River Collective (1974) 'The Combahee River Collective statement', *Freedom Organizing Series*, 1: 1–7. https://americanstudies.yale.edu/sites/default/files/files/Keyword Coalition_Readings.pdf

Coston, B.M. and Kimmel, M. (2012) 'Seeing privilege where it isn't: marginalized masculinities and the intersectionality of privilege', *Journal of Social Issues*, 68(1): 97–111. DOI: 10.1111/j.1540-4560.2011.01738.x.

Crenshaw, K.W. (1991) 'Mapping the margins: intersectionality, identity politics, and violence against women of color', *Stanford Law Review*, 43(6): 1242–99.

Dwyer, P.J., Scullion, L., Jones, K. and Stewart, A. (2019) 'The impact of conditionality on the welfare rights of EU migrants in the UK', *Policy and politics*, 47(1): 133–50. DOI: 10.1332/030557318X15296527346800.

England, K. (1994) 'Getting personal: reflexivity, positionality, and feminist research', *Professional Geographer*, 46(1): 80–9.

Fiałkowska, K. (2019) 'Negotiating masculinities: Polish male migrants in the UK – insights from an intersectional perspective', *Norma*, Taylor & Francis, 14(2): 112–27. DOI: 10.1080/18902138.2018.1533270.

Fleetwood, J. (2014) 'Keeping out of trouble: female crack cocaine dealers in England', *European Journal of Criminology*, 11(1): 91–109. DOI: 10.1177/1477370813491177.

Ford, S. (2018) 'County lines – a national summary of emerging and best practice' [online] https://tce.researchinpractice.org.uk/county-lines-a-national-summary-emerging-best-practice/

Grundetjern, H. and Sandberg, S. (2012) 'Dealing with a gendered economy: female drug dealers and street capital', *European Journal of Criminology*, 9(6): 621–35. DOI: 10.1177/1477370812453103.

Hales, G. and Hobbs, D. (2010) 'Drug markets in the community: a London borough case study', *Trends in Organized Crime*, 13(1): 13–30. DOI: 10.1007/s12117-009-9086-9.

Harding, S. (2020) *County Lines: Exploitation and Drug Dealing Among Urban Street Gangs*, Bristol: Bristol University Press.

Harris, N. (2016) 'Demagnetisation of social security and health care for migrants to the UK', *European Journal of Social Security*, 18(2): 130–63. DOI: 10.1177/138826271601800204.

Hill Collins, P. (2019) *Intersectionality as Critical Social Theory*, Durham: Duke University Press.

Hill Collins, P. and Bilge, S. (2016) Intersectionality. Cambridge: Polity Press.

Holstein, J.A. and Gubrium, J.F. (2011) *Animating Interview Narratives*, Los Angeles: Sage.

Home Office UK (2018) 'Serious violence strategy'. [online] www.gov.uk/government/publications/serious-violence-strategy

Hudek, J. (2018) 'Scoping county lines – a snapshot of challenges and emerging practice'. [online] www.basw.co.uk/resources/county-lines-scoping-report-may-2018

Kimmel, M. (2005) *The History of Men: Essays on the History of American and British Masculinities*, New York: SUNY Press.

Klocker, N. (2007) 'An example of "thin" agency: child domestic workers in Tanzania', in Panelli, R., Punch, S. and Robson, E. (eds) *Global Perspectives on Rural Childhood and Youth: Young Rural Lives*, New York: Routledge, pp 83–94.

McLean, R., Robinson, G. and Densley, J. (2019) *County Lines: Criminal Networks and Evolving Drug Markets in Britain*, London: Springer.

Melrose, M. and Pearce, J. (2013) *Critical Perspectives on Child Sexual Exploitation and Related Trafficking*, London: Palgrave Macmillan. [online] www.ghbook.ir/index.php?name=ناسر و گـن‌هرف=ن‌یون ی‌اه هناسر&option=com_dbook&task=readonline&book_id=13650&page=73&chkhashk=ED9C9491B4&Itemid=218&lang=fa&tmpl=component

Moyle, L. (2019) 'Situating vulnerability and exploitation in street-level drug markets: cuckooing, commuting, and the "county lines" drug supply model', *Journal of Drug Issues*, 49(4)002204261986193. DOI: 10.1177/0022042619861938.

National Crime Agency (2017) 'County lines violence, exploitation and drug supply – national briefing report'. [online] https://nationalcrimeagency.gov.uk/who-we-are/publications/234-county-lines-violen-ce-exploitation-drug-supply-2017/file

National Crime Agency (2019) 'County lines drug supply, vulnerability and harm 2018'. [online] www.nationalcrimeagency.gov.uk/publications/993-nac-19-095-county-lines-drug-supply-vulnerability-and-harm-2018/file

Not in Our Community (2017) 'Grooming and exploitation'. [online] https://notinourcommunity.org/grooming-exploitation/#criminalexploitation

Parmar, A. (2017) 'Intersectionality, British criminology and race: are we there yet?', *Theoretical Criminology*, 21(1): 35–45. DOI: 10.1177/1362480616677496.

Phoenix, J. (2002) 'In the name of protection: youth prostitution policy reforms in England and Wales', *Critical Social Policy*, 22(2): 353–75. DOI: 10.1177/02610183020220020901.

Potter, H. (2015) *Intersectionality and Criminology: Disrupting and Revolutionizing Studies of Crime*, London: Routledge. DOI: 10.16309/j.cnki.issn.1007-1776.2003.03.004.

Richie, B.E. (2012) *Arrested Justice: Black Women, Violence, and America's Prison Nation*, New York: New York University Press. DOI: 10.7591/9780801459429-004.

Robinson, G., McLean, R. and Densley, J. (2019) 'Working county lines: child criminal exploitation and illicit drug dealing in Glasgow and Merseyside', *International Journal of Offender Therapy and Comparative Criminology*, 63(5): 694–711. DOI: 10.1177/0306624X18806742.

Sanchez, G. (2017) 'Beyond the matrix of oppression: reframing human smuggling through instersectionality-informed approaches', *Theoretical Criminology*, 21(1): 46–56.

Scott, S. and Harper, Z. (2006) 'Meeting the needs of sexually exploited young people: the challenge of conducting policy-relevant research', *Child Abuse Review*, 15: 313–25. DOI: 10.1002/car.

Shakur, A. and Chesimard, J. (1981) 'Women in prison: how we are', *Black Scholar*, 12(6): 50–7. DOI: 10.1080/00064246.1981.11414221.

Spicer, J. (2020) 'International journal of drug policy between gang talk and prohibition: the transfer of blame for county lines', *International Journal of Drug Policy*, 87. DOI: 10.1016/j.drugpo.2020.102667.

St Giles Trust (2019) 'Evaluation of the county lines pilot project'. [online] https://stgilestrust.org.uk/general-attachments/view?id=18

Temple, A. (2020) 'Excluded, exploited, forgotten: childhood criminal exploitation and school exclusions,' [online] https://justforkidslaw.org/sites/default/files/fields/download/JfKL%20school%20exclusion%20and%20CCE_2.pdf

The Children's Society (2019) 'Counting lives: responding to children who are criminally exploited.' [online] www.childrenssociety.org.uk/sites/default/files/counting-lives-report.pdf

Truth, S. (1851) 'Ain't I a woman?' [online] www.nps.gov/wori/learn/historyculture/sojourner-truth.htm

Windle, J. and Briggs, D. (2015) '"It's like working away for two weeks": the harms associated with young drug dealers commuting from a saturated London drug market', *Crime Prevention and Community Safety*, 17(2): 105–19.

Wojnicka, K. (2019) 'Men, masculinities and migration processes', in Gottzén, L., Mellström, U., and Shefer, T. (eds) *Routledge International Handbook of Masculinity Studies*, London: Routledge.

7

Navigating Constructions of the 'Ideal Victim' among Men Who Experience Childhood DVA and Gang Involvement

Jade Levell

Introduction

Young men who are on-road and gang-involved are some of the most hidden victims of violence and marginality. Race, class and gender intersect in this context to create a perception of dangerous working-class masculinity, which is then associated with criminal offending and potential perpetration of violence, rather than the nuanced understanding of how they came to be in those circumstances and the vulnerabilities they face while inhabiting that physical and mental space. In this chapter I explore the ways in which an intersectional consideration of gender, race and class can help us understand the complexities of being situated as both victims and perpetrators of violence at the same time. I also consider how blanket labels that are ascribed to young people can create oversimplified constructions of individual experiences. These young people are some of the most hidden victims as their involvement in unruly and potentially criminal activities obscures their experiences of victimization at home. There has been an increased focus on co-existing childhood adversity since the popularity of the Adverse Childhood Experiences (ACEs) framework. However, there is still much work to be done to understand the impact that diverse axes of marginalization can have on young people's lives.

UK Ministry of Justice figures (Williams, Papadopoulou and Booth, 2012) suggest that, of adult prisoners, 41 per cent had experienced violence at home in childhood. Female prisoners were more likely to report that they experienced violence at home (50 per cent) than men (40 per cent). Of these, prisoners who had a minority ethnic background were less likely to report witnessing violence at home (32 per cent) than white British prisoners (42 per cent). This raises several questions: is it the case that white women prisoners are more likely to experience DVA (domestic violence and abuse) at home, or is it the case that they are more likely to identify themselves as vulnerable victims in these circumstances?

The definition of DVA that I use as a foundation to this chapter is the UK government definition (Home Office, 2015). This definition recognizes elements of DVA that include physical violence as well as other forms of abuse including emotional, financial, sexual and psychological. The definition was amended in 2013 to include coercive control in light of Evan Stark's (2007) research. Stark noted that, 'unlike other capture crimes, coercive control is personalized, extends through social space as well as over time, and is gendered in that it relies for its impact on women's vulnerability as women due to sexual inequality' (2007, p 24). This gendered view is also recognized by the Home Office, particularly in noting how wider gender inequality underpins coercive control (Home Office, 2015); however, the main UK government definition of DVA is gender neutral.

The concept of 'on-road' to young people is a complex visceral one that refers both to the physicality of being 'street present' (Pearson, 2011) as well as an on-road headspace. On-road not only refers to gang involvement, but serves more as a broader term that refers to both a physical space of the streets as well as a 'way of being in the world for young people in disadvantaged urban neighbourhoods' (Young, 2016, p 10). Young people themselves use the term on-road to refer to a catch-all of behaviours including gang involvement, but also 'to associate with a group of people who regard the street as a social space in which to "hang out" or the illegal drug economy', and is a phrase that allows for the 'complexity and fluidity of urban street life' (Young, 2016, p 11). Gunter (2010) also characterized on-road as defined by violence, criminality and low-level drug dealing. In this study, I use the term 'on-road' alongside 'gang-involved' throughout. Participants tended to refer to being on-road as being involved with the wider aspects of street culture and low-level criminality including drug dealing. Whereas the gang aspects were those that were group-oriented activities organized or facilitated by elders on the estate, which included organized criminality.

Considering intersectional perspectives

Intersectionality was popularized by 'critical race feminism foremother' Kimberlé Crenshaw (Wing, 2003, p 7). Intersectionality is a lens used to understand how individuals navigate matrices of domination that work through amalgamations of both micro- and macro-level power structures and interrelated systems of oppression (Collins, 2000). The different forms of oppression and subjugation that individuals experience is shaped by ingrained racism, sexism, economic disadvantage, abuse and exploitation that limits an individual's agency at different points in time (Bernard, 2013). The effects of these are overlapping and cumulative, as individuals' experiences change and at times simultaneous intersections of systems of oppressions. Individuals 'stand at the intersection' of different elements of their identity (Grillo, 1995, p 18). It is a framework that allows one to recognize 'simultaneously interlocking oppressions' (Brah and Phoenix, 2004, p 78). This has been an important development in feminist theory as it has created a space where the historic essentialism of white feminism has been critiqued (Phipps, 2020).

In the context of DVA, intersectionality urges us to see that for many families, domestic violence and abuse is not the only violence that shapes their experiences and family life (Bograd, 2005). Traditionally, individual identities have been fragmented, with separate identities of 'woman or a mother, victim or survivor, but not all at once' (Krane and Davies, 2002, p 186). Through using an intersectional analysis, the trauma of violence can be seen as amplified and changed by other co-existing forms of victimization including racism and heterosexism (Sokoloff and Dupont, 2005). Although DVA occurs between individuals in the private sphere, it is *culturally produced* from a range of intersecting relations, which include gender, race, class and sexuality. It is no longer useful to separate experiences of race and gender, and instead 'to focus on the ways in which each is implied in and experienced through the other' (Maynard, 2001, p 131). Dasgputa noted that, in a DVA situation, 'all women are victims of this nexus of culture, institutions, and the individual abuser' (2005, p 60). This model allows one to examine the way that women's wider communities can be involved in legitimizing and contributing to control being used over the individual.

Intersectionality requires us to go beyond single-issue explanations of DVA and what it means to be a victim or survivor. This is pertinent when focusing on the experiences of boy child survivors, who grapple with this experience as well as the complex intersections of gender (including masculinity pressures), class and race. The complexities of intersectionality and a focus on interlocking oppressions come to life when homing in on the narratives of men who have been victimized by violence in childhood, and who then commit violence on-road and in gangs in adolescence. Young men in this position have to navigate a range of marginality, including racial stereotyping, poverty and assumptions about their masculinity. All of this compounds to make them very unlikely to be considered as victims of abuse and crime themselves, but rather perpetrators, offenders and potentially dangerous individuals.

Childhood domestic abuse victimization

Being a direct victim of DVA as a child who experiences it among adults in the home has only just become recognized with the passing of the Domestic Abuse Bill (Home Office, 2020). Prior to this point, children who lived with DVA were seen as on the periphery – exposed to abuse, but not directly victimized. However, they were regarded as experiencing a form of emotional and psychological maltreatment, related to Section 31 of the Children Act 1989: impairment suffered from seeing or hearing the ill treatment of another (LSCB, 2016, l. 28.4.2). Thus, 'seeing or overhearing violence to another person in the home is recognised by law as potentially detrimental to children's welfare' (Radford et al, 2011, p 9). DVA is a complex issue within families as its presence can overlap with a range of other social issues such as substance abuse and mental ill health (Stanley and Humphreys, 2014, p 78). Despite this, children are still witnessing DVA in silence. In a SafeLives study of victims who accessed DVA support services, they found that only half (54 per cent) of the children who were or had been exposed to DVA, and only two thirds (63 per cent) of those exposed to severe DVA, were known to children's social care prior to intake to the specialist children's service (Jones, 2016, p 36).

Research has shown that children are more likely to be abused or neglected in homes where DVA is happening. One study found 34.4 per cent of under-18s who had lived with DVA had been abused or neglected, in comparison with 7 per cent of the general child population (Radford et al, 2011, p 101). Another found a 50 per cent correlation between perpetration of direct child abuse within the same families (NHS Barking and Dagenham, 2016). Thus, DVA cannot be seen as an isolated problem for children where it is occurring. In Mullender et al's (2002) research into children who witness DVA they concluded that the process had 'moved us on from seeing DVA as primarily a child protection issue to seeing it as an educational, health, welfare, civil and criminal justice issue of some complexity' (2002, p 206). This displays the far-reaching nature of the issue within a home environment.

Children who have experienced DVA have been historically overlooked and seen as the add-on to the primary victim, the non-abusing parent. Research has looked to centre the experiences of children who experience DVA and highlight the impact that it has on them (McGee, 2000; Mullender et al, 2002) as well as work into the impact on adult survivors of DVA (Hague, Harvey and Willis, 2012). In recent years there has been a shift in discourse around children, moving from framing them as 'exposed' or 'witnesses' to the DVA, and instead framing them as 'experiencing' the DVA (Överlien and Hydén, 2009; Callaghan et al, 2015). Boys who have experienced DVA have occupied a space of tension within feminist organizing around DVA. In the early days of the second-wave feminist movement, boys were seen as peripheral to the women-focused nature of the movement and its related interventions. This was reflected in the provision of 'women-only spaces' as well as the enduring age limit on refuge provision for sons of DVA survivors (Levell, 2020). This relative invisibility of boys who experience DVA in childhood begs the question, how do boys who live with male violence in childhood navigate emerging manhood in adolescence? For some young people this coincides with a period of on-road and/or gang involvement. In fact, the Children's Commissioner for England (2019) report found that children who were in gangs were 37 per cent more likely to have experienced childhood domestic violence and abuse than other children. In general, there is an awareness of the co-existence of DVA and offending behaviour.

The mix of race, gender and class among men labelled as 'gang-involved'

The external labelling of men assumed to be in gangs is a highly racialized affair in the UK. Since the riots in England in 2011 the Metropolitan Police have been collecting data on young people who are seen to be gang-involved, often despite no evidence or offending, through the gang matrix (Williams, 2015). Amnesty International released a report on this in 2018, claiming that the matrix is a highly racialized process that infringes on the individual's human rights, in particular the right to non-discrimination (Amnesty International, 2018). They noted that it was based on a 'vague and ill-defined concept of "the gang" that has little objective meaning and is applied inconsistently' (Amnesty International, 2018, p 3). This leads back to the overall discussion that is reflected in academic discourse around gangs. Amnesty noted that many of the indicators that the police use to define a gang member reflect more about urban youth culture rather than indication of serious crime. In fact, '78 per cent of individuals on the Gangs Matrix are black, a number which is disproportionate both to the black population of London (13 per cent of the whole) and the percentage of black people among those identified by the police as responsible for serious youth violence in London (27 per cent)' (Amnesty International, 2018, p 3). This disproportionality means that many young people that are on the matrix have not committed a violent offence in the last two years (40 per cent) and some have never committed a serious offence at all (35 per cent). In addition to the gang matrix, there is also evidence of racial bias in the police's use of stop-and-search. In the most recent statistics, there were six stop-and-searches for every 1,000 white people, compared with 54 for every 1,000 black people in the UK (Home Office, 2021). These statistics are not only a reflection of the intersections of race and ethnicity, but also of class, as there is a correlation between the young people identified on the gang's matrix and the most deprived areas. Masculinities are produced from the available cultural resources, 'which includes ideologies, social structures, and boys' and men's particular experiences and social positions' (Phoenix, 1994, p 146).

In the case of black boys this cultural resource includes a significant amount of cultural baggage that associates black masculinities with a range of largely negative associations. These stereotypes endure and are not helped by the way that black males are 'viewed by the dominant society as victimisers' resulting in them becoming 'victims of persistent poverty and racial discrimination in a self-fulfilling cycle deprivation, denied opportunities, and deviant behaviour' (Gibbs and Merighi, 1994, p 64). Therein lies the origin of the reactionary, 'culturalist, blaming-the-victim perspective that is clearly discernible in the media accounts of "the Asian Gang", and also in the account of black masculinity' (Alexander, 2000, p 19). The expectations of embodied masculinity are altered for black men in UK society. As noted by Edley and Wetherell (1995) racism is not just a cultural experience but is also a 'material phenomenon' (p 110). They noted that 'consciousness of masculinity reflects men's material circumstances', thus racial differences directly affect gender experiences (Edley and Wetherell, 1995, p 110). The characterization of black masculinity has been shaped in a context of a range of racist practices. Jefferson noted, in the American context, that the combination of a societal history of slavery and lynching, discrimination and the civil rights movement created a situation where black men were worn down by 'the effects of both restricted opportunities and internalization' (Jefferson, 1998, p 86). This left a legacy that meant that there has become a prevalent stereotype of black young men as 'the "Buck" … the black man as sexual, virile, strong, tough, and dangerous' (Jefferson, 1998, p 86). This so-called 'black macho' is typified in gang warfare, rap music and prominent black sports stars, labelled the 'black-aesthetic commodity' (Singh, cited in Jefferson, 1998, p 86). There is still a racist paradox present in the way that society encourages the 'black macho' ideal. Flores asserted that 'Gangs are rooted in masculine resistance to institutionalized racism' (Flores, 2016, p 591). Glynn noted that 'the narrative space black men do occupy is enabled by a system that supports and encourages notions of hyper-masculinity, and then criminalises it for asserting that position' (Glynn, 2014, p 25). The gang context typifies this contradiction, illustrated in part by the capitalist appropriation of forms of gang culture (particularly clothing brands and in the music industry), which are then sold as urban street culture products despite the criminalization of men who are at the heart of it.

There is a class bias inherent in who is classified as belonging to a gang. Young people who congregate in disadvantaged areas are more likely to have their behaviours criminalized because their areas are more heavily policed (Hine, 2010). The historic definition of the term gang has been said to be 'veiled expressions of bourgeois disapproval' (Ball and Curry, 1995, p 227).

Young people in poor urban areas are more likely to be labelled in this way and this has a direct implication with issues of 'race'. Black youth style and cultures have long been stereotyped as occupying a negative space in popular culture. Where it has presented, black youth style has 'been positioned as defensive, negative and oppositional, with an emphasis on authenticity and exclusion' (Alexander, 2000, p 19). Thus, it is somewhat unsurprising that, firstly, the activities of young black boys are perceived as problematic, and, secondly, if a gang subculture exists then it is perceived as dangerous. This is not to say that it is only black boys who are implicated in the gang's discourse. There has been increasing public concern at working-class white boys too (Jefferson, 1994). Some theorists have downplayed the impact that race has on gang membership, rather attributing it to the demographics of the local area (Pitts, 2008; Harding, 2014). However, Gunter urges theorists to look at the 'ethnic penalty' and focus on why there are disproportionate numbers of young black men in gangs and in prison (2017, p 136). He emphasizes the difficult task of highlighting this, while avoiding essentializing the experience of young black men and reducing their experiences to macro-structural constraints (2017).

The intersection of race and gender has been explored by Vron Ware (2015), who asserted that both gender and race are socially constructed in relation to one another. Due to this, it is imperative to explore the meanings behind these constructions; for example, she insists 'It is not about being a white woman, it is about being *thought of* as a white woman' (Ware, 2015, p xviii). This has been also highlighted in the case of black masculinity, which has been constructed out of an amalgam of white people's fears and projections, which rarely contain truth about black men's existence (Henry, 2013). Masculinity needs to be examined through the lens of sexism as well as racism, classism and other forms of oppression (Chen, 2012). In Glynn's study of masculinities among black men involved on-road, he urged for an intersectional lens to be applied in order to understand the ways in which race, class and gender intersect and change the social realities for the young men. He noted that traditionally, race, class and gender have been separated in criminological research and that 'as race is socially constructed, it seems to be a stronger proposition to expand racialisation, which involved an intersection of class and gender' (Glynn, 2014, p 19).

Marginalized masculinity on-road

Despite masculinity being historically essentialized as being present in males (designated by sex), there exists a hierarchy of masculinities. '"Boys will be boys" differently, depending upon their position in social structures and, therefore, upon their access to power and resources' (Messerschmidt, 1994, p 82). Connell (2000) has argued that masculinities are defined in relation to each other as well as in relation to femininities. If this is the case, then how men view women will form a key aspect of their personal gender construction efforts. All forms of masculinities have been constructed in contrast with a feminine other, with those that are positioned at the bottom of the masculine hierarchy somehow symbolically assimilated to femininity (Swain, 2005, p 221). One discourse around masculine capital lies in a heterosexual assumption. Masculine performativity ('looking hard') has been 'structured around the avoidance of "being seen" as that which is the apotheosis of the "not masculine": being, that is, "homosexual", being "womanly" (being a girl, a "puff", a "fag" and so forth, the routine and pervasive derogations of hetero-masculine culture)' (Collier, 1998, p 77). The concept of a hierarchy of masculinities originated from homosexual men's experiences of abuse, violence and prejudice from straight men. Thus, the emphasis is on the performativity of hegemonic masculinity as a polar opposite to feminine self-presentation. The masculine hierarchy is related to the amount of 'masculine capital' that the performance earns. Indeed, the deconstruction of the monolithic term 'masculinity' and its replacement with understanding of 'masculinities' was largely down to the advancement of the gay liberation movement. It was men in this movement who 'developed a sophisticated analysis of the oppression of men as well as oppression by men' (Connell and Messerschmidt, 2005, p 831).

Within the concept of the hierarchy of masculinities the importance of the local context has been emphasized as important. Structured relations among various local masculinities exist in context, so there is not one formalized presentation of hegemonic masculinity, but rather localized variations. One variation of masculinity that has said to occur within working-class or ethnically marginalized male communities is 'protest masculinity', which 'embodies the claim to power typical of regional hegemonic masculinities in Western countries, but which lacks the economic resources and institutional authority that underpins the regional and global patterns' (Connell and Messerschmidt, 2005, p 847). A key problem with these as markers of masculine capital is that attainment of these becomes 'refracted in the prism of street life' when contextualized in heavily disadvantaged communities (Mullins, 2006, p 75). When situated in a society that values wealth and power as measures of hegemonic masculine success, minority males with limited access to resources can face nearly insurmountable barriers to such success through the traditional routes of financial success, independence and as the patriarch in a nuclear family (Gibbs and Merighi, 1994).

In a gang context, where much of the traditional masculine capital was unavailable, there is often the development of a 'street masculinity' that is 'derived more from the capital available to them (potential and real violence), as well as from participation in the underground economy that provided the financial resources crucial for masculinity performances' (Mullins, 2006, p 75). Similar conclusions have been drawn by Harding (2014) who found that the gang context offered a fitting place to 'do masculinity' in a way that transcends race and class boundaries. This discourse around gang membership as a tool for heightening masculinity capital for young men who have few other means to do so is a reoccurring theme in much gang literature. Pitts (2008) locates an element of this is in the difficult socioeconomic conditions of poorer communities, which produce, 'socio-economically induced gender insecurity', which plays into the idea that financial constraints deny poor men the opportunity to enact masculinity in traditional ways. Phillips noted that those boys who are most likely to be 'bad' and 'kicking against authority' are those 'who recognize early on that society does not provide for them a place in which they can legitimately exhibit their power' (1993, p 28). What we can see here is that it is essential to explore the interlocking oppressions of race, class and gender in order to understand why protest masculinity develops among marginalized men. When the dominant messages of successful hegemonic masculinity in a patriarchal society are unobtainable, some young people react against it and engage in protest masculinity. In this context it is also pertinent to consider how this is compounded by the masculinity messages young people who live with patriarchal violence in the form of DVA grow up with.

In gang-affected communities, the gang structure often becomes institution-like, functioning through generations and 'compounding ontologically "what it means to be a successful man", and crucially how to achieve that "success"' (Baird, 2012, p 185). By looking at the pursuit of gang masculinity as part of gendered ways that society reproduces culture, Baird is placing gender performance as central to the gang issue. Baird asserted that the key to promoting desistance among young men is to offer contexts for them to achieve 'dignified masculine livelihoods' in a context of social exclusion (Baird, 2012, p 187). The links between masculinity and crime have been stated in prior research.

Messerschmidt (1994) theorized that different crimes are utilized by different men in the construction of masculinities. Partaking in crime can also perform a protective function for involved young people and offer hidden benefits. For instance, a young person's peer group may provide them with a net of support that they lack elsewhere (Hine, 2010).

In the context of looking at gang masculinity, various authors have provided different explanations for the way in which men in gangs are somehow doing gender, using the gang as an instrumental context for masculinity achievements. Harding (2014) used the lens of Bourdieu's concept of social capital and social fields to construct the street as a place that offers 'fields of possibilities' through which gender can be achieved, particularly for poor men who may not be able to achieve this masculinity status otherwise. Harding argued that the gang context offered an opportunity for its members to 'do masculinity', through enacting physical violence and material gang via drug dealing. These provide a context where 'the very worst aspects of hegemonic masculinity often become reinforced' (Deuchar, 2018, p 23).

Uncomfortable labels: victims, perpetrators, children, offenders

Being a young man who is on-road or assumed to be gang-involved can result in intersectional discrimination that feeds on stereotypes of racism, classism and sexism. Young boys in this position are further marginalized and labelled through the Criminal Justice System's racist practices. Although there is emerging evidence that many gang-involved young people are also experiencing DVA, they do not sit comfortably constructed as victims, but rather as victimizers. Central to the tension among boys who both experience DVA as well as perpetrate violence in the on-road and gang context is the notion of the *ideal victim* (Christie, 1986). Work within the DVA practice community is predominantly approached from feminist activist perspectives and in this context, the children who live with DVA are considered as victims or 'survivors' (Callaghan et al, 2015). Whereas work with on-road and/or gang-involved young people is located within the criminal justice risk management perspective, which places young people in the position of criminals, offenders or 'at risk'. The conceptualization of young people, which is expressed through language, is significant in the construction of the victims and perpetrators in these cases. The 'ideal victim' role is gendered, classed and racialized (Schwöbel-Patel, 2018). The ideal victim is positioned as female, weak, respectable, small and targeted by a stranger (Christie, 1986). Considering this notion of an ideal victim makes it clearer as to why men in gangs who experienced childhood abuse and adversity are more often constructed as offenders primarily over being victims themselves. As discussed earlier, young black men are more likely to be at the centre of moral panics around youth in crisis than framed as victims. To add complexity to this discussion, what it means to be a 'survivor' is constructed differently between the DVA and gang sectors and is also gendered.

An issue for front-line policy work on DVA and gangs is that the external categorization of young people promotes a one-dimensional view of them and their behaviours. As Yates usefully noted, 'the "young offender" could just as readily be conceptualised as the "child in need" if child welfare assessments and provisions of the Children's Act 1989 were applied' (2010, p 14). This is particularly important since many gang-involved individuals are children, who if positioned *as children* would traditionally be seen as vulnerable and in need of wider societal safeguarding (Motzkau, 2020). In gang discourse this rhetoric is often absent when referring to the problematic behaviours of the young people involved, as here they are positioned as offenders rather than children.

Gadd et al researched young men who had experienced DVA as either victims, perpetrators or both. They highlighted that caution should be taken between the polarized concepts of children, either as 'done-to victims' or 'brave survivors' (Gadd et al, 2015, p 118). This was explored through the in-depth examination of the men's narratives, which showed how close many men are to occupying both roles, almost simultaneously. Gadd et al urge others to 'avoid constructing children's responses to exposure to domestic violence too narrowly, either as negative psychological effects or as positive acts of resilience with little ambiguity in-between' (2015, p 126). They highlight how pertinent this is with the intersecting issue of gender. Gadd and colleagues urge academics to look at the nuanced area between the opposites of victim and perpetrator, and agency and victimization.

Conclusion

Currently, both academic and professional foci on DVA and gangs work operate within distinct professional sectors or 'planets' (Hester, 2011), each with distinct language, assumptions about the young people involved and culture. Work within the DVA community is predominantly pursued from feminist activist perspectives and in this context the children who witness DVA (particularly girls) are traditionally considered as victims or survivors. Whereas work with gang-/on-road-involved young people is located within the criminal justice risk management perspective, which places young people in the position of criminals, offenders or 'at risk' of harm to themselves or to others. The third related professional sector is statutory child protection, which is dominated by discourses that position children as passive and requiring state assistance related to family care deficiencies, but only those who meet high thresholds. Children can be involved with these different sectors concurrently, but their silo existence within professional discourse and academic literature limits connections between them.

So how do we get past these limiting labels such as victim, perpetrator, gang-involved and child in need? How do we recognize in criminological research that these are often the same individuals who are classified differently depending on which service shines a light on their experiences (child protection versus youth offending teams, for instance)? As discussed in this chapter, individual identities are much more than a sum of their parts. Lives are gendered, racialized, classed, and how young men navigate their positions is a complex pathway of navigating their available resources. Using intersectionality as a lens enabled a deeper exploration of the ways in which race, ethnicity and class changed and shaped the men's experiences. The intersections of race and ethnicity are important to understand, as they have great impact on the lives of men on-road and gang-involved. This is due to the highly racialized portrayal of gangs in the media and a targeted (and racially discriminate) police response (Williams, 2015). Men who are on-road and gang-involved are impacted by the structural inequalities and interlocking oppressions that surround the association of masculine criminality.

Young men who experience both DVA in childhood and on-road or gang involvement can occupy an invisible space between victim and perpetrator/ child in need and young offender discourse. They did not fit the 'ideal victim' typology and thus outlets for them to claim this identity have been limited. The concept of the ideal victim is often feminized and infantilized in a way that excludes young, marginalized men, especially those who enact violence and criminality from a young age. Language matters. It is important to consider the predominant labels that are used with young people who may experience both childhood adversity as well as criminality. Children may simultaneously be both victims and perpetrators of differing forms of harm. Using an intersectional perspective enables us to focus on the *interlocking oppressions* that limit their abilities to help seek as well as to recognize their own experiences of victimization.

References

Alexander, C.E. (2000) *The Asian Gang: Ethnicity, Identity, Masculinity*. Oxford: Berg.

Amnesty International (2018) *Trapped in the Matrix: Secrecy, Stigma, and Bias in the Met's Gangs Database* [online] www.amnesty.org.uk/gangs

Baird, A. (2012) 'The violent gang and the construction of masculinity amongst socially excluded young men', *Safer Communities*, 11(4): 179–90. DOI: 10.1108/17578041211271445.

Ball, R.A. and Curry, G.D. (1995) 'The logic of definition in criminology: purposes and methods for defining "gangs"', *Criminology*, 33(1): 225–45.

Bernard, A. (2013) 'The intersectional alternative: explaining female criminality', *Feminist Criminology*, 8(1): 3–19. https://doi.org/10.1177/1557085112445304

Bograd, M. (2005) Strengthening domestic violence theories: intersections of race, class, sexual orientation, and gender. In N.J. Sokoloff (ed), *Domestic Violence at the Margins: Readings on Race, Class, Gender, and Culture*, London: Rutgers University Press, pp 25–38.

Brah, A. and Phoenix, A. (2004) 'Ain't I a woman? Revisiting intersectionality', *Journal of International Women's Studies*, 5(3): 75–86.

Callaghan, J.E.M., Alexander, J.H., Sixsmith, J. and Fellin, L.C. (2015) Beyond "Witnessing"', *Journal of Interpersonal Violence*, https://doi.org/10.1177/0886260515618946

Chen, E.J. (2012) Caught in a bad bromance. *Texas Journal of Women and the Law*, 21.

Children's Commissioner (2019) Keeping kids safe. [online] www.childrenscommissioner.gov.uk/report/keeping-kids-safe/

Christie, N. (1986) 'The ideal victim', in E.A. Fattah (ed) *Crime Policy to Victim Policy*, London: Palgrave Macmillan.

Collier, R. (1998) *Masculinities, Crime and Criminology*, Thousand Oaks, CA: SAGE Publications Ltd.

Collins, P.H. (2000) *Black Feminist Thought: Knowledge, Consciousness, and the Politics of Empowerment*, 2nd Ed., London: Routledge.

Connell, R.W. (2000) *The men and the boys*, Cambridge: Polity Press.

Connell, R.W. and Messerschmidt, J.W. (2005) 'Hegemonic masculinity: rethinking the concept', *Gender & Society*, 19(6): 829–59. DOI: 10.1177/0891243205278639.

Dasgputa, S.D. (2005) 'Women's realities: defining violence against women by immigration, race and class', in N.J. Sokoloff (ed) *Domestic Violence at the Margins: Readings on Race, Class, Gender, and Culture*, London: Rutgers University Press, pp 56–70.

Deuchar, R. (2018) *Gangs and Spirituality: A Global Perspective*, London: Palgrave Macmillan.

Edley, N. and Wetherell, M. (1995) *Men in Perspective: Practice, Power and Identity*, Englewood, NJ: Prentice Hall/Harvester Wheatsheaf.

Flores, E. O. (2016) '"Grow your hair out": Chicano Gang masculinity and embodiment in recovery', *Social Problems*, 63(4): 590–604. DOI: 10.1093/socpro/spw017.

Gadd, D., Fox, C.L., Corr, M.-L., Alger, S. and Butler, I. (2015) *Young Men and Domestic Abuse*, Abingdon: Routledge.

Gibbs, J. T. and Merighi, J.R. (1994) 'Young Black males', in T. Newburn and E.A. Stanko (eds), *Just Boys Doing Business?*, London: Routledge, pp 64–80.

Glynn, M. (2014) *Black Men, Invisibility and Crime*, London: Routledge.

Grillo, T. (1995) 'Anti-essentialism and intersectionality: tools to dismantle the master's house', *Berkeley Women's Law Review*, 10: 16–30.

Gunter, A. (2017) *Race, Gangs and Youth Violence*, Bristol: Policy Press.

Hague, G., Harvey, A. and Willis, K. (2012) *Understanding Adult Survivors of Domestic Violence in Childhood: Still Forgotten, Still Hurting*. London: Jessica Kingsley Publishers.

Harding, S. (2014) *The Street Casino: Survival in Violent Street Gangs*, Bristol: Policy Press.

Hester, M. (2011) 'The three planet model: towards an understanding of contradictions in approaches to women and children's safety in contexts of domestic violence', *British Journal of Social Work*, 41(5): 837–53. DOI: 10.1093/bjsw/bcr095.

Henry, R.C. (2013) *Searching for the New Black Man.* Jackson, MS: University Press of Mississippi.

Hine, J. (2010) 'Young People's "voices" as evidence', in W. Taylor, R. Earle and R. Hester (eds), *Youth Justice Handbook*, 1st Ed., Cullompton: Willan Publishing, pp 168–78.

Home Office (2015) Statutory guidance framework: controlling or coercive behaviour in an intimate or family relationship. [online] www.gov.uk/government/publications/statutory-guidance-framework-controlling-or-coercive-behaviour-in-an-intimate-or-family-relationship

Home Office (2020) Domestic Abuse Bill 2020: overarching factsheet. [online] www.gov.uk/government/publications/domestic-abuse-bill-2020-factsheets/domestic-abuse-bill-2020-overarching-factsheet

Home Office (2021) Stop and search. [online] www.ethnicity-facts-figures.service.gov.uk/crime-justice-and-the-law/policing/stop-and-search/latest

Jefferson, T. (1994) 'Crime, criminology, masculinity and young men', in A. Coote (ed.), *Families, Children and Crime*, London: Institute for Public Policy Research, pp 72–84.

Jefferson, T. (1998) 'Muscle, "hard men" and "Iron" Mike Tyson: reflections on desire, anxiety and the embodiment of masculinity', *Body and Society*, 4(1): 77–98.

Jones, S.K. (2016) A cry for health: why we must invest in domestic abuse services in hospitals. [online] www.safelives.org.uk/node/945

Krane, D. and Davies, L. (2002) 'Sisterhood is not enough: the invisibility of mothering in shelter practice with battered women', *Affilia*, 17: 167–90.

Levell, J. (2020) 'Using Connell's masculinity theory to understand the way in which ex-gang-involved men coped with childhood domestic violence', *Journal of Gender-Based Violence*, 4(2): 207–21. https://doi.org/10.1332/239868020X15857301876812

LSCB (2016) 28. Safeguarding children affected by domestic abuse and violence, in *London Child Protection Procedures* (5th Ed.). [online] www.londoncp.co.uk/chapters/sg_ch_dom_abuse.html#introduction

Maynard, M. (2001) '"Race", gender and the concept of "Difference"', in K. Bhavnani (ed) *Feminism and Race*, Oxford: Oxford University Press, pp 121–33.

McGee, C. (2000) *Childhood Experiences of Domestic Violence*, London: Jessica Kingsley Publishers.

Messerschmidt, J.W. (1994) 'Schooling, masculinities, and youth crime by white boys' in T. Newburn and E.A. Stanko (eds), *Just Boys Doing Business? Men, Masculinities, and Crime*, London: Routledge, pp 81–99.

Motzkau, J. (2020) 'Children as victims', in D.T. Cook (ed) *The Sage Encyclopedia of Children and Childhood Studies*, Canada: Sage.

Mullender, A., Hague, G., Imam, U., Kelly, L., Malos, E. and Regan, L. (2002) *Children's Perspectives on Domestic Violence*, London: Sage.

Mullins, C.W. (2006) *Holding your Square: Masculinities, Streetlife and Violence*, Cullompton: Willan Publishing.

NHS Barking and Dagenham (2016) Domestic violence: a resource for health professionals. [online] www.domesticviolencelondon.nhs.uk/1-what-is-domestic-violence-/8-impact-upon-children.html

Överlien, C. and Hydén, M. (2009) 'Children's actions when experiencing domestic violence', *Childhood*, 16(4): 479–96. https://doi.org/10.1177/0907568209343757

Pearson, G. (2011) 'Perpetual novelty youth, modernity and historical amnesia', in B. Goldson (ed) *Youth in crisis?: 'Gangs', Territoriality and Violence*, Abingdon: Taylor & Francis, pp 20–37.

Phillips, A. (1993) *The Trouble with Boys: Parenting the Men of the Future*, London: HarperCollins.

Phipps, A. (2020) *Me Not You: The Trouble with Mainstream Feminism*, Manchester: Manchester University Press.

Phoenix, A. (1994) 'Practising feminist research: the intersection of gender and "race" in the research process', in M. Maynard and J. Purvis (eds), *Researching Women's Lives From A Feminist Perspective*, Abingdon: Taylor and Francis, pp 49–71.

Pitts, J. (2008). *Reluctant Gangsters: The Changing Face of Youth Crime*, Cullompton: Willan Publishing.

Radford, L., Aitken, R., Miller, P., Ellis, J., Roberts, J. and Firkic, A. (2011) Meeting the needs of children living with domestic violence in London, *Refuge/NSPCC research project* [online] www.refuge.org.uk/files/onlineDVLondon.pdf

Schwöbel-Patel, C. (2018) 'The "ideal" victim of international criminal law', *European Journal of International Law*, 29(3): 703–24. https://doi.org/10.1093/ejil/chy056

Sokoloff, N.J. and Dupont, I. (2005) 'Domestic violence: examining the intersections of race, class, and gender: an introduction', in N.J. Sokoloff (ed) *Domestic Violence at the Margins: Readings on Race, Class, Gender, and Culture*, London: Rutgers University Press, pp 1–13.

Stanley, N. and Humphreys, C. (2014) 'Multi-agency risk assessment and management for children and families experiencing domestic violence', *Children and Youth Services Review*, 47: 78–85. https://doi.org/10.1016/j.childyouth.2014.06.003

Stark, E. (2007) 'Introduction', in *Coercive Control*, Oxford: Oxford University Press, pp 17–47.

Swain, J. (2005) 'Masculinities in Education', in M.S. Kimmel, J. Hearn and R.W. Connell (eds), *Handbook of Studies on Men and Masculinities*, Thousand Oaks, CA: SAGE Publications Inc., pp 213–29.

Ware, V. (2015) *Beyond The Pale – White Women, Racism and History*, New York: Verso Books.

Williams, P. (2015) 'Criminalising the other: challenging the race-gang nexus', *Race and Class*, 56(3): 18–35. https://doi.org/10.1177/0306396814556221

Williams, K., Papadopoulou, V. and Booth, N. (2012) *Prisoners' Childhood and Family Backgrounds Results from the Surveying Prisoner Crime Reduction (SPCR) Longitudinal Cohort Study of Prisoners* (March) [online] www.gov.uk/government/publications/prisoners-childhood-and-family-backgrounds

Wing, A.K. (2003) *Critical Race Feminism*, New York and London: New York University Press.

Yates, J. (2010) 'Structural disadvantage: youth, class, crime and poverty', in W. Taylor, R. Earle and R. Hester (eds), *Youth Justice Handbook*, 1st Ed., Cullompton: Willan Publishing/The OUP, pp 5–22.

Young, T. (2016) *Risky Youth or Gang Members?: A Contextual Critique of the (Re)discovery of Gangs in Britain*, London: London Metropolitan University.

8

Intersectional Studies in Prisons Research: Prisons and Punishment in England and Wales

Saabirah Osman

Introduction

Prison is the most commonly used form of punishment in the UK (Cavadino et al, 2019; Prison Reform Trust, 2019). Lippman (2006) highlights the key debates around the primary goal of punishment, distinguishing between those who believe it should be to aid rehabilitation of those prosecuted, those who believe it should function to keep society safe by removing offenders away from the community or those who believe punishment should serve to compensate the victims of crime. With a specific focus on inmates in prison, this chapter explores the experiences of individuals based on intersecting power structures and documents whether individuals' experiences, with a particular focus on women, are currently accounted for within the penal system.

There are four common philosophies of punishment that sit within two justifications (Cavadino et al, 2019). The first, reductivism, is described as a forward-looking theory and justifies punishment as it is believed to help reduce crime; the philosophies that sit under this are deterrence, incapacitation and rehabilitation, also referred to as reform. Retributivism, on the other hand, looks back at the offender's previous actions, which includes retribution, also known as 'just desserts', and justifies punishment on the grounds that the offender deserves that punishment (Cavadino et al, 2019).

Punishment in the UK is predominately used to rehabilitate and/or incapacitate those found guilty of committing a crime, falling within the former justification. The role of prison in the UK is explained in its mission statement, which states that 'Her Majesty's Prison Service serves the public by keeping in custody those committed by the courts. Our duty is to look after them with humanity and help them lead law-abiding and useful lives in custody and after release' (Joyce, 2013, p 114). Rehabilitation or reform justifies punishment on the grounds that it can reduce the likeliness of reoffending, generally done through a rehabilitative approach or treatment model (Joyce, 2013), and this is the focus of this chapter.

The overall view of criminal behaviour from this perspective is that the individual who has engaged in it is not doing so through their own free will but has other contributing factors out of their control that have pushed them to such behaviours (Blevins, 2017). These contributing factors vary and may include mental health concerns, abusing illicit and/or licit substances and other psychological and sociological factors, such as socially learnt behaviour, environment and poverty, for example. In acknowledging this, the approach of rehabilitating these individuals does not suggest that they should go unpunished, but that punishment should consider a combination of both rehabilitation and either deterrence, incapacitation or retribution, which are equally implemented to avoid recidivism (Cavadino et al, 2019). Evidence through the practices of Nordic prisons supports this in that it has identified a need for these two philosophies of punishment to be implemented to have greater chances of successful outcomes for inmates, and that incarcerating individuals not only protects the victims and the public but also provides the time, space and opportunity to reform or rehabilitate the individual (Dahl and Mogstad, 2020).

Though the approach to rehabilitate individuals while incapacitated has proven to be successful in other parts of the world and in prisons in the UK who take a therapeutic approach, such as HMP Grendon and HMP Dovegate, taking this approach is complex. The current penal system in England and Wales continues to face obstacles, which have resulted in the system being described as in crisis for over a decade (Bennett and Jewkes, 2013). One issue that has negatively impacted the general prison population is the expansion of the penal system in England and Wales. Examples of these drivers include the privatization of prisons, the approach of being 'tough on crime' and the notion that prison works. Corporate Watch (2018) provides some insights on the drivers that push growth for prisons in England and Wales, arguing that state and media justifications on expanding prisons are grounded in arguments built around overcrowding, cost effectiveness, space to reduce violence, drug use and harm, and overall to offer an environment that is more humane. Given the focus on overcrowding, Corporate Watch (2018) propose that the answer is not to expand prisons when trying to address these issues but rather to avoid prison terms for petty or low-level crimes.

Other scholars present similar concerns and propose a review around the privatization of prisons and of its contractors (Shichor, 1995; Cavadino et al,

2019). Privately run prisons in England and Wales were first introduced in the 1990s and 14 continue to be managed by private companies such as G4S Justice Services, Serco and Sodexo Justice Services (HM Prison Service, 2019). This transition to privatization was initially seen to be a preferred alternative and mostly cost effective in providing extra prison places (Prison Reform Trust, 2005). Yet, Cavadino et al (2019) and Shichor (1995) explore the issues of privatizing prisons and argue that this has proven to be problematic, both historically and in current prison systems, which is often the result of the contractor's failures. Issues and risk factors involved in privatization include the potential of exploitation and mistreatment of inmates, corruption among the official agencies involved and lack of sufficient resources for inmates (Shichor, 1995; Cavadino et al, 2019; Politics.co.uk, nd). There continues to be clear evidence indicating that this shift or expansion to privatizing prisons can be very dangerous. Grierson and Duncan (2019) highlight that prisons that are run through private organizations have proven to be far more violent than institutes that are run by the government. Moreover, *The Guardian* (2019) suggests that privately run prisons have shown a rise in violence, self-harm, substance misuse, cell time and overcrowding. Evidently, these issues raise concerns and questions as to whether basic support or treatment is available for the general prison population, and this chapter recognizes that this becomes an even greater concern when considering the experiences of black, Asian and minority ethnic (BAME) people in prison, as highlighted in Brookes et al's (2012) work.

Intersectional identities and prison terms

The notion of being 'tough on crime' has been seen to disproportionately impact individuals who are from poorer backgrounds, women and BAME communities (Goodman and Ruggiero, 2008). Newburn (2016) suggests that there are contrasting penal practices, which generally result in a tougher impact for those experiencing social and economic inequalities. William et al (2013) demonstrate that those who were in prison had or continued to have experienced difficult living circumstances. These include experiences such as abuse within their homes, previously being in foster care, being homeless, exclusion from school, lack of educational qualifications, long-standing illnesses or disabilities, and unemployment.

Further evidence illustrates the disparities in experiences of prison, such as women being more likely to be prosecuted for low-level crime. The Ministry of Justice (2018) documented a considerable percentage of women who were largely prosecuted for crimes such as TV licence evasion, shoplifting and truancy. Moreover, in 2019 there was a higher prison proportion of female offenders who did not have previous convictions (35 per cent) compared with male offenders (22 per cent) who had a long criminal history (Ministry of Justice, 2020). Further statistics suggest prosecution rates were twice as high for black females than for white females (Prison Reform Trust, 2017; Ministry of Justice, 2018). Other findings suggest Asian women are more likely to plead not guilty than white women as they fear the stigma attached to this among their community, which in turn may result to longer sentencing when convicted (Prison Reform Trust, 2017). It is here that we can see the utility that intersectionality has to offer in shaping our understanding of how there is no universal experience of imprisonment and punishment.

While significant attention has been paid to a number of issues affecting prisons such as privatization, overcrowding and, more recently, the impact of cocooning in the context of COVID-19, scholarship has not fully engaged with adopting an intersectional perspective when addressing these concerns. In this chapter, race and gender are considered intersectionally, exploring some of the issues that have been identified in existing research, and demonstrating how an intersectional approach can enhance our understanding of the disproportionate impact that imprisonment has on those who occupy multiple marginalized positions.

Race, prisons and programmes

While various treatment methods in prison have shown some promising results, Shingler and Pope (2018) argue that the idea of therapeutic or rehabilitative approaches are predominantly concepts created by the white middle classes for the white middle class. This begs the question as to the effectiveness of current treatment approaches for marginalized groups. This becomes a larger concern considering the disproportionate number of BAME people in prison. The latest statistics have shown that BAME individuals represent over a quarter of the prison population, at 22,227 inmates – a significantly disproportional number as, if the prison population reflected the general population in England and Wales, there would be 9,000 fewer BAME people in prison (Prison Reform Trust, 2019).

Studies have also highlighted the lack of cultural awareness when incorporating treatment for BAME people in prison. It has previously been reported that many BAME male inmates fear losing their cultural practices and the support they would receive among their community in prison as a result of taking part in treatment programmes (Patel and Lord, 2001; Brookes et al, 2012). Brookes et al (2012) explored the experiences of black men in therapeutic environments. They found that black male inmates often felt they were suppressing their cultural and racialized identities, which included individual practices and language/s, as they feared being misunderstood or stereotyped. This resulted in these individuals feeling disempowered, reporting that their voices were being erased. Other research presents narratives from inmates who stated that they felt a sense of "blackness being 'invisible' in prison"; this invisibility refers to the lack of cultural elements such as food, literature and black staff (Shingler and Pope, 2018, p 16). Sullivan et al (2007) also identify this element of cultural absence within prisons, again resulting in BAME people describing feeling erased, unable to integrate or take part in activities and feeling disempowered. Furthermore, a study by Cowburn et al (2008) on sex offenders in prisons also identified a failure to recognize and understand cultural aspects that may result in a lack of engagement from BAME people, which suggests a lack of cultural awareness in training and facilitation methods.

This sense of erasure may be exacerbated for ethnic minority women in prison who feel 'invisible' as a result of both race and gender combined. Shingler and Pope (2018) stress the importance of maintaining individuals' cultural identities and they argue that treatment methods within prisons should provide relevant cultural activities that will mean a greater chance of BAME people taking part in therapy and as a result achieve the ultimate goal of preventing further recidivism. Given that women are the minority within the prison estate, BAME women may therefore experience a double marginalization, in which their needs are overlooked.

It has been suggested that the current treatment approach in British prisons is taking progressive steps, as programmes seek to minimize harm and offer opportunity for personal growth and development to inmates, as practised in therapeutic prisons like HMP Grendon (Bennet and Shuker, 2017). However, this is often not the experience of inmates who belong to minority groups. The United Nations provide guidance for practice and state in the 'Basic Principles for the Treatment of Prisoners' that 'there shall be no discrimination on the grounds of race, colour, sex, language, religion, political or other opinions, national or social origin, property, birth or other status' (OHCHR, 1990). As highlighted in previous research (Cowburn et al, 2008; Shingler and Pope, 2018), UK prisons often fail to acknowledge and cater to individuals' specific identities and therefore can be seen to be discriminatory to individual needs. Indeed, the UN's guidance reflects a focus on individual identities and does not conclusively consider a combination of intersectional concerns. This chapter recommends that reflection on the language and phrasing of these 'basic principles' is warranted, to explicitly acknowledge the increased risk for those in multiple minority groups.

Recent research provides additional insight into BAME people's experiences in prison as well as the obstacles and mistreatments they face daily. Chistyakova et al (2018) present narratives from BAME and foreign national prisoners in a prison located in the north of England. This research, in a Category B male prison, assessed whether the specific needs of BAME prisoners were being met post-Equality Act (2010). Findings highlighted that all BAME participants felt intimidated, and emotionally and/or physically vulnerable, and they spoke about their constant experiences of being victims of racism while in prison. For example, a participant stated that there were racist slurs written on the prison's walls that read 'All Pakis should be killed. All blacks should be killed' (Chistyakova et al, 2018, p 5).

Research on Muslim and traveller prisoners reported that they felt they were being treated with less respect than white British prisoners; both groups mentioned similar concerns, such as having no prison officer that represented their community or group, and a sense that their cultural and/or religious needs and practices were neglected in prison (Chistyakova et al, 2018). This evidence provides insights into foreign nationals' experiences while in prisons and documents the vulnerabilities and ill treatment they experience. The authors present a list of problematic factors, including being held in prison for longer than their sentences, ignorance around mental health issues, lack of understanding of prisoners' language and limited contact with families (Chistyakova et al, 2018). A worrying discovery is that prison staff did not view racist behaviour among inmates to be a concern, in contrast with BAME inmates' perspectives (Chistyakova et al, 2018). This differing perception by the officers and experience in behaviours among the inmates can be problematic, as it suggests that the staff may be ignorant of such behaviours/attitudes (which may mirror their own).

To expand further on this point, previous scholarly work has shown that an individual's knowledge generally stems from their social positioning (Harding, 2004), which might explain why such behaviours within prisons may not be seen as problematic or addressed at all by prison officers. By drawing upon standpoint theory and its relevance and importance in the functionality of prisons, Du Bois (1999) presents an argument for democracy and concludes 'only the sufferer knows his suffering' (p 83). This suggests that only those who have experienced prison can properly identify with it, and understand those who are incarcerated, and in the case where prison officers are unable to identify racist behaviour among inmates this may indicate that staff are perhaps unable to identify with the experiences of inmates as they have not suffered similarly (Smith, 2017). Considering the proportion of prison staff in the UK who identify as BAME, The Lammy Review (2017) reported that around 6 per cent of prison staff identified as BAME, though a more recent government report suggests a slight growth in 2020 where there were 7.7 per cent BAME prison staff in public sector prisons (Gov.uk, 2021). These figures may explain why racist behaviour and general mistreatment of BAME inmates often goes unseen by staff, as the majority of the prison staff population (over 90 per cent) are white and therefore may fail to recognize the mistreatment of those inmates who are not white. This may further be exacerbated for ethnic minority women in prison, who may experience oppression, discrimination and abuse along lines of race, gender and religion.

Gender and prisons

The numbers of women in UK prisons have grown substantially since 1993 (Prison Reform Trust, 2019b), and while it is evidenced that women are generally the minority within all prisons, recent research highlights an overwhelming rise in numbers, with reports that the statistics of women in prison in England and Wales have increased by over 200 per cent since the turn of the century (van den Bergh et al, 2011). Despite this rise, women continue to be in the minority of prisoners, which may contribute to their relative 'invisibility' and lack of gender-specific approaches to treatment. It is also important to highlight that BAME women make up 11.9 per cent of the female population in England and Wales but occupy a higher percentage within prisons, with statistics showing a population growth of BAME women in prison from around 12 per cent in 2011 to over 18 per cent in 2016 (Prison Reform Trust, 2017). Comparing this with the ratio of prison staff has proven to be difficult due to a lack of available data (Prison Reform Trust, 2017). The Ministry of Justice (2016) documents that in 2016 Her Majesty's Prison and Probation Services (HMPPS) consisted of 32,835 staff in public sector prisons, and women accounted for 46.8 per cent (21,492) of staff in National Offender Management Services (NOMS, now known as HMPPS). It is important to highlight that HMPPS also includes additional penal establishments outside of the prison, such as the probation services, so in this case it is difficult to identify clearly how many female staff work within women's prisons as officers.

BAME women often fear experiencing stigma from their communities and therefore are more likely to plead not guilty, which could result in harsher sentencing if found to be guilty (Prison Reform Trust, 2017). Furthermore, BAME women continue to face disadvantages within the Criminal Justice System, where they are more likely to be imprisoned for a first and/or non-violent offence/s compared with men. The Lammy Review (2017) documents disparities between women of different ethnic backgrounds and highlights how black women are more likely to be tried at the Crown Court than white women. Statistics from 2014/15 show that for those who were charged, there were 163 black women tried at the Crown Court for every 100 white women. Further findings suggest black women are 29 per cent more likely to be remanded in custody at Crown Court and if convicted, black women are 25 per cent more likely to be given a custodial sentence (Criminal Justice Alliance, 2021). This demonstrates the disproportionate criminal justice responses to black women.

The Prison Reform Trust (2017) suggest that while criminal justice agencies continue to attempt to take progressive steps to eliminate discrimination, when doing so there is often a lack of acknowledgement or understanding that the disadvantages women experience in the Criminal

Justice System are multi-layered, especially for women who are from BAME communities. In addition to this, with the efforts to eradicate discrimination there is often the tendency to look to white women when discussing gender inequalities and black men when exploring racial disparities (Prison Reform Trust, 2017), failing to consider an intersectional lens. Hull et al's (1982) publication, titled 'All women are white, all the blacks are men, but some of us are brave', constructs women as white and the black population as male, and can be seen in the treatment of black women within the Criminal Justice System, as well as wider society generally.

The Prison Reform Trust (2017) outline some of the specific circumstances of many women in prison and state that women are more likely to be the primary carers of children, which can have severe repercussions for both the children and the mothers. Corston (2007) noted that around 18,000 children are separated from their mothers each year as a result of imprisonment, which can have catastrophic consequences for children and families. Other research in the gendered experiences in prison (van den Bergh et al, 2011; van Hout et al, 2020) exposed the treatment of women in prison, specifically their health, the lack of gender sensitivity and human rights, arguing that women inmates' health needs are often neglected. These include reproductive health issues, mental health problems, drug misuse, histories of violence and abuse, and the women were often from marginalized and disadvantaged backgrounds.

It must be recognized that, structurally, prisons are generally designed and run to cater for male inmates; therefore, it is unrealistic to expect women to be able to cope or, at best, to rehabilitate and become reformed characters in such circumstances (van den Bergh et al, 2011). While van den Bergh et al (2011) present imperative findings, it is important to recognize that they did not consider women's differing experiences based on intersectional identities in great depth. Their work focused predominantly on women's health and identified issues that often impact women more than men when in prison, such as self-harm. Given the issues of cultural awareness discussed earlier in the chapter, an intersectional approach provides a more nuanced insight into the needs and experiences of BAME women in prison; without taking this approach, any resulting response to women's experiences risks disregarding and silencing those who can be described as most vulnerable, which leaves them to continue to suffer both within prisons and the wider practices and institutes within the Criminal Justice System.

Labhart and Wright (2018) further support this by presenting figures that suggest almost 50 per cent of female inmates need support with mental health compared with under 20 per cent for men. In 2019, it was reported that for every 1,000 prisoners, there were 335 females and 148 males that self-harmed (Ministry of Justice, 2020. Once again, a breakdown of individuals' demographic information is not documented, resulting in a simplistic and one-dimensional presentation of women who self-harm. Given that BAME women's experiences are different to white women, these experiences could further explain the strains, stigmas and disadvantages the population face, which could result in self-harming and which may disproportionally impact BAME women. By applying an intersectional approach to this data, the evidence underlines significant differences and justifies the importance of recording individual women's demographic information. To understand the experiences of BAME women, more data on their experiences must be gathered, or risk essentially ignoring their experiences or applying a white-normative lens to them.

van den Bergh et al (2011) argue that female prisoners suffer far more than male prisoners from mental health problems, self-harming and attempting suicide; but, in addition to this, they also identify that women are more likely to have experienced physical or sexual abuse prior to imprisonment, have a dependency on illicit or licit substances and feelings of further isolation, and are unable to maintain or develop meaningful relationships with inmates and family and/or friends outside of prisons due to the high turnover rate of women in prisons and the distance between the prison and their home. Thus, when one also considers the lack of cultural awareness in prisons identified earlier, in combination with the considerable gender-based obstacles, BAME women who are in prison may therefore be more likely to experience a deterioration in mental health, self-harm or attempted suicide. Given the number of BAME women in prison, this suggests a substantial risk. Once again, taking an intersectional approach will allow researchers and practitioners to identify appropriate and effective measures, provisions and practices to be introduced for better support and treatment for this population.

Women in Prison (nd) proffer narratives from BAME women that suggest they often experienced racism and discrimination while in prison from both staff and other inmates, with comments suggesting their cultural and religious needs were also neglected. Further findings in regard to the mistreatment of BAME women in prison suggest their experiences are significantly worse than white female prisoners (HM Inspectorate of Prisons, 2009). BAME women in prison also reported that they were disliked and abandoned by their communities as a result of being sent to prison (Women in Prison, nd). This is concerning as it is already understood that women in prison are often victims of violent and serious crimes prior to imprisonment and become victims of exploitation within prisons and/or are suffering from anxiety or poor mental health (Labhart and Wright, 2018; Van Hout and Mhlanga-Gunda, 2018). Without the support of their communities or families, which is recognized as a protective factor in prisons (Shingler and Pope, 2018), this suggests that individual BAME women's mental health may deteriorate.

With these specific needs in mind, and reflecting on earlier discussions around the current state of the penal system in the UK, it is clear that women in prison may face additional, more impactful, gender-specific obstacles. Earlier, this chapter addressed some of the structural issues within the penal system including factors such as the crisis in the current penal system (Cavadino et al, 2019), the turn or expansion to privatization (Shichor, 1995; Cavadino et al, 2019) and overcrowding (Corporate Watch, 2018). All of these factors have resulted in negative outcomes such as the poor treatment and general negative experiences of inmates. As highlighted earlier, we look to white women and black men when exploring gendered and racial disparities (Prison Reform Trust, 2017). It is important to acknowledge that intersectional discrimination is experienced in the lives of all BAME women (Imkaan and Ascent, 2016); they face additional obstacles such as difficulty in seeking support as a victim of violence, are more likely to live in poverty and earn less than white women and BAME men (Barnard and Turner, 2011; Imkaan and Ascent, 2016; Fawcett Society, 2017).

Bosworth and Carrabine (2001) argue that while there is an over-representation of BAME people in prison, who are often guarded by white prison officers, this relationship between people of different ethnic backgrounds can often guide or shape the power hierarchy within the walls. However, they also propose that existing power hierarchies are not fixed along racialized lines, but also structured through an individual's class and geography, regardless of their race. This supports Bosworth's (1999) previous evidence that women in prison develop alliances with others who were from similar backgrounds, which includes their class and geographical area. Furthermore, Bosworth and Carrabine (2001) state that, while they wish not to minimize the experiences of individuals, they found that 'prisoners often draw on ideas and practices of race, gender and sexuality in their performances of self to create alternative meaning' (p 513), in attempts to resist institutional power and create their own spaces and empowerment among their fellow inmates.

Public Health England (2018) provides guidance for prisons to help make them more inclusive of individuals' religious or cultural practices, such as providing specific dietary requirements and improved professional awareness of cultural and religious practices that may impact on whether or not an individual takes part in health screening. While this document paints a picture of a progressive approach, it is important to acknowledge that there are external factors not yet considered; as mentioned earlier in this chapter, the expansion of prisons go hand in hand with economic development (Simon and Sparks, 2012; Corporate Watch, 2018). Providing such support proposed by Public Health England (2018) requires significant amounts of time, staff and money, all of which have the potential to lessen the capital produced through this system.

Conclusion

This chapter has demonstrated the poor treatment of inmates within prisons, with a specific focus on BAME women. There are multiple factors that may determine whether someone will be a victim of mistreatment while incarcerated, such as an individual's race, class, gender and sexuality. While significant research has been conducted that explores gender or race within the context of prison, intersectional approaches are lacking. As a result, the experiences of *BAME women* in prison are often overlooked within wider research, often treating them in isolation. However, considering both gender and race in combination, it becomes clear that BAME women experience additional obstacles to what white women and BAME men do. BAME women's specific experiences are often not documented by official agencies and this may be the result of too much focus on women's experiences generally rather than exploring gendered disparities. Therefore, reflecting upon an intersectional approach when exploring these issues is imperative. Intersectionality enables researchers to acknowledge the nuances of specific identify characteristics in interaction with each other, illustrating the unjust and unrecognized experiences of those who are most often marginalized.

The lack of criminological research within this field, specifically in the UK, is criticized by Cheliotis and Liebling (2006), who suggest this area has been surprisingly inert. This chapter therefore calls for further empirical work to be done that engages with intersectionality as a framework within UK prisons. This shift of engaging with intersectionality will allow policies and guidance to be better informed, potentially resulting in improved experiences of BAME women in prison and, ultimately, taking the right steps in rehabilitating and preventing recidivism or more harm for those individuals.

References

Barnard, H. and Turner, C. (2011) 'Poverty and ethnicity: a review of evidence', Joseph Rowntree Foundation. [online] www.jrf.org.uk/sites/default/files/jrf/migrated/files/poverty-ethnicity-evidence-summary.pdf

Beard, J. (2018) 'Transgender prisoners: briefing paper', House of Commons Library [online] https://researchbriefings.files.parliament.uk/documents/CBP-7420/CBP-7420.pdf

Bennett, J. and Jewkes, Y. (2013) *Dictionary of Prisons and Punishment*, Devon: William Publishing.

Bennett, J. and Shuker, R. (2017) 'The potential of prison-based democratic therapeutic communities', *International Journal of Prisoner Health*, 13(1): 19–24. https://doi.org/10.1108/IJPH-08-2016-0036

Bosworth, M. (1999) *Engendering Resistance: Agency and Power in Women's Prisons*, Aldershot: Ashgate.

Bosworth, M. and Carrabine, E. (2001) 'Reassessing resistance: race, gender and sexuality in prison', *Punishment & Society*, 3(4): 501–15. DOI: 10.1177/14624740122228393.

Blevins, K.R. (2017) 'Positivism', in A. Brisman, E. Carrabine, and N. South (eds) *The Routledge Companion to Criminological Theory and Concepts*, London: Routledge.

Brookes, M., Glynn, M. and Wilson, D. (2012) 'Black men, therapeutic communities and HMP Grendon', *Therapeutic Communities: The International Journal of Therapeutic Communities*, 33(1): 16–26.

Burnett, R. and Farrell, G. (1994) *Reported and Unreported Racial Incidents in Prisons*, Oxford: Centre for Criminological Research, University of Oxford.

Buncy, S. and Ahmed, I. (2014) *Muslim Women in Prison. Second Chance Fresh Horizons: A Study into the Needs and Experiences of Muslim Women at HMP & YOI New Hall & Askham Grange Prisons during Custody and Post-Release*, Bradford: HPCA and Khidmat Centres, [online] https://muslimhands.org.uk/_ui/uploads/kqe5a9/MWIP_Report.pdf

Cavadino, M., Dignan, J., Mair, G. and Bennett, J. (2019) *The Penal System: An Introduction*, London: Sage.

Cheliotis, L.K. and Liebling, A. (2006) 'Race matters in British prisons', *The British Journal of Criminology*, 46(2): 286–317.

Chistyakova, Y., Cole, B. and Johnstone, J. (2018) 'Diversity and vulnerability in prisons in the context of the Equality Act 2010: the experiences of Black, Asian, Minority Ethnic (BAME), and Foreign National Prisoners (FNPs) in a northern jail', *Prison Service Journal*, 235: 10–16.

Corporate Watch (2018) *Prison Island: Prison Expansion in England, Wales & Scotland*, London: Corporate Watch Co-operative Ltd.

Corston, J. (2007) *The Corston Report: A Review of Women with Particular Vulnerabilities in the Criminal Justice System*, London: Home Office.

Cowburn, M., Lavis, V. and Walker, T. (2008) 'BME sex offenders in prison: the problem of participation in offending behaviour groupwork programmes – a tripartite model of understanding', *British Journal of Community Justice*, 6(1): 19–34.

Crenshaw, K. (1989) 'Demarginalizing the intersection of race and sex: A black feminist critique of antidiscrimination doctrine, feminist theory and antiracist politics', *University of Chicago Legal Forum*, 1(8): 139–67.

Criminal Justice Alliance (2021) Coalition warns new policing and sentencing bill will deepen racial inequality, [online] www.criminaljusticealliance.org/blog/coalition-warns-new-policing-and-sentencing-bill-will-deepen-racial-inequality/

Dahl, G. and Mogstad, M. (2020) 'The benefits of rehabilitative ncarceration', National Bureau of Economic Research [online] www.nber.org/reporter/2020number1/benefits-rehabilitative-incarceration

Du Bois, W. (1999) *Darkwater: Voices from Within the Veil*, New York: Dover Publications.

Fair Play for Women (2018) 'How many transgender prisoners are there and where?' [online] https://fairplayforwomen.com/trans_prison_stats_2018/

Fawcett Society (2017) *Gender Pay Gap by Ethnicity in Britain – Briefing*, London: Fawcett Society.

Goodman, A. and Ruggiero, V. (2008) 'Crime, punishment, and ethnic minorities in England and Wales', *Race/Ethnicity: Multidisciplinary Global Contexts*, 2(1): 53–68.

Gov.uk (2021) *Prison Officer Workforce*. [online] www.ethnicity-facts-figures. service.gov.uk/workforce-and-business/workforce-diversity/prison-officer-workforce/latest

Grant, J.M., Mottet, L., Tanis, J.E., Harrison, J., Herman, J. and Keisling, M. (2011) 'Injustice at every turn: a report of the national transgender discrimination survey', [online] www.transequality.org/sites/default/files/docs/resources/NTDS_Report.pdf

Grierson, J. and Duncan, P. (2019) 'Private jails more violent than public ones, data analysis shows', *The Guardian*, [online] www.theguardian.com/society/2019/may/13/private-jails-more-violent-than-public-prisons-england-wales-data-analysis

The Guardian (2019) '*The Guardian view on private jails: flaws in the system: Editorial*', [online] www.theguardian.com/commentisfree/2019/may/13/the-guardian-view-on-private-jails-flaws-in-the-system

Harding, S. (2004) *The Feminist Standpoint Theory Reader*, New York: Routledge.

HM Government (2019) '*The care and management of individuals who are transgender*', [online] www.gov.uk/government/publications/the-care-and-management-of-individuals-who-are-transgender

HM Inspectorate of Prisons (2009) *HM Chief Inspector of Prisons for England and Wales Annual Report 2007–08*, London: The Stationery Office.

HM Prison Service (2019) 'Contracted-out prisons', [online] www.justice.gov.uk/about/hmps/contracted-out

Hull, G.T., Bell Scott, P. and Smith, B. (eds) (1982) *All the Women are White, all the Blacks are Men, but some of us are Brave*, New York: The Feminist Press.

Imkaan & Ascent (2016) *Safe Pathways? Exploring an Intersectional Approach to Addressing Violence against Women and Girls*, London: Imkaan & Ascent.

Joyce, P. (2013) *Criminal Justice: An Introduction*, 2nd Ed., London: Routledge.

Kleinig, J. (2016) *Prisoners' Rights*, London and New York: Routledge.

Kleinig, J. (ed) (2017) 'United Nations rules for the treatment of women prisoners and non-custodial measures for women offenders (the Bangkok rules)', in J. Kleinig (ed) *Prisoners' Rights*, London: Routledge, pp 435–57.

Labhart, J. and Wright, L. (2018) 'Why doesn't prison work for women?', [online] www.bbc.co.uk/news/uk-england-45627845

The Lammy Review (2017) '*The Lammy review: an independent review into the treatment of, and outcomes for, Black, Asian and Minority Ethnic individuals in the Criminal Justice System*', [online] https://assets.publishing.service.gov.uk/government/uploads/system/uploads/attachment_data/file/643001/lammy-review-final-report.pdf

Lippman, M. (2006) *Contemporary Criminal Law: Concepts, Cases, and Controversies*, London: Sage.

McAvinchey, C. (2011) *Theatre and Prison*, London: Red Globe Press.

Ministry of Justice (2016) 'National offender management service staff equalities annual report', [online] https://assets.publishing.service.gov.uk/government/uploads/system/uploads/attachment_data/file/571721/noms-staff-equalities-report.pdf

Ministry of Justice (2018) *Statistics on Women and the Criminal Justice System 2017: A Ministry of Justice Publication under Section 95 of the Criminal Justice Act 1991*, London: Ministry of Justice.

Ministry of Justice (2020) *Statistics on Women and the Criminal Justice System 2019: A Ministry of Justice Publication under Section 95 of the Criminal Justice Act 1991*, [online] https://assets.publishing.service.gov.uk/government/uploads/system/uploads/attachment_data/file/938360/statistics-on-women-and-the-criminal-justice-system-2019.pdf

Newburn, T. (2016) 'Social disadvantage, crime, and punishment', in H. Dean and L. Platt (eds) *Social Advantage and Disadvantage*, Oxford: Oxford University Press, pp 322–40.

OHCHR (1990) 'Basic principles for the treatment of prisoners', [online] www.ohchr.org/en/professionalinterest/pages/basicprinciplestreatmentofprisoners.aspx

Patel, K. and Lord, A. (2001) 'Ethnic minority sex offenders' experiences of treatment', *Journal of Sexual Aggression*, 7(1): 40–50.

Politics.co.uk. (nd) 'Private prisons', [online] www.politics.co.uk/reference/private-prisons/

Prison Reform Trust (2005) *Private Punishment: Who Benefits?*, London: Prison Reform Trust.

Prison Reform Trust (2017a) *Counted Out Black, Asian and Minority Ethnic Women in the Criminal Justice System*, London: Prison Reform Trust.

Prison Reform Trust (2017b) *Why Focus on Reducing Women's Imprisonment?*, London: Prison Reform Trust.

Prison Reform Trust (2019a) *Prison: The Facts*, [online] www.prisonreformtrust.org.uk/Portals/0/Documents/Bromley per cent20Briefings/Prison per cent20the per cent20facts per cent20Summer per cent202019.pdf

Prison Reform Trust (2019b) *Why Focus on Reducing Women's Imprisonment? England and Wales Fact Sheet*, [online] www.prisonreformtrust.org.uk/Portals/0/Why per cent20Women per cent20England per cent20and per cent20Wales.pdf

Public Health England (2018) *Gender Specific Standards to Improve Health and Wellbeing for Women in Prison in England*, London: PHE Publications.

Reality Check Team (2018) 'Reality check: how many transgender prisoners are there?', [online] www.bbc.com/news/uk-42221629

Shichor, D. (1995) *Prisons for Profit: Private Prisons/Public Concerns*, Thousand Oaks, CA: Sage.

Shingler, J. and Pope, L. (2018) *The Effectiveness of Rehabilitative Services for Black, Asian and Minority Ethnic People: A Rapid Evidence Assessment*, London: Ministry of Justice, [online] https://nls.ldls.org.uk/welcome.html?ark:/81055/vdc_100063276672.0x000001

Simon, J. and Sparks, R. (2012) The Sage Handbook of Punishment and Society, London: Sage.

Smith, A. (2017) '*From where she stands: standpoint theory as a significant predictor of diversity in academia*', [online] https://cogsci.yale.edu/sites/default/files/files/Thesis2017Smith.pdf

Stotzer, R.L. (2014) 'Law enforcement and criminal justice personnel interactions with transgender people in the United States: a literature review', *Aggression and Violent Behavior*, 19(3): 263–77.

Sturge, G. (2020) *UK Prison Population Statistics*, London: House of Commons Library.

Sullivan, E., Assante, Z., Gyamfi, E., Joyce, J. and Pamphile, P. (2007) 'Straight from the horse's mouth', *Prison Service Journal*, 173: 9–14.

Uhrig, N. (2016) *Black, Asian and Minority Ethnic Disproportionality in the Criminal Justice System in England and Wales*, London: Ministry of Justice.

van den Bergh, B., Gatherer, A., Fraser, A. and Moller, L. (2011) 'Imprisonment and women's health: concerns about gender sensitivity, human rights and public health', *Bulletin of the World Health Organization*, 89(9): 689–94.

Van Hout, M.C., Kewley, S. and Hillis, A. (2020) 'Contemporary transgender health experience and health situation in prisons: a scoping review of extant published literature (2000–2019)', *International Journal of Transgender Health*, 21(3): 258–306.

Van Hout, M.C. and Mhlanga-Gunda, R. (2018) 'Contemporary women prisoners' health experiences, unique prison health care needs and health care outcomes in sub-Saharan Africa: a scoping review of extant literature', *BMC International Health and Human Rights*, 18(1): 31.

Williams, K., Papadopoulou, V. and Booth, N. (2012) *Prisoners' Childhood and Family Backgrounds: Results from the Surveying Prisoner Crime Reduction (SPCR) Longitudinal Cohort Study of Prisoners*, Ministry of Justice Research Series 4/12, [online] www.justice.gov.uk/publications/research-and-analysis/moj

Williams, K., Poyser, J. and Hopkins, K. (2013) *Accommodation, Homelessness and Reoffending of Prisoners: Results from the Surveying Prisoner Crime Reduction (SPCR) Survey*, London: Ministry of Justice.

Women in Prison (nd) '*BAME women face "double disadvantage" in Criminal Justice System*', www.womeninprison.org.uk/news/double-disdvantage

PART III

New Frontiers in Hate
Crime Research

9

Intersectional Oppression and Transgender People's Experiences of Discrimination

Ben Colliver

Introduction

Despite Home Office (2019) reports indicating an annual increase of police-recorded transphobic hate crimes, criminologists have been slow to investigate, interrogate and respond to this social and criminal phenomenon. Although academic interest in hate crime has flourished, particularly within the last two decades, research has tended to focus on racist, Islamophobic and homophobic hate crime (Bowling, 1999; Mason, 2005; Awan and Zempi, 2017; James and Smith, 2017). Less is known about the experiences of transgender and non-binary people and their experiences of hate crime. While there is a growing attention being paid to transphobic hate crime (Jamel, 2018; Colliver and Silvestri, 2020), this is often through a white, Eurocentric lens (Jamel, 2018). Resultantly, the experiences of those who occupy multiple minoritized social positions are often overlooked. Indeed, in 2006, Stryker (p 15) noted 'the overwhelming (and generally unmarked) whiteness of practitioners in the academic field of transgender studies'. In this chapter I challenge current knowledge around transphobic hate crime and pay attention to the ways in which experiences of transphobic hate crime are understood and responded to by diverse, heterogeneous communities. In doing so, I explore how a 'master identity' is often imposed on people, that may not coincide with how they understand and interpret their own identity. To do this, I draw upon data collected through semi-structured interviews that were part of a larger research project exploring the 'everyday' and 'mundane' nature of transphobic hate crime.

Understanding transphobic hate crime

Hate crimes are gaining significant political and social attention, with successive governments being called upon to provide more effective protection to minoritized groups (Chakraborti, 2018). Hate crimes are a subset of crimes that the Home Office (2020) collects data on, and figures suggest they constitute approximately 2 per cent of overall recorded crime in England and Wales. Transphobic hate crime accounts for the smallest amount of officially recorded hate crime, making up only 2 per cent of police-recorded hate crimes (Home Office, 2020). However, this category of hate crime saw the largest annual increase in 2018–2019, up 37 per cent from the previous year, totalling 2,333, to a record number of crimes (Home Office, 2019). 2019–2020 saw a further significant increase to a total of 2,540 recorded transphobic hate crimes (Home Office, 2020). While it is not the purpose or in the scope of this chapter to provide a detailed interrogation of these statistics, it is important to note that these figures likely underestimate the reality of how much transphobic hate crime takes place. Home Office (2019) statistics rely on police-recorded crime, and therefore do not include incidents of crime that are not reported to the police, or those that are not correctly identified as being 'hate'-motivated. Other studies have shown significantly higher rates of hate crime targeting transgender and non-binary people (Chakraborti et al, 2014; METRO Charity, 2014).

While the Home Office (2019) largely explain annual increases in hate crime through better reporting systems, it is unlikely that this accounts for the total increase. In the UK, issues affecting transgender and non-binary communities have become central in political 'debates'. In 2017, the then Conservative government announced that they intended to review the current process for gaining legal recognition of an individual's gender, with the purpose of streamlining and demedicalizing the process to reflect that being transgender is not an illness. In 2018, a public consultation was launched that was intended to inform the reform of the Gender Recognition Act 2004. This act has considerably 'improved the protocols ... [that] protect the rights of transgender people' (Jamel, 2018, p 43). The introduction of this legislation enabled people to gain legal recognition of their gender identity by obtaining a gender recognition certification. In order to acquire this certification, a 'gender recognition panel' must have agreed that certain criteria had been met, including that the individual was at least 18 years old, had lived as their gender for a minimum of two years prior to legal recognition being granted and that the individual had been diagnosed with gender dysphoria.

The proposed reform of the Gender Recognition Act (2004) intended to demedicalize this process to make it easier for transgender people to gain legal recognition of their self-declared gender. The outcome of the public consultation was announced in September 2020, when Liz Truss, Minister for Women and Equalities, made a public statement that self-identification would not be introduced. Instead, a number of other amendments would be made including reducing the financial requirements of obtaining legal recognition and moving the application process online. These amendments are intended to address some of the bureaucratic issues associated with the process. The continued reliance on medical diagnosis perpetuates the pathologization of transgender people. As such, a deficit model of understanding trans people is reinforced in which they are positioned as inferior, and therefore become legitimate targets for hatred, discrimination and oppression.

Throughout the public consultation, social media platforms have become a hotbed for 'debate', which has primarily focused on the implications self-identification has for single-sex spaces (including refuges and public toilets) and the 'authenticity' of transgender people (specifically transgender women). My previous work has explored the ways in which transgender people are constructed in online discourse and identified a range of motifs that are regularly used to construct transgender people as unnatural, inauthentic and as a potential risk to the safety of cisgender women and children (Colliver et al, 2019; Colliver and Coyle, 2020). The key issue identified in relation to 'self-identification' is the potential for cisgender men to abuse the system in order to gain access to 'vulnerable' cisgender women and children, and as such, a conflict emerged in which one must choose whether to protect 'women's rights' or 'transgender rights' and positioned these as exclusively in opposition.

Before I present any empirical data and key findings, it is important to define some key concepts used throughout this chapter. The racially aggravated murder of Stephen Lawrence in 1993, and the subsequent Macpherson Report (1999), propelled the term 'hate crime' into the public arena. Government definitions tend to define hate crimes as individual incidents of victimization, thereby overshadowing the often ongoing and repetitive nature of much hate crime, and also ignoring the social and political context within which hate crimes occur. Additionally, the term 'hate crime' does not appear in any legislative context. Despite the lack of legislative definition, in the UK hate crime has been defined by the Home Office (2012) as 'any criminal offence which is perceived, by the victim or any other person, to be motivated by a hostility or prejudice based on a personal characteristic'.

The personal characteristics that require annual monitoring by all police forces include race, religion, disability status, sexual orientation and transgender identity (Home Office, 2020). Section 146 of the Criminal Justice Act (2003) imposes a duty upon courts to increase the sentence imposed on an offender for any criminal offence that is motivated by hostility or prejudice against an individual's transgender identity, or perceived transgender identity.

However, it is important to note that the initial introduction of this act did not offer legislative protection for transgender people. Instead, the Legal Aid, Sentencing and Punishment of Offenders Act (2012) amended the Criminal Justice Act (2003) to include transgender identity as a characteristic to be considered during sentencing. The current process for considering whether a criminal incident was motivated by prejudice or hostility does not recognize multiple marginalizations or oppressions and only one characteristic can be considered at sentencing. Resultantly, a perpetrator motivated by a matrix of prejudice will only have one form of prejudice considered when sentenced. This has resulted in a simplistic perception of identity and does not recognize or acknowledge the intersectional nature of oppression, marginalization and othering.

On the other hand, academics and researchers have attempted to acknowledge the complex social structures that create a climate in which marginalized and oppressed groups become seen as legitimate targets for hate (Perry, 2001). In hate crime scholarship, it is Perry's (2001) conceptualization that has emerged as key when discussing victimization, and she claims that:

> Hate crime ... involves acts of violence and intimidation, usually directed towards already stigmatised and marginalised groups. As such, it is a mechanism of power and oppression, intended to reaffirm the precarious hierarchies that characterise a given social order. It attempts to re-create simultaneously the threatened (real or imagined) hegemony of the perpetrator's group and the 'appropriate' subordinate identity of the victim's group. It is a means of marking both the Self and the Other in such a way as to re-establish their 'proper' relative positions, as given and reproduced by broader ideologies and patterns of social and political inequality. (2001, p 10)

Perry's definition of hate crime provides a more nuanced account of it, directly linking individual incidents into the wider social, cultural and political structures that dominate societies. While this definition generally provides a more holistic picture of hate crime, this may be less useful in practice for those responsible for policing hate crime. It is also key to note that the language associated with 'hate crime' has been identified as problematic (Gerstenfeld, 2004; Hall, 2005). While the term 'hate' has connotations of extreme emotion, it has been argued that not all perpetrators of hate crime are motivated by 'hate', and that to fully understand the nature of hate crime we must consider it in relation to less emotionally charged language (Sullivan, 1999; Chakraborti and Garland, 2012).

Throughout this chapter I also use a number of words that relate to gender identity and expression. Language associated with gender identity and expression is continually evolving, representative of the fluid nature of gender. As with many terms, there is no universally agreed definition of 'transgender'; however, for this chapter I draw upon the work of Hines (2010, p 1) who has defined 'transgender' as denoting:

> a range of gender experiences, subjectivities and presentations that fall across, between or beyond stable categories of 'man' and 'woman'. 'Transgender' includes gender identities that have, more traditionally, been described as 'transsexual', and a diversity of genders that call into question an assumed relationship between gender identity and presentation and the 'sexed' body.

I draw specifically on this definition as it acknowledges gender identities and expressions that fall between and beyond the gender binary of 'man' and 'woman'. While gender is not a binary, rather a spectrum, dominant Western conceptualizations of gender are intrinsically attached to a perceived sex binary, and therefore gender is often understood in oversimplistic, binary terms. As I aim to consider intersectional oppressions, it is key to challenge the Western gender binary that classifies sex and gender into distinct categories of 'male' and 'female'. In challenging this, I can better reflect the experiences of non-binary participants and the issues of oppression and discrimination they discussed. The term 'non-binary' refers to individuals whose gender identity falls between, or outside of, normative and binary categories (Richards et al, 2016). This also serves as an umbrella term encapsulating gender identities including gender-queer, gender-fluid and bi-gender (Vijlbrief et al, 2020). While non-binary identities are gaining considerable social recognition, there is currently no legal recognition of non-binary identities within the UK.

The final term I want to define is 'cisgender', which describes an individual whose gender identity is consistent with the sex they were assigned at birth (Stryker, 2008). A significant amount of research into issues that impact transgender people allows 'cisgender' to be the unspoken norm by failing to recognize this as an identity category (Johnson, 2015). As such, naturalized assumptions about the relationship between sex assigned at birth and gender identity are not challenged. In this sense, the term cisgender challenges the privilege of people who claim a gender based on a biological basis from birth. Cisnormativity refers to the social expectation that all members of a society are cisgender, and that individuals will live their entire lives as the sex they were assigned at birth (Bauer et al, 2009).

It is important to acknowledge the subjective nature of all language, and while I try to be as inclusive as possible throughout this chapter, there is some contention regarding the use of 'transgender' as an umbrella term. Monro (2003) argues that the term is inherently problematic, as the inclusion of such a wide range of social groupings has a homogenizing effect, in which a range of needs and interests are neglected. It is in this chapter that I seek to address this by demonstrating empirically how issues of hate crime, discrimination and prejudice are not experienced uniformly by all transgender people. Instead, I will argue that intersecting oppressions and marginalizations significantly impact the ways in which people engage with their transgender identity.

Notions of 'transnormativity' have been engaged with academically (Johnson, 2016; Bradford and Syed, 2019). Transnormativity refers to a framework that creates a hierarchy of authenticity relating to transgender identities. It privileges those who conform to the gender binary, and holds transgender people accountable to a legal and medical model of transition (Johnson, 2016). While I have previously written about the delegitimization and othering of those who do not conform to this ideological framework (Colliver, 2021), in this chapter I address other issues that also contribute to the marginalization and exclusion of some trans people.

Drawing on research specific to transgender community groups, medicalization and legal transition, I argue that transnormativity structures transgender experience, identification and narratives into a hierarchy of legitimacy that is dependent upon medical status, the specific framework to which transgender people's presentations and experiences of gender are held accountable.

Methodology

The data presented within this chapter were collected as part of a larger research study that was specifically interested in what might be termed 'low-level', or mundane, incidents of transphobic hate crime. As part of this project, 396 online surveys, 31 semi-structured interviews and an analysis of comments posted on YouTube in relation to 'gender-neutral' toilets were completed (Colliver et al, 2019; Colliver and Coyle, 2020; Colliver and Silvestri, 2020). This chapter draws upon the data collected from 31 semi-structured interviews with trans people who live within the UK and were aged 16 and over at the time of interview. The interviews focused on participants' experiences of hate crime targeting their gender identity with a specific emphasis on incidents of verbal abuse, harassment and online victimization. Participants were also asked to speak of other forms of oppression they experienced, either separately from their trans identity or simultaneously. There was a strong focus on oppression, discrimination and hate experienced *within* trans communities, in order to avoid the pitfall of locating issues of oppression solely outside of trans communities. Thematic analysis was conducted on the transcribed data, guided by the six steps outlined by Braun and Clarke (2006). The lack of existing research into 'everyday' and mundane experiences of transphobic hate crime meant that an inductive approach to analysis was adopted.

Participants were recruited for this research project through organizations offering services and support for trans communities, and also through social media. Of the total sample of interview participants, 23 per cent of participants were non-binary, while 31 per cent and 44 per cent were male or female respectively. The majority of participants identified as white British (54.8 per cent); however, a range of ethnic backgrounds were represented within the sample including black British (10 per cent), Asian British (3.2 per cent), black African and white British (3.2 per cent), black Caribbean and white British (3.2 per cent), South American (3.2 per cent), Bangladeshi (3.2 per cent), Irish Traveller (6.4 per cent), Thai (3.2 per cent) and Pakistani (3.2 per cent). Participants' ages ranged from 17 to 67 years old with an average age of 32 years old. Additionally, 30.3 per cent of participants indicated that they lived with a disability, including sensory, mobility and long-term health conditions. Several participants also identified as Christian, Sikh and Muslim and a smaller number identified as Buddhist and Pagan. All participants spoke English, and for most participants English was their first language, to varying degrees of fluency, and four participants spoke English as a second language. This does mean that trans people within the UK who did not speak English at the time of interviews are not represented in this study.

As a researcher, I also have many years' experience in the third sector supporting young LGBTQ people around a number of sensitive, personal issues. This experience also meant that I was able to develop a national network of organizations that could fast-track participants into relevant support services, if appropriate. All participants have been assigned pseudonyms in this chapter.

As a cisgender researcher working with trans communities, personal reflection was paramount throughout the research project. While my identity as a white, gay, cisgender man meant that I may be considered to belong to the broader LGBTQ community, I was aware that the demographic I belong to traditionally dominates these communities and spaces and tends to hold more social power. Resultantly, it was important to continually interrogate my own assumptions, which are often rooted from places of privilege. I was conscious not to represent myself as a voice, or a spokesperson of trans communities. As others have argued, 'no one should ever 'speak for' or assume another's voice … it becomes a form of colonisation' (Sinister Wisdom Collective, 1990, p 4). The development of this research project was initially as a result of many of the young trans people I had worked with in a professional capacity who felt that they had never had the opportunity to participate in research. I therefore worked with organizations and individuals when developing the interview schedule to ensure that the key issues highlighted by trans communities were considered. To engage participants throughout the research process and to gain a greater level of clarity regarding their experiences, all participants were invited to review their interview transcripts, codes and themes developed throughout the analysis of the data.

I was also conscious of not wanting my research to exploit people's hardships, trauma and lives for an academic or research agenda (Arber, 2006). To minimize this risk, I left decisions regarding participation, time of participation and location of participation up to those who had expressed an interest in the research. Emphasizing participants' autonomy was an important aspect when conducting the research, offering regular reminders of participants' right to withdraw from the study at any time without reason.

In adopting an intersectional framework throughout the research process, I maintained the position of asking 'the other question' (Matsuda, 1991, p 1189). Matsuda (1991) describes this as looking for other forms of privilege, oppression and dominance when focusing in on one issue. Participants were therefore asked to discuss their experiences of oppression, discrimination and hate crime more generally in order to avoid participants feeling that they could only discuss one form of discrimination. As such, when participants described incidents of transphobia, I consciously questioned whether issues of patriarchy, racism, heteronormativity, ableism and classism were also present, although this was not an exhaustive list. Participants often reflected on the multiple and interlocking forms of oppression they experienced without prompting, situating their experiences within the context of multiple social hierarchies. In adopting this approach, it became possible to appreciate the social and cultural context within which trans identities are understood, often symbolized by whiteness. This is central to advancing hate crime literature, which often adopts a single-axis framework.

In the next section, I focus on the qualitative findings to provide a critical analysis of the ways in which intersecting oppressions influence the experiences and lives of trans people.

Transnormativity, transphobia and exclusion

A central theme that was developed from the data related to a sense of 'belonging'. Finding a sense of 'belonging' was often perceived to be difficult for trans people who were not white, atheist, able-bodied and did not identify within the Western gender binary. Many participants described a sense of having "nowhere to belong". I focus primarily here on the role that religion and faith play in establishing a dominant, normative trans identity. When accessing social spaces created by, and for, trans people, Isa, a 58-year-old woman, describes how she is often excluded and ridiculed from and within these spaces:

'The couple of times I have been to social events for trans people, I have normally left quite quickly. I don't force my religion on people, but I wear a St. Christopher, and I am happy to talk about my faith if it comes up in conversation. When I do, I normally get comments like "oh, who invited the God squad along". It's like there is a stereotype about Christians all being these crazy preacher people who want to force religion in others' faces.' (Isa)

Despite Isa being a trans woman, and accessing these social events to build a network of support, her religious identity is often imposed on her by others as a 'master identity' (Hughes, 1945). While her religion may not be the motivating reason she attended these spaces, it becomes the central aspect of her identity when interacting with others. As a result, when trying to engage in an 'inclusive' space, she experiences further exclusion and marginalization, and this results from her 'difference' to other trans people who are non-religious, or perceived to be non-religious. This may result from historic and contemporary tensions between some religious sectors and trans people that contribute to the social exclusion and marginalization of trans people (Bolich, 2008). Simon, a 47-year-old man, highlights how he often conceals his faith when engaging with other trans people. In times when he has disclosed his religious beliefs, he describes being met with suspicion and uncertainty from other trans people as to why he was accessing these spaces. Similarly for Simon, his religious identity is imposed on him as a 'master identity', in which he is seen as a person of faith first, and as transgender second. In this sense, an individual's 'difference' is perceived to be a more significant identity marker than the similarities he shares with trans people.

In these situations, notions of 'exclusivity' become apparent, in which individuals must identify as either trans or religious, but not both simultaneously. Therefore, complex and multifaceted identities are reduced to a single-axis framework in which those who do not conform to the groups' dominant ideals face marginalization. It is also clear in Isa's narrative that harmful stereotypes about Christianity and Christians are drawn upon to ridicule and belittle her. The phrase "who invited" also speaks directly to other trans people's discomfort, confusion or disdain towards Isa because of her religious identity. Similarly to Simon, Isa went on to describe how at subsequent events she should would try to conceal her religious identity to avoid these experiences. It is important to recognize how these practices of concealing an identity marker can be harmful and concealment has been linked to stress-related physical symptoms (Cole et al, 1996) and low self-efficacy (Barreto et al, 2006). However, similar feelings of exclusion may be felt within religious spaces, in which cisnormative ideals dominate. Simon describes an incident he experienced after he had recently disclosed their trans identity to some members of the church they regularly attended:

'It was early morning, I was running late. I arrived to Church, walked in and sat at the back. Even just sitting there, I have never felt so humiliated. I felt every pair of eyes on me, burning through me. I couldn't work out if it was because I was late, or because the news had spread ... Afterwards, the Priest came to speak with me. Apparently there had been a lot of talk about me and a lot of people not comfortable with me being there. I was very subtly invited to leave and find somewhere else to worship.' (Simon)

The exclusion from trans-inclusive spaces, and from religious spaces, speaks to participants' feelings of there being 'nowhere to belong'. Similar to the experiences of exclusion from trans-inclusive spaces, trans people may also have their trans identity imposed on them as a 'master identity' within religious spaces. In this sense, cisnormative ideals permeate these spaces, and those who do not conform to these experience further marginalization as a result of their 'difference', with identities being reduced to a simplistic, single-axis framework. This is unsurprising, as previous research has shown that transgender people are often constructed as in contradiction with religious values (Colliver et al, 2019). These experiences demonstrate some of the dangers with describing transgender communities as a homogenous group. It is clear that religion plays a significant part in trans people's experiences of exclusion and marginalization.

Religion also contributes to the ways in which transphobic hate crime is experienced. This was particularly the case for participants who felt they were 'visibly' religious (Colliver and Silvestri, 2020). Participants' religious identity often interacted with the visibility of their trans identity to create unique experiences of hate crime. This reiterates claims made by Woods (2014) that experiences of marginalization and oppression are shaped by more than just an individual's gender identity, and that other identity markers such as race, religion and disability status influence these experiences. Deena, a 34-year-old woman, explains how she regularly experiences Islamophobia. She says that "I have always been surprised at how much racism and Islamophobia I receive from other trans people, not just outsiders of that community. It shocked me, I feel very isolated because I feel like I don't fit in to any particular community or group."

Deena's narrative also highlights a sense of 'nowhere to belong', which was recurrent. In this excerpt, Deena describes the interplay of racism and Islamophobia that she experiences from other trans people, although not transphobia. Issues of racism within spaces for lesbian, gay, bisexual and trans people have been documented (McKeown et al, 2010). In this sense, LGBT spaces are symbolized by whiteness, by which people's inclusion within these spaces is judged by. Resultantly, access to 'safe spaces' is not feasible for all trans people, and there are a number of social hierarchies that interact simultaneously that influence an individual's access to these spaces. It is here that we are able to see how whiteness operates to dominate these spaces, and further marginalize people who are already subordinated on a number of social hierarchies. Arguably, hierarchies of race that dominate society more broadly also operate within trans communities, assigning privilege to trans people who do not experience marginalization based on their racial identity. In adopting an intersectional framework, it is possible to challenge dominant hate crime narratives that locate issues of power solely outside of marginalized groups, and a more nuanced interrogation of how power hierarchies operate within and between marginalized groups can occur. Failure to do so may exacerbate the invisibility and erasure that multiply marginalized groups experience. Overlooking how whiteness operates in the configuration of 'trans-inclusive' spaces risks privileging the experiences of white transgender people.

Interlocking axes of race and religion do not only impact trans people's access to trans-inclusive spaces. When discussing experiences of hate crime perpetrated by cisgender people, racial and religious identities often interacted and overshadowed the visibility of participants' trans identity. Sam, a 31-year-old male, describes his experiences of racism:

'I do find that I experience more racism than transphobia. I am so visibly Asian and I can't hide that. I can walk with my head down so people can't see my face, but I can't disguise my colour and I think that is what stands out instantly about me, my brownness.' (Sam)

As Sam describes, it is his Asian heritage that is the most 'visible' identity marker, and this results in him experiencing more racism than transphobia. However, Sam's experiences are more complex than this, as he later describes how people assume he "is Muslim, because they just assume that everyone who is brown is Muslim". In this sense, conflations are made between race and religion, and it results in Sam experiencing a matrix of oppression and hate, in which both his racial and religious identity are targeted. Furthermore, Sam later describes how he sometimes "experience[s] transphobia because [his] race has attracted attention, and people start off being racist and then it moves to transphobia when they realise". A similar experience was shared by Ty, a 21-year-old non-binary individual, who felt as though they "stood out from all of the other black boys on the estate", putting them at risk of experiencing transphobia. However, in other spaces, they experienced "transphobia with racism", particularly within spaces where whiteness is the norm.

Western culture and thereby cultural expectations of gender presentation and identity are rooted within white-normative ideals (Collins, 2000). Heteronormativity and cisnormativity are central features of white-normative ideals of masculinity and femininity, and, therefore, trans people who are white, or perceived as white, may be able to occupy these spaces more safely, as they will not have to contend with subordination or marginalization in relation to hierarchies of race. This demonstrates the ways in which race, religion and gender identity interact to create unique experiences for trans people who occupy multiple marginalized positions. When considering how people negotiate their gender identity, particularly in public spaces where they may be subject to higher levels of social policing, it is therefore essential to consider how other identity characteristics influence these negotiations. It is clear how intersecting oppressions, marginalizations and expectations associated with gender identity, religion and faith, and race influence trans people's experiences of hate crime and discrimination. In challenging the 'whiteness' of research into experiences of transphobia, adopting an intersectional framework is imperative to better understand the ways in which multiple marginalizations impact access to spaces.

Conclusion

Not all trans people have the same social access to various spaces, and experiences of marginalization, exclusion and ridicule are dependent on how other aspects of their identity are perceived. In this chapter, I have highlighted the ways in which transgender people's experiences of transphobia, and other forms of discrimination, are not isolated, separate incidents. Rather, issues of racism, and anti-religious sentiment, manifest simultaneously to transphobia to create distinctive experiences of oppression, marginalization and hate. While it is important to understand how these hierarchies of oppression interact, there is still significant work to be done in relation to the policing and prosecution of hate crime. While the police have the capacity to record hate crimes motivated by more than one form of prejudice, and therefore recognize complex identities, this does not extend to prosecution. This is compounded by varying levels of legislative protection, with more punitive criminal justice responses in relation to race and religion. Therefore, hate crimes motivated by multiple forms of prejudice are often reduced to a single-axis framework at prosecution, in which only a single identity characteristic can be considered.

As such, it is recommended that future research into trans people's experiences of hate crime adopts an intersectional framework to continue to interrogate the ways in which different identity characteristics interact. Applying this approach will allow for a more nuanced understanding of the ways in which multiple marginalizations may be experienced simultaneously and in conjunction with each other, rather than adopting a silo approach that sees transphobia, racism and anti-religious sentiment as three distinct forms of prejudice. This approach risks excluding the experiences of those who may be the most marginalized and excluded from social life and social spaces, and privileges the experiences of those who are white and non-religious.

References

Arber, A. (2006) 'Reflexivity: "A challenge for the researcher as practitioner"', *Journal of Research in Nursing*, 11: 147–57.

Awan, I. and Zempi, I. (2017) '"I will blow your face OFF" – virtual and physical world anti-Muslim hate crime', *British Journal of Criminology*, 57(2): 362–80.

Barreto, M., Ellemers, N. and Banal, S.R. (2006) 'Working under cover: performance related self-confidence among members of contextually devalued groups who try to pass', *European Journal of Social Psychology*, 36: 337–52.

Bauer, G.R., Hammond, R., Travers, R., Kaay, M., Hohenadel, K.M. and Boyce, M. (2009) 'I don't think this is theoretical; this is our lives: how erasure impacts health care for transgender people', *Journal of the Association of Nurses in AIDS Care*, 20: 348–61.

Bolich, G.G. (2008) *Transgender Realities: An Introduction to Gender Variant People and the Judgments about Them*, North Carolina: Psyche's Press.

Bowling, B. (1999) *Violent Racism: Victimisation, Policing and Social Context*, Oxford: Oxford University Press.

Bradford, N.J. and Syed, M. (2019) 'Transnormativity and transgender identity development: a master narrative approach', *Sex Roles*, 81(5–6): 306–25.

Braun, V. and Clarke, V. (2006) 'Using thematic analysis in psychology', *Qualitative Research in Psychology*, 3(2): 77–101.

Chakraborti, N. (2018) 'Responding to hate crime: escalating problems, continued failings', *Criminology and Criminal Justice*, 18(4): 387–404.

Chakraborti, N. and Garland, J. (2012) 'Reconceptualizing hate crime victimization through the lens of vulnerability and "difference"', *Theoretical Criminology*, 16(4): 499–514.

Chakraborti, N., Garland, J. and Hardy, S.-J. (2014) *The Leicester Hate Crime Project: Findings and Conclusions*, Leicester: University of Leicester.

Cole, S.W., Kemeny, M.E., Taylor, S.E. and Visscher, B.R. (1996) 'Elevated physical health risk among gay men who conceal their homosexual identity', *Health Psychology*, 15: 243–51.

Collins, P. (2000) *Black Feminist Thought: Knowledge, Consciousness, and the Politics of Empowerment*, 2nd Ed., New York: Routledge.

Colliver, B. (2021) *Reimagining Hate Crime: Transphobia, Visibility and Victimisation*, London: Palgrave Macmillan.

Colliver, B., Coyle, A. and Silvestri, M. (2019) 'The 'online othering' of transgender people in relation to "'gender neutral toilets'", in K. Lumsden and E. Harper (eds) *Online Othering: Exploring Digital Violence and Discrimination on the Web*, London: Palgrave Macmillan, pp 215–38.

Colliver, B. and Coyle, A. (2020) 'Risk of sexual violence against women and girls in the construction of "gender-neutral toilets": a discourse analysis of comments on YouTube videos', *Journal of Gender-Based Violence*, 4(3): 359–76.

Colliver, B. and Silvestri, M. (2020) 'The role of (in)visibility in hate crime targeting transgender people', *Criminology and Criminal Justice*, 22(2), 235–53.

Gerstenfeld, P. (2004) *Hate Crimes: Causes, Controls and Controversies*, London: Sage Publications.

Hall, N. (2005) *Hate Crime*, Cullompton: Willan Publishing.

Hines, S. (2010) 'Introduction', in S. Hines and T. Sanger (eds) *Transgender Identities: Towards a Social Analysis of Gender Diversity*, New York: Routledge, pp 1–22.

Home Office (2012) *Challenge It, Report It, Stop It: The Government's Plan to Tackle Hate Crime*, London: Home Office.

Home Office (2019) *Hate Crime, England and Wales, 2018–2019*, London: Home Office.

Home Office (2020) *Hate Crime, England and Wales, 2019–2020*, London: Home Office.

Hughes, E.C. (1945) 'Dilemmas and contradictions of status', *The American Journal of Sociology*, 50(5): 353–359.

Jamel, J. (2018) *Transphobic Hate Crime*, London: Palgrave Macmillan.

James, Z. and Smith, D. (2017) 'Roma inclusion post Brexit: a challenge to existing rhetoric?', *Safer Communities*, 16(4): 186–95.

Johnson, A. (2015) 'Beyond inclusion: thinking toward a transfeminist methodology', in V. Demos and M. Segal (eds) *At the Center: Feminism, Social Science and Knowledge*, Bingley: Emerald Group Publishing Ltd, pp 21–42.

Johnson, A. (2016) 'Transnormativity: a new concept and its validation through documentary film about transgender men', *Sociological Inquiry*, 86(4): 465–91.

Macpherson, W. (1999) '*The Stephen Lawrence Inquiry*', [online] www.gov.uk/government/uploads/system/uploads/attachment_data/file/277111/4262.pdf

Mason, G. (2005) 'A picture of hate crime: racial and homophobic harassment in the United Kingdom', *Current Issues in Criminal Justice*, 17(1): 79–95.

Matsuda, M.J. (1991) 'Beside my sister, facing the enemy: legal theory out of coalition', *Stanford Law Review*, 43(6): 1183–92.

McKeown, E., Nelson, S., Anderson, J., Low, N. and Elford, J. (2010) 'Disclosure, discrimination and desire: experiences of black and South Asian gay men in Britain', *Culture, Health and Sexuality*, 12(7): 843–56.

Metro Charity (2014) *Youth Chances: Summary of First Findings*, London: METRO Charity.

Monro, S. (2003) 'Transgender politics in the UK', *Critical Social Policy*, 23(4): 433–52.

Perry, B. (2001) *In the Name of Hate: Understanding Hate Crimes*, London: Routledge.

Richards, C., Bouman, W.P., Seal, L., Barker, M.J., Nieder, T.O. and T'Sjoen, G. (2016) 'Non-binary or genderqueer genders', *International Review of Psychiatry*, 28(1): 95–102.

Sinister Wisdom Collective (1990) 'Editorial', *Sinister Wisdom*, 42(4): 1–6.

Stryker, S. (2006) '(De)subjugated knowledges: an introduction to transgender studies', in S. Stryker and S. Whittle (eds) *The Transgender Studies Reader*, New York: Routledge, pp 1–18.

Stryker, S. (2008) *Transgender History*, Berkley, CA: Seal Press.

Sullivan, A. (1999) What's so bad about hate? The illogical and illiberalism behind hate crime laws, *New York Times Magazine* [online] www.nytimes.com/1999/09/26/magazine/what-s-so-bad-about-hate.html

Vijlbrief, A., Saharso, S. and Ghorashi, H. (2020) 'Transcending the gender binary: gender non-binary young adults in Amsterdam', *Journal of LGBT Youth*, 17(1): 89–106.

Woods, J. (2014) 'Queer contestations and the future of a critica "queer" criminology', *Critical Criminology*, 22(1): 5–19.

10

Hateful Subjectivities: Using Intersectionality to Inform a Critical Hate Studies Perspective

Katie McBride and Zoë James

Introduction

This chapter explores the role of neo-liberal capitalism, as the prevailing socioeconomic and political grammar of our contemporary society, in the construction and proliferation of hate throughout society today. Hate is not a modern-day phenomenon (Petrosino, 1999). Imperialist colonialism and the bludgeoning 'success' of Empire has indelibly shaped social relations (see, for example, Bowling and Phillips, 2012), enabling and sustaining increasing disparities between the 'haves' and the 'have nots'. The critical hate studies perspective (James and McBride, 2018) acknowledges how historic inequalities according to structures including class, gender and race continue to inform who gains access to power and privilege today. Critical hate studies build upon this existing knowledge base to consider how and why hate happens in contemporary society. In doing so, critical hate studies stress the significance of processes of identity formation as acknowledged within ultra-realist criminology (Winlow and Hall, 2015) to provide a full appreciation of both the extent of hate harms experienced by victims as well as what informs the motivations of those who are responsible for inflicting harm against others.

This chapter engages with intersectionality as a framework capable of capturing the complex and dynamic nature of contemporary social relations in a way that questions the capacity of accepted criminological categorization and traditional criminological domain assumptions to explain hate. Hate crime agendas, as signified through legal statutes, government policies and practices, have to date relied heavily upon popular notions of social identity characteristics of victims and the underlying prejudices of identifiable offenders to explain the hate crime phenomenon. The discussion that follows asserts the significance of conceiving the process of identity formation as embedded within the contemporary neo-liberal capitalist context. Intersectionality is 'critically attuned to how interlocking systems of power operate and come to bear on notions of crime and deviance' (Henne and Troshynski, 2013, p 457), and critical hate studies are attuned to the nature of the contemporary neo-liberal capitalist context and its role as a formative force in producing multiple, messy and overlapping personal and social identities, which operate in tension with one another resulting in harmful victim and offender subjectivities. Experiences of gypsies, travellers and transgender people illuminate a wider set of harmful experiences associated with the tensions between our personal and social identities. Utilizing a critical hate studies perspective in combination with the concept of intersectionality, this chapter extends the discussion of hate and harm beyond the confines of traditionally narrow conceptualizations of prejudice and hate based on a singular identity, which produce limited analytical insight into the problem of hate in society (Crenshaw, 1991; Meyer, 2004; Marchetti, 2008).

This chapter presents a theoretical discussion informed by empirical research, undertaken within the UK over the past 20 years, that captures the lived experiences of gypsies, travellers and transgender people to extend our understanding of hate in society. The authors' approach to research is participatory in its efforts to develop knowledge, power and capacity within the communities within which they conduct their research. The methods are immersive, generating thick ethnographic data to raise new questions and find 'more fruitful ways of speaking about' everyday life (Rorty, 1980, p 360) that are representative of, often alternative, lived experiences and ways of being in the world (Dilley, 1999). In doing so, the chapter identifies key tensions in existing theoretical positions on hate harms in late modernity and provides evidence of their impact on praxis and people. The focus of the discussion here emanates from the delivery of a hate crime agenda in the UK, but its theoretical points may be applied more widely to other Western democratic states as well as burgeoning democracies that embrace neo-liberal capitalist norms.

Neo-liberal capitalism and hate

Neo-liberal capitalism has been broadly acknowledged as the prevailing political ideology of our contemporary times (Harvey, 2005). It is defined as a set of financial market-based principles that have been absorbed within the social governance of Western societies. The underpinning principles of neo-liberal capitalism simultaneously favour the privatization of public services alongside principles of deregulation that effectively dismantle the processes and opportunities through which service providers can be held accountable for any failures or inequalities in their provision[1]. This shift has been justified by unsubstantiated claims of a 'trickle-down' economy/social support system whereby those who have accumulated power and wealth will use their position to ensure the sustenance and success of others less fortunate (Duggan, 2012). Embedded within this contemporary discourse of neo-liberal capitalist society is the underlying notion of human agency.

Within a meritocratic (Bell, 1973) society, economic inequality is justified and normalized on the premise that everyone has equal opportunity to succeed and individuals are responsible for personal risks and rewards. Those that assimilate through the adoption of neo-liberal capitalist terms and reasoning are perceived as those who 'work the hardest' and thus will reap the greatest rewards. Those who fail to succeed under these terms are held equally accountable and responsible for their plight. Through this lens public issues such as poverty, exclusion and discrimination are constructed as personal troubles (Wright Mills, 1959) detached from the social structures and systems that present real barriers to individuals achieving success (Duggan, 2012; Waquant, 2009). An output of the punitive 'tough on crime' rhetoric produced under the conditions outlined earlier was the push to construct hate crime agendas through which errant behaviours were defined, and some *successful* victims could be rewarded with recognition and offenders punished. Therefore, that agenda was itself indelibly marked by its emergence through the economic and political modifications representative of contemporary neo-liberal capitalism (Duggan, 2012; Meyer, 2014). We challenge the capacity of hate crime agendas to address the wider concern as they have been constructed through neo-liberal capitalist terms, which facilitate a primary concern with the identification and punishment of offenders. Their capacity to adequately define the scope and scale of hate in contemporary society, and indeed the apparent progress made via expanded hate legislation, further entrenches existing systems of oppression which, in reality, present an obstacle to human flourishing for those impacted by the harms of hate. This approach to hate in society could be described as invoking a 'cruel optimism' (Berlant, 2011, p 24) that misdirects our concern and desire for a safe and equal society towards punishment, and in doing so weakens our capacity to forge effective solidarity within and between our communities to effectively challenge the true generative forces of hate today. Of primary concern for this chapter is how the socioeconomic political discourse of neo-liberal capitalism has instructed the mode and terms under which hate is defined, who can make legitimate claims to experiencing hate and who or what is considered the driving force behind hate. As such we can conceive of these issues through the intersectionality lens outlined by Crenshaw (1991), particularly in regards to how intersectionality can be seen as structural, political and representational. The prevailing contemporary socioeconomic and political grammar produced by neo-liberal capitalism intersects with the process of the formation of the self, which in turn takes place within a context that is imbued by historic structural, political and representational exclusion and marginalization of a range of identity characteristics.

Legal hate protections and identity

Interpretations of experiences of hate are most regularly approached through the lens of identity and hate laws seek the recognition and protection of 'group-specific' cultural identity (Fraser, 2003, p 166) from hateful speech, behaviours and targeted crimes. Groups who experience hate must organize and construct an argument that engenders their recognition by state bodies as worthy of protection. Groups seek inclusion based on aspects of a collective social identity that is ascribed to them or to which they ascribe themselves. However, if the concept of identity in late modern usage can be bisected into the personal and the social (Moran, 2014), the tensions between ascribed and aligned identity can be extrapolated. Appiah (2006) has defined ascription as a criterion used to categorize individuals. For example, infants are 'ascribed' a sex at birth. Ascription of an individual to a category is not as simple as the attributes associated with that category, as these will not always hold true for all individuals capable of making that judgement. For example, an infant may be ascribed as female on the basis of this anatomically led categorization, but a personal gender identity is achieved via a complex process of regulated socialization and role-modelled performativity, which is far more complex than the essentialized notion that gender automatically reflects an externally ascribed sex categorization. This difficulty may be seen in the well-documented and divisive debate over who should be ascribed as a 'woman'. As such, this form of identity generates an identity politics that gives rise to a process of negotiation regarding where the boundaries of a given social category begin and end. Here, social identities are realized via processes of negotiation whereby unworthy or unappealing aspects of personal identities are denied or 'traded' (to apply the economic language of neo-liberal capitalism) for reductive and commodified aspects of social identity in the pursuit of acceptance and inclusion. This process gives rise to competition within social groups to have their narrative authenticated via external recognition such as that afforded through inclusion within the recognized characteristics protected through equality legislation and reinforced through hate crime statutes. For trans people, whose personal gender identity differs from their ascribed sex category, this context instructs them to perform and conform to a representation of trans identity that is defined within legal and medical structures that do not necessarily relate to the complex lived realities of being trans.

155

Others argue (and we would agree) that there is an important place and role for legal protections and the associated policy frameworks that prohibit both direct forms of hate crime and the broader discrimination that some groups experience in accessing and receiving services and support. For example, hate crime legislation holds symbolic value (Mason, 2013, p 2014), and as Chakraborti (2012, p 3) points out, the 'process of criminalizing actions or expressions which violate the core values of a diverse society can convey an equally powerful message of solidarity to victims of hate'. However, hate crime legislation and its associated political discourse has also been criticized for its divisiveness by favouring certain minority groups over others (Garland, 2011), which has had the effect of creating a hierarchy of victims (Mason-Bish, 2010) where some are recognized as more deserving of legal protections than others (Richardson and May, 1999). This approach to hate crime distorts perceptions of lived experiences of hate and of those who experience it and creates a system whereby 'the interests of more privileged individuals' (Meyer, 2012, p 850), and specifically those who lack the social capital required to garner political support have their personal and social identities disregarded and their experiences of hate erased from view. Meyer (2014) argues that while there may be some deterrent impact on the reduction of public displays of targeted abuse, this impact does not permeate into private spaces and leaves those vulnerable to harms within the private sphere among family members. This illuminates the potential for harm to be generated at the intersections of lived realities that exist in tension with structural, political and representational intersectionality as conceived of by Crenshaw.

Contemporary research with trans individuals (McBride, 2019) and gypsies and travellers (James, 2020) has demonstrated lived experiences of harm at the hands of family members who regulate the personal identities of their family members against the accepted norms they have associated with permitted social identities. Hence, parents of trans individuals may repress their child's expression of gender as a protective mechanism for themselves and their child, neither of whom the parents wish to live outside accepted norms. Ultimately, that child has been harmed by that protective behaviour as their personal identity formation is negatively impacted by their incapacity to express themselves truly. Further, harm occurs as a direct response to the digression personal identities represented from the socially ascribed identities deemed as worthy and unworthy in public space. Gypsies and travellers commonly hide their identity for fear of discrimination on school application forms or in health care settings. Again, this act of protection serves to augment the cognitive dissonance that young gypsies and travellers then experience as their personal identity and social identity do not cohere (Heaslip et al, 2016).

Despite their limitations, legal sanctions have been proposed and deployed as an appropriate response to particular groups' negative experiences in our society, but the necessary operationalization of these complex social issues for legal processing necessitates the drawing of fixed boundaries related to individuals' identity characteristics, thus perpetuating harms associated with this form of representational intersectionality that deny the existence of alternative lived realities. The ongoing failures of this framework to address the complex and nuanced experiences of all those who experience hate are evident in contemporary society. For example, despite the inclusion of transgender people within legal protections in England and Wales, the legal framework (Whittle, 2002) and associated social policy approaches inadequately account for the diversity and particularities of trans individuals' lived realities and associated support needs (Hines, 2006; 2007). As noted by James (2020) elsewhere, in the case of gypsies and travellers, it is only those communities that have achieved legal recognition on the basis of their ethnicity, specifically Irish travellers and Romany gypsies, who are afforded protection from hate. Whereas new travellers and show people have no recourse to legal protection against such experiences, despite their lived experiences and acknowledgement of their traveller identities within planning legislation and policy.

Hate crime is often explained as a tool in the maintenance of social 'hierarchies of difference' (Perry, 2001, p 49) between victim and offender groups. In the examples previously discussed, though, it is possible to see how the hate crime agenda and legal framework itself also contributes to and serves to perpetuate 'hierarchies of acceptability' (Warner, 2000, p 67), and creates points of tension within and between socially defined identity groups. Here, we can see 'legal declarations of "equality" are often tools for maintaining and stratifying [historically founded] social and economic arrangements' (Spade, 2011, p 14). For example, Ward (2008) argues that LGBT activist organizations often fail to acknowledge the experiences and associated needs of low-income LGBT people and in doing so administer a form of inclusion fit for only the 'worthy' middle classes with disregard for the consequences of such intersectionality in peoples' lived experiences of harm. Intersectionality theory was established as a means to intervene in these ways in which normative discourses emerging from historic archetypes reinforce historic power relations and indeed how contemporary discourses of resistance also serve to reproduce and legitimize exclusion and marginalization (Crenshaw, 1991). Within the ethnographic empirical research, which informed this chapter, this issue was exemplified by the lived experiences of Bird, a trans woman in her late 50s who lived a precarious existence reliant on social support and without independent means to support herself and isolated from family or social support networks. Bird's experiences were characterized by physical violence and aggression that differed from those of other research participants who occupied privileged social positions because of their occupational status, secure housing tenure and financial independence. These factors provided a buffer from some of the day-to-day interactions that brought Bird into more interaction with others in public spaces (McBride, 2019). Similarly, Irish travellers also experience increased hate harms due to the precarious nature of their lives as they are more likely to suffer the detriments of extremely poor accommodation and associated social, economic and political marginalization than other gypsies and travellers (notwithstanding the overarching exclusion of gypsies and travellers generally) (James, 2020).

Intersectionality and the hate crime agenda

Acknowledging the propensity for oversimplified conceptualizations of hate victimization to advance the interests of some identity characteristics over others, intersectionality theory seeks to redress this harm through its emphasis on the interplay between multiple identity characteristics that allow for representation of both personal and social identities. Arising out of black feminist scholarship, intersectionality theory has a long history of challenging essentialist paradigms (Han, 2006; Hong, 2008). Intersectionality theory introduces and embraces a level of complexity that more readily speaks to the lived realities of experiences of hate for many.

Butler (1990, p 42) contends that to deny the influence of the external environment on our understanding of identities erases from view the processes by which social identities are subjective positions that are actually being actively (re)produced within the broader regulatory social context; thus, our personal and social identities may conflict in this context (James, 2020). This is a fundamental sticking point that, for critical hate studies, needed to be overcome in order for it to offer a fruitful addition to our understanding of hate in society. As such, critical hate studies emphasize and seek to extend what Hong (2008) suggests as intersectionality theory's capacity to also acknowledge how intersections and their consequences occur '… *within* the context of global colonial capitalism' [emphasis added] (Hong, 2008, p 100).

The alternative domain assumptions utilized by critical hate studies assert that human subjectivity actually arises through an interplay between the individual and the external social world. Social politics of the late 20th century has been dependent upon fixed categories of identity. Duggan (2012, p xvi) argues that the neo-liberal capitalist economic agenda cannot be detached in real terms from human relations and in fact 'neoliberalism has assembled its projects and interests from the field of issues saturated with race, with gender, with sex, with religion, with ethnicity and nationality' In this way, we can see how neo-liberal capitalism's economic and political regime is not distinct and separate from the historic inequalities that continue to run through Western societies but instead, contemporary manifestations rely upon and actively elicit these issues and social tensions to justify and further its pursuit of financial reward for the few. Neo-liberal capitalism should therefore be considered in relation to these existing structures of power to critique the ways in which these have been shaped into modes of activism that have actively contributed to the distribution of resources upwards (Duggan, 2012). It is the intersection of these structures, politics and systems of power that now instruct the lived experiences of harm in contemporary society. A social harm approach offers the potential to expose the harms generated by social, political and economic values and systems integral to neo-liberal capitalist ideology that privileges individualism and promotes meritocracy and competition (McCarthy and Prudham, 2004). For critical hate studies, intersectionality serves as a useful companion in deconstructing essentialist categorizations that oversimplify and erase the complexities of lived experiences of hate and in exposing the social, political and economic modes through which identities are constructed and associated harms produced in the pursuit of unattainable inclusion and acceptance via individualistic means.

In the same way that gender- or race-focused social movements can negate the intersectional experiences of black women, so too do mainstream movements for the inclusion of trans people erase the lived experiences of some of these people. Specifically, of those trans women that do not wish to (or cannot) conform to the medicalized conceptualization of acceptable and recognized (in law at least) trans identities, non-binary people and trans men. Similarly, gypsy and traveller social movements have negated the experiences of new travellers and show people. This is enacted based on their not achieving the required ethnic status and as such weakens or damages an argument for recognition and protection based upon a minority ethnic status (a well-trodden and successful route to this form of inclusion for other black and ethnic minority groups). There are numerous examples of how these externally generated hierarchies of acceptability and recognition are actively regulated and perpetuated within minority groups. For example, the derogation of 'transvestites' by other trans women who have ascribed to the medical model of trans identity in their performance of their compliance with this externally imposed narrative of trans identities as a matter of medically facilitated alignment of the body with the mind in order to achieve authentic alignment (Garrison, 2018). Their approach upholds the Cartesian relationship that underpins the Western binary gender order and provides justification for medical intervention as the accepted route to achieving a 'natural' state (Salamon, 2010). Another example would be the perpetuation of the myth of the authentic Romany gypsy by Romany scholars and activists who have, according to Gheorge (1997, p 158), 'found promise in the ethnic discourse and in a national minority politics' and thus created an intellectual Romany elite that has consequently fed in to the process of ordering gypsies and travellers within a hierarchy. That hierarchy has placed Irish travellers in a denigrated position relative to Romany gypsies, despite their legislatively acknowledged ethnic identity, and as such, as previously noted, they are far more likely to lack a political voice, be socially included or have access to fiscal wealth. What these examples explicate are hidden hate harms that are not acknowledged within the mainstream hate crime agenda or by recourse to strand-based explanations of experiences of prejudice. In light of these sentiments, the endeavours of intersectionality theory in combination with the underpinning theoretical domain assumptions of critical hate studies afford us a more nuanced appreciation of these lived realities as occurring *within* the context of contemporary neo-liberal capitalism.

Taking a critical hate studies approach

The reductive focus on experiences that are shaped by normative stereotypical categorizations of an individual's social identity/ies falls short of fully acknowledging the depth and breadth of harms evident in individuals' lived experiences of hate that occur within and as a result of the space between their personal and social identities. The ascription or alignment of an individual with a social identity is mediated by its acceptability, visibility and viability within neo-liberal capitalist norms. In order to appreciate the space between the personal and social aspects of identity and the harms engendered therein, a critical hate studies approach initially considers how human subjective experience develops by using a transcendental materialist approach (Zizek, 2006, developed by Johnston, 2008). This approach in turn utilizes a Lacanian interpretation of the psychosocial development of human subjectivity, which posits that human subjectivity develops from an internal lack or void that necessitates our active elicitation of the signs and symbols presented to us throughout the various facets of our social world in order to fill that void and make sense of our existence. Within neo-liberal capitalism there is an absence of any effective symbolic order for our subjectivity to find root within as the social world is oriented around notions of liberal freedom that are defined within the confines of capital accumulation. Thus, the human subject can only satiate its sense of lack, or the void, through individual progression and consumption, rather than via a framework of communal experience and shared moral values. Within this environment individuals either search out a communal framework by aligning their identity with some form of dogma, be that a religion or political interest group, or they compete alongside everyone else to progress as an individual within consumerist society as defined by late modern neo-liberal capitalism.

Having established how subjectivity is developed within neo-liberal capitalism, it is then possible to appreciate why hate has become ubiquitous. Those individuals aligning themselves with a dogma such as far-right ideology, for example, commit hateful actions based on that belief system. Others commit hateful actions as they compete in society to reach their individual goals. Given that, as Young (1999) noted, the social world's playing field is not level due to the global destruction wrought by colonialism (Andrews, 2019), those people most likely to experience hate harms are those who have been placed in the poorest and most excluded spaces of society.

Our analysis of hate in these terms has been informed by empirical research with individuals from some of the most excluded and marginalized communities within our society: gypsies and travellers, and transgender people. The harms of hate experienced by participants in our research have included crimes such as criminal damage of gypsy and traveller homes and violent physical attacks of gypsies, travellers and trans people. Gypsies and travellers, and trans people, have reported to us their experiences of hate incidents, speech and discrimination in their everyday lives that have ranged from explicit prejudice to microaggressions (Sue, 2010). Further, as noted earlier, the harms of hate that occur systemically and symbolically through processes of categorization, a lack of recognition of personal and social identity and the tension therein are also important to acknowledge as outcomes of our research. The breadth of hate harms suffered by gypsies, travellers and trans people can best be appreciated by shifting the lens of hate studies to more clearly see how each of these harms occurs in late modernity. The myopic nature of hate crime agendas limits our attention and concern to a specific set of behaviours enacted against a defined identity characteristic of a given victim and asserts that the solution lies in identifying and punishing the individuals responsible. Such an approach particularly reinforces the dyadic focus of adversarial Criminal Justice Systems upon victims and offenders (Freeman, 1978) and further reduces consideration of a complex interaction that is situated within a social context to a dualistic and detached interaction between individuals. Bound up within this approach to understanding the problem of hate in society is an unwillingness to explore the role of wider social conditions on the persistence and contemporary manifestations of hate in individuals' lives. The political rhetoric underpinning these interpretations and responses reinforces a divisive society, creating 'evil others' (see Baumeister and Campbell, 1999, for a review of the psychology of evil) as individually responsible for morally abhorrent actions and prejudices, that informs hate crime agendas' legal focus on offenders. The pursuit of the assumption that individual offenders are acting with autonomy and free will in some form of rejection of otherwise positive social values influences our analysis of harm in our society.

This analysis informs what we decide to do about it in a way that fails to acknowledge that we are, first of all, each members of the same moral society (Coleman, Deutsch and Marcus, 2014) and therefore each capable of instigating hate as harm on one another in pursuit of individually framed success. Thus, a politics focused on inclusion in this sense not only poses challenges associated with who should be included and who is left excluded but also, and most importantly for the quest of critical hate studies, what we are seeking to be included within (Duggan, 2012; Brandzel, 2016). Inclusion within a system that normalizes harms by its alignment with, and promotion of, competitive individualism has resulted in the commodification of the self and unattainable notions of the ideal citizen as a hard-working individual who is project and risk manager of their own lives. Within this context there is no reference to the impact that systemic barriers have for those who cannot achieve that ideal by their own means and the vilification of those people as irresponsible and accountable for their own plight. Systemic barriers to inclusion are ever-present in the lives of gypsies, travellers and trans communities whose lack of access to resources, support and welfare has placed them within the precariat (Standing, 2014) wherein they have also experienced over-policing as offenders and under-policing as victims, including as victims of hate crime (Spade and Willse, 2000; Moran, 2001; James 2007; 2020).

Ludwig (2016) contended that the political rationality of neo-liberalism is key to revealing the violent form of governance it represents. This mode of political power does not rely upon the coercion of its citizens; instead, it has achieved its goals through a willing consensus (see Hall, 1988). A backdrop characterized by a political rhetoric of scarce resources provides justification for austerity measures that cut public spending and permit the retraction of the welfare state. This political and cultural discourse keys into the depths of human anxiety and thus resonates from a subjective level, manipulating that anxiety to construct others as 'a potential real threat to anyone else's livelihood, status and identity' (Hall and Winlow, 2015, p 114; see also Hall et al, 2008). This individualistically framed anxiety serves to foster competition and associated tensions within and among communities in a fight for recognition as a means of survival.

A sociopolitical economy that is shaped by neo-liberal capitalist values of competitive individuality fosters divisions within and between groups in society, as noted earlier. This social context also legitimizes hateful behaviours as fair pursuits of 'special liberty' where 'one is entitled to do whatever it takes to participate in profitable market activity and achieve economic security and social status, even if it risks the infliction of harm on others and their social and physical environments' (Hall and Winlow, 2015, p 120). To construct hate victimization and offending as the result of idiosyncratic misfortune and rogue behaviour serves processes of pacification inherent within neo-liberal capitalism's success (Fisher, 2009) and in doing so belies an interpretation of the problem as one that is generated within and by that context. Further, this misdirection and diminishing of the problem to an individual risk or responsibility extinguishes the potential for collective action aimed at challenging this context and expanding normative configurations of how recognition can be achieved (Honneth, 1996) in contemporary and future society. Research has demonstrated how hate crime discourse that presents and shapes responses along the lines of social identities serves a limited number of people within a given identity category better than it does others (Spade and Wilce, 2000).

Conclusion

This chapter does not wish to detract from the impact of behaviours that are informed by prejudiced stereotyping of historically marginalized minority groups, but it does question the capacity of such a limited lens to confront the reality of the breadth of contemporary manifestations of hate and the associated harms that permeate individuals' lived realities. We propose that hate studies would benefit from a more thorough and critical analysis of the social context of contemporary neo-liberal capitalism in order to mount more effective responses to the perpetuation of hate within contemporary society. Through the application of intersectional theorizing, our data illuminates a range of experiences of harm that exist outside of popular conceptualizations of the hate crime paradigm. These experiences are not necessarily the result of interpersonal attacks, derived from bigotry and prejudice, and are instead experienced more implicitly at a psychological level associated with individuals' experiences of themselves as viable and worthy human beings. The critical hate studies perspective then asserts that these harms manifest as a result of the failings of the contemporary neo-liberal capitalist regime to provide a framework within which individuals and communities are supported to flourish. Instead the contemporary imbuing of the social world, and our relations to one another within it, with the values and rationale of economic free markets has produced 'harmful subjectivities' (Raymen, 2016) primarily concerned with the individualistic pursuit of freedom and fiscal success. Our approach would extend the interpretation and use of intersectionality theory further as a tool to explore lived experiences of hate that occur at the nexus of the interplay between personal and social identities that are both constructed within and through neo-liberal capitalist late modern society.

Note

[1]   See, for example, Flynn and Hodgson, 2017, for discussion of the impact of de-investment of legal aid on some of the most vulnerable in society.

References

Andrews, K. (2018) *Back to Black: Retelling Black Radicalism for the 21st Century.* London: Zed Books.

Appiah, K.A. (2010) *The Ethics of Identity*, Princeton, NJ: Princeton University Press

Baumeister, R.F. and Campbell, W.K. (1999) 'The intrinsic appeal of evil: sadism, sensational thrills, and threatened egotism', *Personality and Social Psychology Review*, 3(3): 210–21.

Bell, D. (1973) *The Coming of Post-Industrial Society: A Venture in Social Forecasting*, New York: Basic Books.

Berlant, L. (2011) *Cruel Optimism*, Durham: Duke University Press.

Bowling, B. and Phillips, C. (2012) 'Ethnicities, racism, crime and criminal justice', in: M. Maguire, R. Morgan and R. Reiner (eds), *Oxford Handbook of Criminology*, 5th Ed., Oxford: Oxford University Press.

Butler, J. (1990) *Gender Trouble: Feminism and the Subversion of Identity*, New York: Routledge.

Brandzel, A.L. (2016) *Against Citizenship: The Violence of the Normative*, Champaign, IL: University of Illinois Press.

Chakraborti, N. (2012) 'Introduction: hate crime victimization', *International Review of Victimology*, 18(1): 3–6.

Coleman, P.T., Deutsch, M. and Marcus, E.C. (eds) (2014) *The Handbook of Conflict Resolution: Theory and Practice*, 3rd Ed., San Franscisco: Jossey-Bass.

Crenshaw, K. (1991) 'Mapping the margins: intersectionality, identity politics and violence against women of colour', *Stanford Law Review*, 43(6): 1241–99.

Dilley, P. (1999) 'Queer theory: under construction', *International Journal of Qualitative Studies in Education*, 12(5): 457–72.

Duggan, L. (2012) *The Twilight of Equality? Neoliberalism, Cultural Politics, and the Attack on Democracy*, Boston: Beacon Press.

Fisher, M. (2009) *Capitalist Realism: Is there No Alternative?* Ropley: Zero Books.

Flynn, A. and Hodgson, J. (2017) *Access to Justice and Legal Aid: Comparative Perspectives on Unmet Legal Need*, Oxford: Hart Publishing Ltd.

Fraser, N., Honneth, A. and Golb, J. (2003) *Redistribution or Recognition? A Political-Philosophical Exchange*, London: Verso.

Freeman, A.D. (1978) 'Legitimizing racial discrimination through antidiscrimination law: a critical review of supreme court doctrine', *Minnesota Law Review*, 62: 1049–119.

Garland, J. (2011) 'Difficulties in defining hate crime victimization', *International Review of Victimology*, 18(1): 25–37.

Garrison, S. (2018) 'On the limits of "trans enough": authenticating trans identity narratives', *Gender & Society*, 32(5): 613–37.

Gheorge, N. (1997) 'The social construction of Romani identity', in T. Acton (ed.), *Gypsy Politics and Traveller Identity*, Hatfield: University of Hertfordshire Press.

Hall, S. (1988) 'The toad in the garden: Thatcherism among the theorists', in C. Nelson and L. Grossberg (eds), *Marxism and the Interpretation of Culture*. Basingstoke: Macmillan, pp 35–57.

Hall, S. and Winlow, S. (2015) *Revitalizing Criminological Theory: Towards a New Ultra-Realism*. London: Routledge.

Hall, S., Winlow, S., Ancrum, C. (2008) Criminal Identities and Consumer Culture: Crime, Exclusion and the New Culture of Narcissm. Cullompton: Willan.

Han, S. (2006) 'Intersectional sensibility and the shudder', in R. Heberle (ed.), *Feminist Interpretations of Theodor Adorno*, University Park, PA: Pennsylvania State University Press, pp 173–91.

Harvey, D. (2005) *A Brief History of Neoliberalism*, Oxford: Oxford University Press.

Heaslip, V., Hean, S. and Parker, J. (2016) 'Lived experience of vulnerability from a gypsy Roma traveller perspective', *Journal of Clinical Nursing*, 25(13–14): 1987–98. DOI: 10.111/jocn.13223.

Henne, K. and Troshynski, E. (2013) 'Mapping the margins of intersectionality: criminological possibilities in a transnational world', *Theoretical Criminology*, 17(4): 455–73.

Hines, S. (2006) 'What's the difference? Bringing particularity to queer studies of transgender', *Journal of Gender Studies*, 15(1): 49–66.

Hines, S. (2007) '(Trans) Forming gender: social change and transgender citizenship', *Sociological Research Online*, 12(1): 1–14.

Honneth, A. (1996) *The Struggle for Recognition*, Cambridge: Polity Press.

Hong G.K. (2008) '"The future of our worlds": black feminism and the politics of knowledge in the university under globalization', *Meridians*, 8(2): 95–115.

James, Z. and McBride, K. (2018) 'Critical hate studies: a theoretical perspective', Australia and New Zealand Criminology Conference, 4–7 December 2018, University of Melbourne, Australia.

James, Z. (2007) 'Policing marginal spaces: controlling gypsies and travellers', *Criminology and Criminal Justice*, 7(4): 367–89.

James, Z. (2020) *The Harms of Hate for Gypsies and Travellers: A Critical Hate Studies Perspective*, London: Palgrave Macmillan.

Johnston, A. (2008) *Žižek's Ontology: A Transcendental Materialist Theory of Subjectivity*, Evanston, IL: Northwestern University Press.

Ludwig, G. (2016) 'Desiring neoliberalism', *Sexuality Research and Social Policy*, 13(4): 417–27.

Marchetti, E. (2008) 'Intersectional race and gender analysis: why legal processes just don't get it', *Social and Legal Studies*, 17(2): 155–74.

Mason, G. (2013) 'Victim attributes in hate crime law: difference and the politics of justice', *British Journal of Criminology*, 54(2): 161–79.

Mason-Bish, H. (2010) 'Future challenges for hate crime policy: lessons from the past', in N. Chakraborti (ed) *Hate Crime: Concepts, Policy, Future Directions*, Cullompton: Willan, pp 58–77.

McBride, K. (2019) A Critical Analysis of Harms Experienced by Transgender Individuals, Doctoral dissertation, Plymouth: University of Plymouth.

McCarthy, J. and Prudham, S. (2004) 'Neoliberal nature and the nature of neoliberalism', *Geoforum*, 35(3): 275–83.

Meyer, M.D. (2004) 'Looking toward the interSEXions: examining bisexual and transgender identity formation from a dialectical theoretical perspective', *Journal of Bisexuality*, 3(3–4): 151–70.

Meyer, D. (2012) 'An intersectional analysis of lesbian, gay, bisexual, and transgender (LGBT) people's evaluations of anti-queer violence', *Gender & Society*, 26(6): 849–73.

Meyer, D (2014) 'Resisting hate crime discourse: queer and intersectional challenges to neoliberal hate crime laws', *Critical Criminology*, 22(1): 113–25.

Mills, C.W. (1959) *The Sociological Imagination*, Oxford: Oxford University Press.

Moran, L.J. (2001) 'Affairs of the heart: hate crime and the politics of crime control', *Law and Critique*, 12(3): 331–44.

Moran, M. (2014) *Identity and Capitalism*, London: Sage.

Perry, B. (2001) *In the Name of Hate: Understanding Hate Crimes*, London: Routledge.

Petrosino, C. (1999) 'Connecting the past to the future: hate crime in America', *Journal of Contemporary Criminal Justice*, 15(1): 22–47.

Raymen, T. (2016) 'Designing-in crime by designing-out the social? Situational crime prevention and the intensification of harmful subjectivities', *The British Journal of Criminology*, 56(3): 497–514.

Richardson, D. and May, H. (1999) 'Deserving victims? Sexual status and the social construction of violence', *The Sociological Review*, 47(2): 308–31.

Rorty, R. (1980) *Philosophy and the Mirror of Nature*, Oxford: Blackwell.

Salamon, G. (2010) *Assuming a Body: Transgender and Rhetorics of Materiality*, New York: Columbia University Press.

Spade, D. (2011) *Normal Life: Administrative Violence, Critical Trans Politics, and the Limits of Law*, Brooklyn, New York: South End Press.

Spade, J. and Willse, C. (2000) 'Confronting the limits of gay hate crimes activism: a radical critique', *Chicano-Latino Law Review*, 21: 38–52.

Standing, G. (2014) *A Precariat Charter: From Denizens to Citizens*, London New York: Bloomsbury Academic.

Sue, D.W. (2010) *Microaggressions in Everyday Life: Race, Gender, and Sexual Orientation*, Hoboken, NJ: John Wiley & Sons.

Thiara, R.K. and Hague, G. (2013) 'Disabled women and domestic violence: increased risk but fewer services', in A. Roulstone and H. Mason-Bish (eds) *Disability, Hate Crime and Violence*, London: Routledge, pp 106–17.

Wacquant, L.J. (2009) *Prisons of Poverty*, Contradictions Series Vol. 23, London: University of Minnesota Press.

Walfield, S.M., Socia, K.M. and Powers, R.A. (2017) 'Religious motivated hate crimes: reporting to law enforcement and case outcomes', *American Journal of Criminal Justice*, 42(1): 148–69.

Walklate, S. (2011) 'Reframing criminal victimisation: finding a place for vulnerability and resistance', *Theoretical Criminology*, 15(2): 179–94.

Ward, J. (2008) *Respectably Queer: Diversity Culture in LGBT Activist Organizations*, Nashville, TN: Vanderbilt University Press.

Warner, M. (2000) *The Trouble with Normal: Sex, Politics, and the Ethics of Queer Life*, Cambridge, Massachusetts: Harvard University Press.

Whittle, S. (2002) *Respect and Equality: Transsexual and Transgender Rights*, Abingdon: Routledge Cavendish.

Yar, M. (2012) 'Critical criminology, critical theory and social harm', in S. Hall and S. Winlow (eds) *New Directions in Criminological Theory*, London: Routledge.

Young, J. (1999) *The Exclusive Society*, London: Sage.

Žižek, S. (2006) *How to Read Lacan*. London: Granta Books.

11

'Why Do You Hate Me So Much?' Examining Disability Hate Crime Experiences through an Intersectional Lens

Jane Healy

Introduction

Disabled people have experienced repeated and ongoing forms of discrimination, isolation, differentiation and inequality throughout history (Petersilia, 2001; Hollomotz, 2013). This has included segregation, social isolation and restrictions to work and residence, and has been utilized as a means of differentiation in contemporary societies (Barton, 1996). It is only since the turn of the 21st century, however, that these forms of discrimination and prejudice towards disabled people have been recognized and labelled as *hate crimes*.

In England and Wales, disability[1] hate crimes were introduced into legislation through Section 146 of the Criminal Justice Act 2003. This advocates for an increase in sentencing for perpetrators where offences are shown to have been motivated by or demonstrative of hostility towards someone with a disability, or perceived disability. Currently, this enhanced sentence provision is the only legal route to prosecuting disability hate crime perpetrators. However, the Law Commission is reviewing all hate crime legislation in 2020–21, including the possibility of introducing a separate, aggravated offence for disability-motivated crimes.

The introduction of this legal provision for offences motivated by hostility or prejudice towards disabled people was welcomed by disabled people's movements, given the scale of purported disablist violence and abuse reported by them (Quarmby, 2008; Sin et al, 2009). Not only were campaigners concerned with extreme acts of violence and murder towards many disabled people, they also highlighted a pattern of ongoing victimization and abuse at the 'lower' end of the offending scale. Reports by disabled victims of hate crime regularly include name calling, bullying, harassment and various other unpleasant targeting and abuse of disabled people, their homes and their vehicles (Chakraborti et al, 2014a; Williams and Tregidga, 2014; Richardson et al, 2016). A pattern of repeated 'low-level' offending towards disabled people has been identified amid concerns that, left unchecked, these would elevate to more serious harms.

The potentiality of disability hate crime victimization is considerable in the context of numbers of people recognized as having a disability, impairment or health condition. Approximately 15 per cent of the world's population lives with some form of disability (Hughes et al, 2012). In the UK, the Office for Disability Issues estimates as many as 11 million people are living with a disability or impairment, equivalent to 29 per cent of the adult population (ODI, 2011; 2014). This prevalence of disability within our society puts a significant proportion of the population at risk of victimization.

This chapter explores the experiences of disabled victims of hate crimes with specific regard to gendered differences. In doing so, it considers experiences of male and female disabled participants who took part in a research study on hate crimes to identify distinct methods of victimization, using intersectionality as a research framework. The chapter begins with an overview of current disability hate crime research, before expanding on the methodology. It then presents contrasting experiences of disability hate crime by the research participants. The chapter concludes by acknowledging the additional contribution to knowledge gained by utilizing an intersectionality framework, despite its operational challenges, and recommends continued intersectional analyses in this field in future.

Conceptualizing disability hate crimes through disablism

Within disability hate crime literature, the term 'disablist crime' emerged as an alternative and potentially more suitable method of encapsulating disabled people's experiences of hate crime. Disablism is defined as 'discriminatory, oppressive or abusive behaviour arising from the belief that disabled people are inferior to others' (Quarmby, 2008, p 8)[2]. Disablism challenges the perceived essentialism of disabled people, placing greater emphasis on the prejudice of the perpetrator (Mason-Bish, 2015; Sin, 2015). A disablist definition also aligns with the social model of disability, with its emphasis on existing structural and environmental barriers and conditions that, combined with impairment, produce disability and links to wider social processes beyond individual perpetrator actions.

Disablism emerges from a permissive social or cultural context that allows disabled people to become easy targets of hate crimes (Balderston, 2013). It is associated with the misperception that disabled people are inferior to non-disabled people, which may be an underlying motivation for disability hate crimes. Disablism, in this manner, is about prejudice *against* disabled people. Consequently, disability hate crimes are an extreme articulation of the prejudice, discrimination and marginalization that disabled people thus face daily and are, therefore, a manifestation of disablism (Richardson et al, 2016) or *disablism in action.*

With specific regard to disability hate crime, College of Policing (2014) guidance define disability hate crime as 'any criminal offence which is perceived, by the victim or any other person, to be motivated by a hostility or prejudice based on a person's disability or perceived disability'. Disablism is therefore a cause of or contributing factor to disability hate crimes, rather than an alternative term for disability hate crime. It enables, justifies and engenders disability hate crimes through its expression of hostility or prejudice. This research recognizes the broader conceptualization of disablism as a contributing factor for disability hate crimes.

Prevalence of disability hate crimes

Disability is one of five legally protected characteristics, or 'strands', of hate crime in England and Wales. Disabled victims reported an estimated 50,000 disability hate crimes per year according to the Crime Survey for England and Wales (the second highest strand after race hate crimes), but only 8,469 were recorded by the police during the last 12 months of available data (Home Office, 2020). This research investigated the factors involved in this explicit under-reporting of disability hate crimes.

Research by academics, charities and third-party organizations provides significant evidence that disabled people are at greater risk of being victims of violent crimes and theft than non–disabled people (for example, Sin et al, 2009; Walker, 2009; ODI, 2011; Emerson and Roulstone, 2014). Disabled victims also report multiple forms of abuse, including name calling, verbal abuse, physical attacks, theft, vandalism and attacks on property (Scope, 2011). Chakraborti et al (2014b) found that disabled people were more likely to experience multiple forms of victimization than any other marginalized group. As such, the majority of victims of disability hate crime are repeat victims, or at greater risk of becoming repeat victims. These experiences can involve repeat targeting by the same perpetrator and also by different perpetrators, often over a prolonged period. Incidents often escalate in severity and frequency, with victims experiencing verbal and physical violence, abuse and harassment over several months and years (Chakraborti et al, 2014a; Williams and Tregidga, 2014; Richardson et al,

2016). Furthermore, evidence suggests that hate crime victimization involves higher levels of threatening and intimidating behaviour and abusive language when compared with other hate strands (Macdonald et al, 2017). The impact of this repeat victimization can be long-lasting and have devastating effects on mental and physical health (Sin et al, 2009; Pettitt et al, 2013), including premature deaths (Mikton and Shakespeare, 2014) and suicidal ideation (Chakraborti et al, 2014a). Examples of the ongoing and repetitive nature of repeat victimization can be evidenced from recent cases such as Fiona Pilkington and Bijam Ebrahimi, highlighting how early identification and response to reports of repeat victimization is crucial. Reported incidents need to be recognized as hate crimes because of the risk of persistent and escalating abuse (Richardson et al, 2016).

Disability hate crimes occur on a continuum (Hollomotz, 2013) in that victim reports can vary from so-called 'low-level' incidents, often in the form of harassment or intimidation (Berzins, Petch and Atkinson, 2003; Wood and Edwards, 2005; Gillen, 2007; Sin et al, 2009; Piggott, 2011), to extreme manifestations of excessive violence, torture, sexual assault and rape (Hughes et al, 2012; Khalifeh et al, 2013; Levin, 2013; Pettitt et al, 2013). Although some incidents may be perceived as 'minor' phenomena, these incidents can escalate into serious violence and significant harm if they are not reported or resolved (Mason, 2005).

Numerous studies have found that disabled women are at greater risk of victimization than non-disabled women and disabled men, are more likely to experience domestic/interpersonal violence and are at increased risk of sexual violence, sexual assault and stalking (for example, Smith et al, 2011; Hughes et al, 2012; Balderston, 2013; Thiara and Hague, 2013; McCarthy, 2017). A number of studies have also found significant numbers of perpetrators were known to their disabled victims, either as friends, family members, in relationships or caring roles (Chakraborti et al, 2014b; Williams and Tregidga, 2014; Sin, 2015; Richardson et al, 2016). This has led to disabled women being particularly vulnerable to victimization from those they are in a relationship with (Magowan, 2003), often exacerbated by the lack of service provision for disabled women at refuges and shelters when they wish to leave (Thiara and Hague, 2013; McCarthy, 2016).

Higher levels of disability hate crime have been reported in areas of poverty or deprivation, though this is not surprising given there are relatively more disabled tenants in local authority housing, an area also associated with poverty levels (Hunter et al, 2007; Sin et al, 2009; Clayton et al, 2016). Disabled people face increased financial hardship compared with non-disabled people (ODI, 2011; 2014) and as such they are often housed in areas of high deprivation (Macdonald et al, 2017), suggesting that social housing contributes to disabled people's risk of victimization. Not only do areas with high levels of deprivation tend to have higher numbers of disabled tenants, they also tend to have larger ethnic minority populations, and thus the intersections of race, class and disability may combine to increase the likelihood of victimization for already-marginalized groups. Resultingly, tensions emerge that can potentially result in increased violence and hostility in a fast-changing social, economic and cultural landscape. Thus, research must consider the structural violence of disproportionate relative poverty experienced by disabled people (Perry, 2013).

The evidence presented earlier demonstrates how disability hate crimes are associated with ongoing, repeated and multiple incidents which, in combination with many disabled people being encouraged to ignore and accept negative behaviour towards them (Sin, 2013), can lead to greater risk of re-victimization. A disabled person's likelihood of being targeted is associated with a number of factors, including their gender, socioeconomic disadvantage and poverty levels. The next section outlines the methodology applied to the research study.

Methodology

The research is part of a wider study that included a survey, interviews and focus groups with disabled people, key informants and activists working in the field. This included 12 narrative interviews with disabled people, eight women and four men, all of whom had been a victim of hate crime (Healy, 2020) (see Table 11.1). An additional 14 people took part in semi-structured interviews as key informants or experts in their field ('stakeholders') and 62 participants indicated through an online survey that they had experienced disability hate crimes (n=83). Analysis was conducted with the aid of an NVivo software package (QSR NVivo 10.0) and SPSS. Given the exploratory nature of the research, an inductive approach to data analysis was initially taken. Analysis followed the principles of 'open coding' within a constructivist perspective, and data was developed into key themes (Bryman, 2004). Full ethical approval was received in advance of all data collection. During the early stages of the interview process, multiple and overlapping categories of identity within participants' stories were exposed through the narrative interview process, which led to the research design adapting an intersectional approach to analysis. Intersectionality requires more than simple separate analysis and a move away from traditional theories to interpret results (Horvath and Kelly 2007; Cole, 2009). It endeavours to construct new theories and methodological approaches that address this complex process through which social categories shape and determine individuals, although its complexity can make analysis difficult if it includes a wide range of dimensions and categories.

Intersectionality within research thus involves the concurrent analyses of multiple, overlapping sources, based on the principle that any impact on one

Table 11.1: Participant interview details

Participants	Pseudonym	Type of disability, impairment or condition OR related area of expertise	Interview in person (IP) or by phone/skype (PS)
1	Amy	Physical impairments and a wheelchair user *and* disability activist	IP
2	Anne Marie	CDG, congenital disorder and physical impairments	IP
3	Ciara	Learning and physical disabilities	IP
4	Daniel	Sensory impairment (blind) and medical conditions	IP
5	Gemma	Sensory impairment (blind) and medical conditions	PS
6	Grace	Auto-immune disease with physical impairments and a wheelchair user	PS
7	Hayley	Medical conditions and genetic disorders	PS
8	Martin	Multiple sclerosis and a wheelchair user	PS
9	Ruby	Cerebral palsy, Asperger's syndrome, PTSD and a brain tumour	PS
10	Sarah	Myalgic encephalomyelitis (ME), physical and mental health conditions	IP
11	Stuart	Amputee (right leg)	PS
12	Zane	Learning and physical disabilities	IP
Stakeholder/Key informant interviewees			
13	Denzil	Head of Cohesion, Council 'N'	IP
14	Emily	Community Safety Officer, housing organization	IP
15	Freya	Lived Experience Officer, disabled people's user-led organization (DPULO)	IP
16	George	Senior Service Delivery Manager, victim support, area 'S'	IP
17	Jayne	Hate Crime Officer, international organization	PS
18	Leah	Detective Constable, police force 'A'	IP
19	Max	Senior Advisor, CPS	IP
20	Patrick	Hate Crime Sergeant, neighbourhood policing, police force 'S'	IP

(continued)

Table 11.1: Participant interview details (continued)

Participants	Pseudonym	Type of disability, impairment or condition OR related area of expertise	Interview in person (IP) or by phone/skype (PS)
21	Phoebe	Hate Crime Caseworker, council 'H'	IP
22	Riley	Learning Disability Coordinator	PS
23	Sally	Hate Crime Project Worker, victim support, area 'L'	IP
24	Susie	Project Leader, third-party reporting agency, area 'A'	IP
25	Teagan	People, Confidence and Equality Officer, police force 'D'	IP
26	Tom	Neighbourhood Policing Chief Inspector, police force 'N'	IP

form of subordination may differ depending on its combination with other potential sources. Liasidou (2013) and Balderston (2013) advocate that it is a suitable method for interpreting experiences of disability hate crime, as consideration of multiple, intersecting layers of oppression or subordination enables the researcher to understand how the impact of experiences of hate crime can vary. Identities should not be regarded as fixed, but should be understood in conjunction with the ways in which ethnicity, gender, socioeconomic status and so on intersect with disability. By applying an intersectional approach to disability, there is a shift away from individual pathology towards a framework bent on tackling wider socially and culturally systemic regimes, which is sympathetic to the social model of disability.

Given the focus of the study on disability hate crimes, the researcher applied McCall's (2005) intracategorical approach to intersectional analysis, which enabled an explicit recognition of a 'master category' (p 1777, but see Healy (2019) for an in-depth discussion on this methodological process). Disability/impairment was identified as the master category or predominant element of identity. Through the narrative interview process, participants naturally and authentically indicated how multiple dimensions of identity shaped their experiences and some of the distinguishing features from the data analysis are presented in this chapter.

Reflections on the research process

There is ongoing debate within disability research, particularly by those in support of the social model, around non-disabled researchers being able to investigate disability with any authenticity (Fawcett and Hearn, 2004).

Drawing on standpoint theory (Dewsbury et al, 2004), this suggests that unless researchers possess the same frameworks of meaning or experience, they cannot appreciate the reality of disability and their research is correspondingly flawed. This argument assumes that disabled people share a culture that is different to others and homogenous across all forms of impairments, however. It fails to consider that 'insiders' are not always recognized as 'inside' the community or that their experiences may differ markedly from those of their research participants (Fassinger and Morrow, 2013). I argue that such cultural differences are not quite as homogenous as previously thought. The experience of disability is not unitary and the range of disabilities and impairments is vast. Effectively, having an impairment does not always provide someone with an affinity with other disabled people, nor the inclination to do disability research (Shakespeare, 1996; Balderston, 2013a). Notwithstanding, it is a concern for non-disabled researchers like myself to contextualize disability research with authenticity (Stone, 1997; Dupont 2008). Like Barnes (1992) I was keen to contribute to a working dialogue between the research community and disabled people. By being non-disabled, I stood in the 'space' between disabled users and the disabling system that may be working around them.

Experiences of disability hate crimes: intersecting gender and disability

As discussed in Healy (2019), an intersectional framework identified two interwoven trends in the findings. The first is that of intersecting hate *strands*. Both victim participants and stakeholders recognize that hate crimes can overlap different minority strands and that individual victims are often targeted for multiple reasons. Many stakeholders and victim participants identified this as a layering of multiple identities. For example, Patrick (police) acknowledges that a number of incidents and crimes have multiple hate crime 'markers' and are recorded as such. He sees this as a positive outcome of recording hate crime as it recognizes the multiple elements to any individual's identity. However, although he can record more than one strand of hate crime on the case management system used by police forces[3], in most incidents there exists a 'hierarchy' of strands, with one perceived as more serious than the other(s) and thus a lack of recognition of the unique experiences of the victim as a result of their intersecting identities (Mason-Bish, 2015). Given the limited legislation available to disability hate crimes when compared with, say, race hate crimes, it is not surprising that the strand with the greater legislative impact will take the lead in prosecutions.

This hierarchical effect is also evident in other fields. Emily (a community safety officer for a housing company) cites several cases of domestic violence where disability was a contributing factor. Because of the constraints of her employer's in-house recording system, cases had to be logged with one primary classification, resulting in the majority of cases being logged as domestic violence, rather than as disability-motivated, events. Emily emphasizes that regardless of how a case is logged, her priority is to address *all* contributing factors to her residents' victimization and any support will target multiple areas, according to need. However, although she concedes that disability is potentially involved in a number of cases, during her interview Emily did not consider the increased risk that *disabled* women are placed at in terms of domestic and interpersonal violence.

These points relate to the complimentary intersection of gender and disability, which was a particularly strong theme within the research findings. This is not surprising given the evidence that disabled women are doubly disadvantaged as a consequence of their gender and disability, making them particularly vulnerable to sexual violence and exploitation (Balderston, 2013; Sherry, 2013b). Unfortunately, at the time of writing, gender (or sex) is not a protected hate crime characteristic and therefore nuanced experiences of disabled women are difficult to distinguish from all disabled people in published hate crime statistics.

The survey data provided a useful contribution to this complex issue. The survey asked if respondents had been a victim of disability hate crime and if so, how often. Findings suggested that slightly more men than women were likely to experience disability hate crime, with 24 men (80 per cent of males who responded) and 38 women (73.1 per cent) having experienced victimization. This contrasts with many studies that show that disabled women are at greater risk of victimization than disabled men (for example, Balderston, 2013; Coleman, Sykes and Walker, 2013; McCarthy, 2017). However, female survey respondents reported two thirds of the total *number* of hate crimes. Women respondents reported being threatened and bullied more than men, as well as reporting more name calling, verbal abuse and physical assaults (see Figure 11.1). In comparison, male respondents reported experiencing slightly more cases of 'withdrawal of support' than females, although the survey did not determine what specific forms of support survey participants may have experienced. Thus, women reported more types of violence and abuse than their male counterparts. This research is cautious not to claim that all women experience a greater variety of abuse than men, given the small numbers involved. Additionally, men may be less likely to recognize or report certain types of abuse than women, but the results contribute to the literature around women's increased risk of victimization.

Shakespeare (1996) suggests that gender identity and disabled identity interact in different ways for men and women; masculinity is traditionally bound to strength and a denial of weakness or frailty. It is noteworthy that, with the exception of Zane, the disabled male interviewees had not reported

Figure 11.1: A comparison of types of abuse by gender

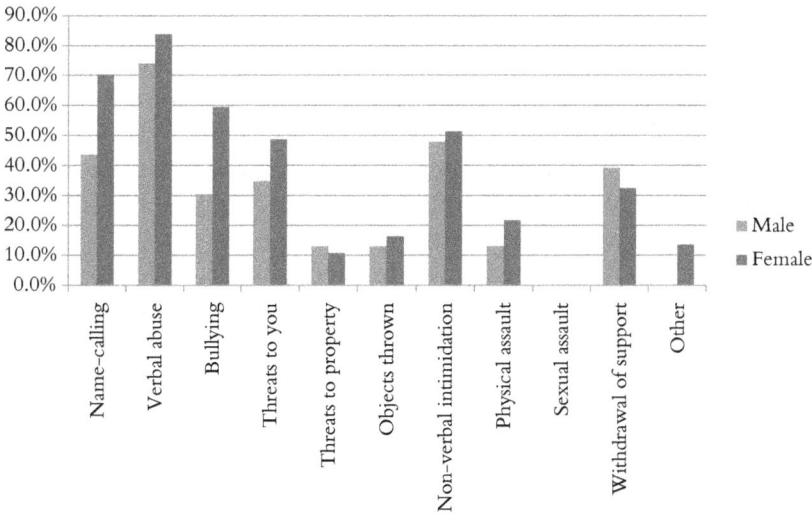

their experiences to police, although all of the disabled female interview participants had (n=8). This may be a coincidence in terms of the small numbers who agreed to take part in the study or perhaps indicative of the type of people who are willing to talk to researchers about their experiences. Alternatively, it raises concerns as to whether there are gender-specific factors involved in how men and women respond to their experiences or the types of experience they are confronted with. Both Stuart and Martin say that they did not see any point in reporting their encounters to police, and Daniel's priority was reporting his neighbours' abusive behaviour to his local council, rather than consulting the police. In addition, female participants who recognized their experiences as disability hate crime believed they were of such a serious nature that they warranted reporting, although consideration must be given to the types of experiences they chose not to report also. Three female interview participants recounted experiences of sexual violence and abuse, supporting current evidence on sexual assault as a method of disability hate crime (Barclay and Mulligan, 2009; Coleman, Sykes and Walker, 2013; Sherry, 2013b).

The narrative interview design allowed for further examination of potential gender differences. Stuart says he never experienced physical assault but has experienced numerous incidents of verbal abuse, none of which he reported to police. He is a white male in his 50s with a prosthetic leg, who is married with two young children. He describes how he uses strategies to reduce tension and apologizes to those who confront him. It may be that his compliant behaviour is reducing the likelihood of an incident *escalating* to physical abuse, or that he is simply fortunate that he has not been physically attacked. It must be considered whether his gender, or masculinity, reduces his risk of physical violence. Being a less visibly disabled man also reduces his risk of being a victim of physical violence, as previous studies have identified how the more visible an impairment, the greater the likelihood of victimization (for example, Action for Blind People, 2008). Furthermore, the perpetrators that Stuart encounters tend to be older men and women, rather than groups of young men or adolescents who are reported by female victims.

Waxman (1991) described how disabled women were perceived as morally suspect and more dangerous than disabled men because disability is perceived as preventing women from embracing traditional female roles such as nurturing and sexual desirability. In addition, sexual stereotypes of women exist around the assumed passivity of disabled people and of women generally; dependency, vulnerability and frailty are dominant, and women are represented in negative and passive ways (Hague et al, 2008; Barclay and Mulligan, 2009; Murray and Powell, 2009). This is acknowledged by Amy (an activist), who says that women in certain minority groups are 'not getting the knowledge of how to report and what experiences are hate crime' because they are *women*. Most of the research participants were of white ethnicity, and these findings can therefore not be applied to women from all ethnic groups, but they underline the desire and importance for further intersectional studies on minority ethnic disabled women's experiences.

Another distinguishing feature was the treatment of two male participants by the police. Zane described being arrested by police for verbally confronting a relative about their behaviour towards his partner, aligning with the literature around stereotypes about learning difficulties, leading to some disabled people being perceived as perpetrators rather than victims (Sin, 2013). Martin described being threatened with arrest for reacting to the verbal abuse he received from a stranger. Roulstone and Sadique (2013) suggest that police tend to align hate crimes with mental ill health or learning disabilities, such that Martin, in a wheelchair, may not have been perceived to be a possible victim. Martin, however, interpreted this as a consequence of his disabled status. He "felt [the police] were accusing me rather than him cos I was an easier target".

Perhaps by responding to and reacting against their abusers these male participants failed to meet social expectations of disabled people as vulnerable or weak (similar findings are reported by Balderston, 2013). Their manifestation as less-than-ideal victims because they refuse to be vulnerable or blameless may have presented them as less deserving of victim status (Brown, 2004; Mason, 2014), when compared with their female counterparts.

Conclusion

Research studies have shown how the experience of disability is compounded when disabled individuals belong to multiple minority groups, including sexual orientation, gender or ethnicity (Clement et al, 2011; Coleman et al, 2013). Intersectionality acknowledges this compounding as it advocates awareness that every individual occupies multiple categories simultaneously and that those individuals can be members of majority and minority communities concurrently. These intersecting categories of identity can move up and down in terms of priority or positioning of identities, like layers that can be worn in a different order, at different times (Anthias, 1998). The challenge for researchers is to be able to identify and interpret these experiences without reductive results.

Researching hate crime through a wider lens, beyond simple constructions of identity, acknowledges the roles other elements have to play in experiences of victimization, including that of socioeconomic conditions and gender. Disabled women are at greater risk of domestic violence (Brownridge, 2006), and thus the experiences of all disabled people will not be the same. Disabled men may be less likely to report hate crimes and less likely to be recognized as victims of hate crime. In addition, strand-based approaches draw attention to those left out of hate crime protection and victim groups are presented in simplistic forms. However, the concept of intersectionality has its limitations in terms of practical and policy questions as to how many aspects of identity should be considered (Mason-Bish, 2015).

A hate crime model informed by intersectionality thus needs to engage on a multi- rather than single-strand level and reduce the 'real risks of oversimplifying the victim experience' (Perry, 2009, p 9). There have been calls for further intersectional analysis of disability hate crimes to identify and explore how other elements of identity can impact upon experiences (Sherry, 2013b; Sin, 2014; Healy, 2019). To date, however, there have been limited attempts to understand the experiences of those who occupy multiple positions of inferiority such as women with disabilities, which is evidenced in the longevity of some of the literature included within this chapter, although there are some exceptions (Brownridge, 2006; Barclay and Mulligan, 2009; Williams and Tregidga, 2014). There is also a dearth of research on ethnic minority women's experiences of disability hate crime. This research reflects upon the experiences of disabled men and women and, in combination with other identity strands, demonstrates how difficult it is to categorize one element of identity as being of greater risk or significance than others. For the male participants, they were at more risk of being labelled or identified as a perpetrator than a victim. For the female participants, they were more likely to experience sexual violence and abuse. Women in this study report more frequent victimization than men, but it is unknown whether this is because men do not experience as much victimization or do not recognize or report it as such.

Hate crime does not occur in a social or cultural vacuum and theorizing hate crime must consider the cultural, social and political processes that underlie these events. Hate crimes are more than bigoted acts and rather demonstrative of embedded violence that occurs within the structural and cultural contexts within which groups interact (Perry, 2002). Violence and hate crimes are therefore a response to those who are outside of socially and culturally accepted boundaries. Hate crime is accordingly a tool for maintaining the social norm and for offenders to reinforce their dominance (Perry, 2005). It is not simply about an individual victim and an individual perpetrator but is a result of a structured and hierarchical society that relies heavily on the history and persistence of relations of advantage and disadvantage. As Perry (2003) argues, systemic violence questions not only the victim's identity but also a national commitment to tolerance and inclusion. The persistence of disability hate crime in our society lays bare 'the bigotry that is endemic' within each of us (p 21).

To conclude, this chapter demonstrates that a strand-based approach to hate crime disguises the variety of intersecting elements of identity that could not only increase their risk of victimization, but also reduce a victim's likelihood of reporting their experiences. Efforts must be made to engage with harder to reach groups and, if reported, to record these experiences adequately and accurately to reflect all of their experiences. As Mason-Bish (2015) suggests, policy needs to adapt to be able to consider the risks involved in more complex identities. We need to be able to record data to take account of these if we want to fully understand the extent of disablist violence and abuse.

Notes

[1] For the purposes of this research, the term 'disability' is understood as a physical, mental, psychological or sensory impairment or health condition that, in interaction with an individual's social environment, has a long-term adverse effect on the daily activities of that individual.

[2] The concept of disablism was first suggested by Abberley in 1987 in response to the absence of any historical experience of disability (Oliver, 1996) although Quarmby (2008) is regularly cited with reference to its definition.

[3] Despite efforts by UK policing generally to position itself as a 'service' rather than a 'force' (Giannasi, 2014), literature continues to refer to police 'forces' (for example, Corcoran and Smith, 2016). In addition, all four police officers and one former police officer who were interviewed specifically referred to the police as a 'force'. For these reasons, whilst acknowledging the attempted re-positioning and cultural shift in policing, the term 'force' is used throughout.

References

Action for Blind People (2008) *Report on Verbal and Physical Abuse Towards Blind and Partially Sighted People Across the UK*, London: Action for Blind People, [online] www.actionforblindpeople.org.uk/abuse-survey,484,SA. html

Anthias, F. (1998) 'Rethinking social divisions: some notes towards a theoretical framework', *Sociological Review*, 46(3): 505–35.

Balderston, S. (2013) 'Victimized again? Intersectionality and injustice in disabled women's lives after hate crime and rape', in M. Texler Segal and V. Demos (eds) *Gendered Perspectives on Conflict and Violence: Part A (Advances in Gender Research, Volume 18A)*, Bingley: Emerald Group Publishing Limited, pp 17–51.

Barclay, H. and Mulligan, D. (2009) 'Tackling violence against women – lessons for efforts to tackle other forms of targeted violence', *Safer Communities*, 8(4): 43–50.

Barnes, C. (1992) 'Qualitative research: valuable or irrelevant?', *Disability, Handicap & Society*, 7(2): 115–24.

Barton, L. (1996) *Disability & Society: Emerging Issues and Insights*, Harlow: Pearson Education Limited.

Berzins, K., Petch, A. and Atkinson, J.M. (2003) 'Prevalence and experience of harassment of people with mental health problems living in the community', *British Journal of Psychiatry*, 183(12): 526–33.

Brown, H. (2004) 'A rights-based approach to abuse of women with learning disabilities', *Tizard Learning Disability Review*, 9(4): 41–4.

Brownridge, D.A. (2006) 'Partner violence against women with disabilities: prevalence, risk, and explanations', *Violence Against Women*, 12(9): 805–22.

Chakraborti, N., Garland, J. and Hardy, S.-J. (2014a) 'The Leicester hate crime project: briefing paper 1: disablist hate crime: victims' perspectives', University of Leicester, [online] www2.le.ac.uk/departments/criminology/ hate/documents/bp1-disablist-hate-crime/view

Chakraborti, N., Garland, J. and Hardy, S.-J. (2014b) 'The Leicester hate crime project: findings and conclusions', University of Leicester, [online] www2.le.ac.uk/departments/criminology/hate/documents/fc-full-report

Clayton, J., Donovan, C. and Macdonald, S.J. (2016) 'A critical portrait of hate crime/incident reporting in North East England: the value of statistical data and the politics of recording in an age of austerity', *Geoforum*, 75: 64–74.

Clement, S., Brohan, E., Sayce, L., Pool, J. and Thornicroft, G. (2011) 'Disability hate crime and targeted violence and hostility: a mental health and discrimination perspective', *Journal of Mental Health*, 20(3): 219–25.

Cole, E.R. (2009) 'Intersectionality and research in psychology', *American Psychologist*, 64(3): 170–80.

Coleman, N., Sykes, W. and Walker, A. (2013) 'Crime and disabled people: baseline statistical analysis of measures from the formal legal inquiry into disability-related harassment', Research report 90, London: EHRC/ Independent Social Research.

College of Policing (2014) *Hate Crime Operational Guidance 2014*, Coventry: College of Policing Limited.

Corcoran, H. and Smith, K. (2016) *Hate Crime, England and Wales, 2015/ 16. Statistical Bulletin 11/16*. London: Home Office, Crown Copyright [online] www.gov.uk/government/uploads/system/uploads/attachment_ data/file/559319/hate-crime-1516-hosb1116.pdf

Dewsbury, G., Clarke, K., Randall, D., Rouncefield, M. and Sommerville, I. (2004) 'The anti-social model of disability', *Disability & Society*, 19(2): 145–58.

Dupont, I. (2008) 'Beyond doing no harm: a call for participatory action research with marginalized populations in criminological research', *Crit Crim*, 16: 197–207.

Emerson, E. and Roulstone, A. (2014) 'Developing an evidence base for violent and disablist hate crime in Britain: findings from the life opportunities survey', *Journal of Interpersonal Violence*, 29(17): 3086–104 [online] http://jiv.sagepub.com/content/29/17/3086

Fawcett, B. and Hearn, J. (2004) 'Researching others: epistemology, experience, standpoints and participation', *International Journal of Social Research Methodology*, 7(3): 201–18.

Fassinger, R. and Morrow, S. L. (2013) 'Towards best practices in quantitative, qualitative, and mixed-methods research: a social justice perspective', *Journal for Social Action in Counselling and Psychology*, 5(2): 69–83.

Gillen, S. (2007) 'Targets of hate crime', *Community Care*, 1692: 28–9.

Giannasi, P. (2014) 'Academia from a practitioner perspective: a reflection on the changes in the relationship between academia, policing and government in a hate crime context', in N. Chakraborti and J. Garland (eds) *Responding to Hate Crime: The Case for Connecting Policy and Research*, Bristol: Policy Press, pp 27–38.

Hague, G., Thiara, R.K., Magowan, P. and Mullender, A. (2008) 'Making the links: disabled women and domestic violence: summary of findings and recommendations for good practice', Women's Aid [online] www. womensaid.org.uk/wp-content/uploads/2015/12/Disabled-women-Making_the_Links_-_full_length_report_large_print11.pdf

Healy, J. (2019) 'Thinking outside the box: intersectionality as a hate crime research framework', *Papers from the British Criminology Conference*, 19: 60–83, [online] www.britsoccrim.org/pbcc2019/

Healy, J.C. (2020) '"It spreads like a creeping disease": experiences of victims of disability hate crimes in austerity Britain', *Disability & Society*, 35(2): 176–200.

Hollomotz, A. (2013) 'Disability and the continuum of violence', in A. Roulstone and H. Mason-Bish (eds) *Disability, Hate Crime and Violence*, London: Routledge, pp 52–63.

Home Office (2020) 'Hate crime, England and Wales 2019/20, statistical bulletin 29/20', [online] www.gov.uk/government/statistics/hate-crime-england-and-wales-2019-to-2020

Horvath, M.A.H. & Kelly, L. (2007) 'From the outset: why violence should be a priority for the Commission for Equality and Human Rights', A briefing paper by the End Violence Against Women Campaign and the Roddick Foundation, [online] www.edf.org.uk/blog/wp-content/uploads/2007/06/From-the-outset-.pdf

Hughes, K., Bellis, M.A., Jones, L., Wood, S., Bates, G., Eckley, L., McCoy, E., Mikton, C., Shakespeare, T. and Officer, A. (2012) 'Prevalence and risk of violence against adults with disabilities: a systematic review and meta-analysis of observational studies', *The Lancet*, 379(9826): 1621–9.

Hunter, C., Hodge, N.S., Nixon, J., Parr, S. and Willis, B. (2007) *Disabled People's Experiences of Anti-Social Behavior and Harassment in Social Housing: A Critical Review*, London: Disability Rights Commission.

Khalifeh, H., Howard, L., Osborn, D., Moran, P. and Johnson, S. (2013) 'Violence against people with disability in England and Wales: findings from a national cross-sectional survey', *PLoS One*, 8(2): e55952. DOI: 10.1371/journal.pone.0055952.

Levin, J. (2013) 'Disablist violence in the US: unacknowledged hate crime', in A. Roulstone and H. Mason-Bish (eds) *Disability, Hate Crime and Violence*, London: Routledge, pp 95–105.

Liasidou, A. (2013) 'Intersectional understandings of disability and implications for a social justice reform agenda in education policy and practice', *Disability & Society*, 28(3): 299–321.

Macdonald, S., Donovan, C. and Clayton, J. (2017) 'The disability bias: understanding the context of hate in comparison with other minority populations', *Disability and Society*, 12(4): 483–99.

Magowan, P. (2003) 'Nowhere to run, nowhere to hide: domestic violence and disabled women', *Safe: Domestic Abuse Quarterly*, 5: 15–18.

Mason, G. (2005) 'Hate crime and the image of the stranger', *British Journal of Criminology*, 45(6): 837–59.

Mason, G. (2014) 'The symbolic purpose of hate crime law: ideal victims and emotion', *Theoretical Criminology*, 18(1): 75–92.

Mason-Bish, H. (2015) 'Beyond the silo: rethinking hate crime and intersectionality', in N. Hall, A. Corb, P. Giannasi and J.G.D. Grieve (eds) *The Routledge International Handbook on Hate Crime*, Oxon: Routledge, pp 24–33.

McCall, L. (2005) 'The complexity of intersectionality', *Journal of Women in Culture and Society*, 30(3): 1771–800.

McCarthy, M. (2016) 'What are the support needs of women with learning disabilities who have been abused?', *Tizard Learning Disability Review*, 21(1): 39–42.

McCarthy, M. (2017) '"What kind of abuse is him spitting in my food?": reflections on the similarities between disability hate crime, so-called "mate" crime and domestic violence against women with intellectual disabilities', *Disability & Society*, 32(4): 595–600.

Mikton, C. and Shakespeare, T. (2014) 'Introduction to special issue on violence against people with disability', *Journal of Interpersonal Violence*, 29(17): 3055–62.

Murray, S. and Powell, A. (2009) ' "What's the problem?" Australian public policy constructions of domestic and family violence', *Violence Against Women*, 15(5): 532–52.

Office for Disability Issues (ODI) (2011) *Life Opportunities Survey*, Wave one results, 2009/11, London: ODI/HM Govt.

Office for Disability Issues (ODI) (2014) *Disability Facts and Figures*, [online] www.gov.uk/government/publications/disability-facts-and-figures/disability-facts-and-figures

Perry, B. (2002) 'Hate crime and identity politics', *Theoretical Criminology*, 6(4): 485–91.

Perry, B. (2003) 'Where do we go from here? Researching hate crime', *Internet Journal of Criminology*, 1–59 [online] www.internetjournalofcriminology.com/Where per cent20Do per cent20We per cent20Go per cent20From per cent20Here. per cent20Researching per cent20Hate per cent20Crime.pdf

Perry, B. (2005) 'A crime by any other name: the semantics of "hate"', *Journal of Hate Studies*, 4(1): 121–37.

Perry, B. (2009) 'The sociology of hate: theoretical approaches', in B. Levin (ed) *Hate Crimes Volume I: Understanding and Defining Hate Crime*, Westport, CT: Praeger, pp 55–76.

Perry, J. (2013) 'The wrong war? Critically examining the "fight against disability hate crime"', in A. Roulstone and H. Mason-Bish (eds) *Disability, Hate Crime and Violence*, London: Routledge, pp 40–51.

Petersilia, J. (2001) 'Invisible victims: violence against persons with developmental disabilities', *Human Rights*, 27(1): 9–13.

Pettitt, B., Greenhead, S., Khalifeh, H., Drennan, V., Hart, T., Hogg, J., Borschmann, R., Mamo, E. and Moran, P. (2013) *At Risk, yet Dismissed: The Criminal Victimisation of People with Mental Health Problems*, London: Victim Support & Mind.

Piggott, L. (2011) 'Prosecuting disability hate crime: a disabling solution?', *People, Place & Policy Online*, 5(1): 25–34.

Quarmby, K. (2008) *Getting Away with Murder: Disabled People's Experiences of Hate Crime in the UK*, London: Scope, Disability Now and UKDPC.

Richardson, K., Beadle-Brown, J., Bradshaw, J., Guest, C. Malovic, A. and Himmerich, J. (2016) '"I felt that I deserved it" – experiences and implications of disability hate crime', *Tizard Learning Disability Review*, 21(2): 80–88.

Roulstone, A. and Sadique, K. (2013) 'Vulnerable to misinterpretation: disabled people, "vulnerability", hate crime and the fight for legal recognition', in A. Roulstone and H. Mason-Bish (eds), *Disability, Hate Crime and Violence*, London: Routledge, pp 25-39.

Scope (2011) '*Deteriorating attitudes towards disabled people*', [online] www.scope.org.uk/news/attitudes-towards-disabled-people-survey

Shakespeare, T. (1996) 'Power and prejudice: issues of gender, sexuality and disability', in L. Barton (ed) *Disability & Society: Emerging Issues and Insights*, Harlow: Pearson Education Limited, pp 190–214.

Sherry, M. (2013b) 'Feminist reflections on disability hate crime: Gendered Perspectives on Conflict and Violence, Part A', *Advances in Gender Research*, 18(A): 53–66.

Sin, C.H. (2013) 'Making disablist hate crime visible: addressing the challenges of improving reporting', in A. Roulstone and H. Mason-Bish (eds) *Disability, Hate Crime and Violence*, London: Routledge, pp 147–65.

Sin, C.H. (2014) 'Using a "layers of influence" model to understand the interaction of research, policy and practice in relation to disablist hate crime', in N. Chakraborti and J. Garland (eds) *Responding to Hate Crime: The Case for Connecting Policy and Research*, Bristol: Policy Press, pp 99–112.

Sin, C.H. (2015) 'Hate crime against people with disabilities', in N. Hall, A. Corb, P. Giannasi and J.G.D. Grieve (eds) *The Routledge International Handbook on Hate Crime*, Oxon: Routledge, pp 193–206.

Sin, C.H., Hedges, A., Cook, C., Mguni, N. and Comber, N. (2009) 'Disabled people's experiences of targeted violence and hostility', EHRC Research Report 21, EHRC & Office for Public Management.

Smith, K. (ed), Coleman, K., Eder, S. and Hall, P. (2011) *Homicides, Firearm Offences and Intimate Violence 2009/10: Supplementary Volume 2 to Crime in England and Wales 2009/10*, Home Office Statistical Bulletin: 01/11, London: Crown Copyright, [online] www.homeoffice.gov.uk/publications/science-research-statistics/research-statistics/crime-research/hosb0111/hosb0111?view=Binary

Stone, E. (1997) 'From the research notes of a foreign devil: disability research in China', in C. Barnes and G. Mercer (eds), *Doing Disability Research*, Leeds: The Disability Press, pp 207–28.

Thiara, R.K. and Hague, G. (2013) 'Disabled women and domestic violence: increased risk but fewer services', in A. Roulstone and H. Mason-Bish (eds) *Disability, Hate Crime and Violence*, London: Routledge, pp 106–17.

Walker, P. (2009) *Charity says 9 per cent of disabled people have been victims of hate crime, The Guardian*, p 12.

Waxman, B.F. (1991) 'Hatred: the unacknowledged dimension in violence against disabled people', *Sexuality and Disability*, 9(3): 185–99.

Williams, M.L. and Tregidga, J. (2014) 'Hate crime cictimization in Wales: psychological and physical impacts across seven hate crime victim types', *British Journal of Criminology*, 54(5): 946–67.

Wood, J. and Edwards, K. (2005) 'Victimization of mentally ill patients living in the community: is it a life-style issue?', *Legal and Criminological Psychology*, 10: 279–90.

12

Using Intersectionality to Understand Abuse against Elders: A Conceptual Examination

Emma Finnegan

Introduction

Feminist research has long been at the forefront of examining violence in women's lives (Stanko, 1990). However, this largely focused on younger women. Consequently, the experiences of older women have been somewhat ignored (Bows, 2019), and there has been scant regard afforded to older male victims (Melchiorre et al, 2016). As a result, there is a dearth of research exploring abuse against elders (EA). Further, despite recent calls for researchers to consider adopting an intersectional lens when exploring EA (Bows, 2018), there is an absence of literature highlighting the potential of intersectionality to examine it. By providing a conceptual examination of the potential of intersectionality to analyse the connection between older age and abuse, this chapter addresses this lacuna.

To ground the discussion, first, this chapter details the histories and identities of older people in the UK, relating this to them as potential victims. It then teases out the key elements of intersectional theory and applies it to EA. It demonstrates that it is a beneficial approach because it provides a nuanced understanding of EA that is obscured by focusing on gender alone. It also offers a more progressive way to advance social justice goals. Further, it is also contended that support services should adopt an intersectional approach because it encourages giving older victims choice and control over the services they receive. This chapter then advocates that combining intersectionality with social constructivist epistemology is beneficial because it promotes listening to the voices of marginalized victims and takes a critical approach that highlights the root causes of EA. Lastly, the chapter provides concluding thoughts and emphasizes the potentiality of intersectionality in advancing knowledge of EA.

Context: older people as victims in the UK

In the UK, there are nearly 12 million people aged 65 and over and this amount is estimated to increase by 8.6 million by 2068 (Office for National Statistics (ONS), 2018a). Ageing is also gendered: in the UK, 55 per cent of people aged 65 and over are women (ONS, 2018b). Also, older women are often poor, with recent UK figures showing that 23 per cent of single female pensioners live in poverty, compared with 18 per cent for single male pensioners (Women's Budget Group (WBG), 2018). This is a result of how family circumstances impact on women's employment and lives more severely than men. Many women who work undertake most of the care for children and other relatives and are more likely to work part-time (Centre for Ageing Better (CFAB), 2019). The situation is more acute when gender intersects with disability and race, because women with disabilities and those from black and minority ethnic[1] backgrounds face a higher risk of poverty (WBG, 2018). When considering domestic abuse and/or violence (DVA) this is somewhat concerning, as poverty can intensify incidents of DVA by increasing or lengthening women's exposure to it, and hinder their capacity to escape (Women's Aid, 2019).

Many older people are extremely active (Minocha et al, 2013). However, as people age, they tend to develop long-term health conditions and require more health and social care (National Health Service (NHS), nd). Numerous health problems are more prevalent when older people are less wealthy. Elders who are less well-off financially have been shown to have one or more health problems and are significantly more likely to be frail (CFAB, 2019). Health problems, physical disabilities and mental health issues can present additional barriers to disclosure, which may prevent older victims from gaining support (Safe Lives, 2016). For instance, due to care and support needs, older people may be reticent to remove themselves from an abusive partner who is providing their main care (Blood, 2004). Further, a physical impairment may create a barrier because leaving home to access services is hindered (Safe Lives, 2016). Alongside these barriers, generational differences may hinder older women from seeking support because historically the home was considered private, and thus what happens there should remain concealed (McGarry et al, 2011). Further, for many women born before the Second World War, financial dependency on their husbands was a socio-cultural norm (Adult Directors of Adult Social Services (ADASS), 2015). Consequently, they are less likely to have their names on mortgage deeds, have little or no control over household finances and are reliant on their partners' pensions. This can prevent them from disclosing EA (Nerenberg, 2002). Further, older women are more likely to hold traditional values and attitudes regarding gender roles, marriage and the family unit (Safe Lives, 2016). Prevalent traditional social norms dictated that they would care for their partners and children, which when combined with strong taboos regarding divorce may cause many older women to stay in abusive relationships (ADASS, 2015). Safe Lives (2016) argue this might be exacerbated for older black, Asian and minority ethnic (BAME)[2] women, particularly those from a religious background, as they may face additional cultural, family and personal pressures to remain in an abusive relationship. It seems clear that there are several factors that augment elders' silence, including generational differences, shame, health and disabilities. There are also cultural and religious barriers. These can intersect and create significant obstacles to speaking out and accessing specialist services.

At the time of writing this chapter, UK research examining EA is mainly limited to abuse that occurs between white heterosexual partners living in the community (Scott et al, 2004; McGarry et al, 2011; Lazenbatt et al, 2014). When wider victims, perpetrators and settings are included, there is no analysis of the possible differences in their experiences, or what different factors may prevent disclosure (Pritchard, 2000; Mowlam et al, 2007; Naughton et al, 2010). Further, while it is recognized that EA occurs in nursing and residential facilities and is likely to be rife (Krug et al, 2002), research examining abuse against older groups tends to exclude institutional settings (Yon et al, 2018). Consequently, little is known about its extent or how it manifests. It seems even less is known about how EA in institutional settings compares with abuse against elders who live in the community. Highlighting the possible differences between EA perpetrated by partners and others is thus somewhat difficult at present. Teasing out comparisons when it is committed within institutional settings is even harder.

With greater longevity and an ageing population, EA will continue to grow at a rapid rate (Aday, 2017), thus leading to an increase in victims who are more likely to be women. Furthermore, EA is a systemic, widespread and pervasive violation of the human rights and dignity of older people (Help Age International (HAI), 2017a; 2017b). Its consequences are dramatic and long-lasting. Older victims can experience a decline in physical and mental capacities, and sometimes develop feelings of rejection and exclusion (Age Platform Europe, 2017). In serious cases, it can lead to homicide (Bows, 2018). Nevertheless, despite evidence that EA occurs and awareness of some of the impacts, the interconnection between older age and abuse has yet to be explored through an intersectional framework (Bows, 2019).

The potential benefits of intersectionality for understanding elder abuse

It has long been accepted that violence against women is a manifestation of male power and privilege (Kelly, 1998). It has thus been acknowledged that it is crucial to account for gender to understand and respond to abuse, and later recognized that other sites of inequality require acknowledgement too (Crenshaw, 1991). Nevertheless, despite recognition of the importance of intersectional approaches to understanding DVA, research and academic observations have, in the main, ignored the overlap of age and gender (Bows, 2019). However, the connection between abuse and age has not been entirely disregarded. O'Brien (2016) used intersectional analysis to examine the discursive relationship between age, gender and class, and the high level of risk for survivors and perpetrators of DV. While this was limited to adolescents, this application shows how intersectionality can be used to explore the connection between DV (domestic violence) and age. Academic observations have stressed the importance of considering age and ageism when examining EA. Nerenberg (2002) argues that it is essential because EA represents a convergence of gender and age-related factors, which together compromise older women's ability to achieve or uphold self-sufficiency. Penhale (2003) suggested that it is important to consider ageism when examining EA as it may increase its risk:

> Of importance also within the field of elder abuse are the societal views and attitudes, which are commonly held concerning older people. The discrimination and lowered social status experienced by older people; the routinized devaluation which elders experience from living in an ageist society can exacerbate vulnerability which may already exist due to deterioration in physical and mental health. The risk of abuse may thus be increased for individuals. (p 179)

Recognition of the impact of age and ageism is thus necessary to establish the extent these both perpetuate abusive situations and act against their resolution (Penhale, 2003). An intersectional lens is beneficial because it can be used to explore how the inequalities of age and gender increase the risk of EA and prevent older women from gaining independence. Without an intersectional lens, the factors that increase risks, and barriers older victims face, may continue to be hidden.

Older women victims

When examining EA, it is necessary to consider how age and gender, and the associated inequalities of both, intersect with victimization (Nerenberg,

2002; Penhale, 2003). However, the aetiology of EA is complex and can involve a multiplicity of factors beyond sexism and ageism. It may also include the intersection of various characteristics due to accumulated discrimination across the life course (HAI, 2017a). In a consultation by HelpAge, older women discussed how various intersecting characteristics placed them at higher risk. These included lower literacy levels, being single or widowed, disability, living in rural areas, being a migrant or a refugee, or receiving care and support for independent living (HAI, 2017b). Further, older women are more likely to live in poverty and have a higher chance of being socially isolated, badly housed and unhealthy (CFAB, 2019). These socio-structural factors are recognized as contributing to many aspects underpinning EA (World Health Organization (WHO) and International Network for the Prevention of Elder Abuse (INPEA), 2002). It is thus essential to allow for consideration of the complex interplay of these various factors, as they set the context for abuse to occur and can prolong exposure to it. Therefore, when analysing EA, a framework that enables exploration of the economic, social and political status of women and elders, alongside the cumulative impacts of sexism and ageism, is needed (Nerenberg, 2002). Intersectionality has the potential to achieve this. It can examine gender, alongside other variables such as age, ethnicity and disability, and draws attention to the root causes of abuse (Crenshaw, 1991; Burgess-Proctor, 2006). A failure to adopt an intersection lens obscures a nuanced understanding of EA, and there is likely to be a continued failure to challenge the multiple inequalities that increase its risk and contribute to its continuance.

Older male victims

Intersectionality arguably has the potential to help us understand abuse against older men (Edstrom et al, 2016). While research and official figures indicate that older women are more likely to be victims than older men (Bows et al, 2017; NHS Digital, 2019; ONS, 2019; Naughton et al, 2010), the gender divide is not as clear when compared with abuse against younger groups. O'Keeffe et al (2007) found prevalence for financial abuse was similar for both sexes. Also, recent data indicates that for partner abuse (non-sexual), family abuse (non-sexual) and sexual assault or stalking, the gender divide is more equal in the 55–59 and 60–74 age brackets when compared with younger groups, particularly the 20–24 age bracket (ONS, 2019). Despite these prevalence statistics, very little is known about men's experiences of EA and what augments their silence (Melchiorre et al, 2016). However, it is acknowledged that socio-structural factors such as poverty contribute to many aspects underpinning EA against men and women (WHO and INPEA, 2002). Intersectionality allows for investigations into how individuals can experience both inclusion and exclusion (Yuval-Davis, 2006). This structural pattern affects access to institutional power and privileges (Anderson et al, 2004). The emphasis on power and privilege allows for an examination of how women and men can simultaneously experience both privilege and oppression (May, 2015), and how some benefit from the oppression of others who occupy lower social positions (Burgess-Proctor, 2006). This framework could therefore be used to ascertain how intersecting inequalities such as poverty and disability place some older men more at risk of abuse. It could also reveal if their perpetrators occupy a higher privileged status. By demonstrating how men can get manipulated in hierarchically gendered power orders, intersectionality can be used to contest dominant understandings of masculinity and reveal how men are often harmed by inequalities (Edstrom et al, 2016). The challenge to the social construction of manhood and cultural male stoicism may also help older men report EA and seek support (Melchiorre et al, 2016). The potential of intersectionality to contest traditional notions that men are not abused (Barber, 2008) is beneficial. This is because it helps break down barriers that prevent older men from disclosing abuse and facilitates the reduction of inequalities that perpetuate abusive situations. A continued ignorance to use intersectionality to help us understand abuse against older men potentially leaves many older male victims at risk.

Power within relationships and power relations within society

EA involves an imbalance of power relations, with those at higher risk often being in relatively less powerful positions than perpetrators (Yon et al, 2014). People who abuse elders do so because they have the power to (Brandl et al, 2003). Older victims either lack the power to stop abuse or due to age-related dependence, disability and other possible sites of inequality are unable to exercise power to prevent abusive situations or escape them (Westwood, 2018). Consequently, consideration must be given to the effects of power within relationships, and the complex interplay of structural power relations throughout society (Penhale et al, 1999). Such an approach would facilitate establishing the extent to which these aspects both perpetuate abusive situations and act against their resolution (Penhale, 2003). Intersectionality acknowledges that social categories are both properties of individuals and characteristics of the social context (Else-Quest et al, 2016). Each of these categories is embedded with inequality and power. The emphasis on power helps to uncover the dynamics that shape victimization (Chaplin, 2019). From an intersectional understanding, how different individuals experience EA depends on their position in context-specific power structures, based on social categorizations. Thus, the application of intersectionality enables a more comprehensive picture of the context and intricacies of EA and fosters a better understanding of the differences between EA that is committed by partners compared with friends, for example. It also has the potential to explore EA within institutional settings. Without this approach, arguably the experiences of many EA victims will continue to be hidden.

Intersectionality acknowledges that the cross-cutting social relations in society, and the way power operates, are products of global socioeconomic relations (Rahamn et al, 2010). It recognizes that the social hierarchies through which we are socially situated are different from each other: they do not all share the same ontological basis, and they are not all founded on the same social relations (Yuval-Davis, 2006). As such, it has the capacity to consider all individuals, accounting for their social, political, economic and cultural experiences across their life course. Its ability to consider individuals' whole histories and identities is potentially fruitful for exploring how abuse against elders intersects with race, disability, sexualities and gender identities. When EA intersects with these characteristics, little is known about the nature and characteristics of abuse (Westwood, 2018; Safe Lives, 2016). When there are overlapping inequalities, the nature and characteristics of EA are even further obscured; for example, the connection between EA and lesbian, gay, bisexual and transgender (LGBT) black African American[3] survivors (Woody, 2014). Intersectionality could be used to examine how EA intersects with these characteristics. For instance, many LGBT elders have experienced horrific treatment by various institutions and society, including discrimination and abuse due to their sexuality and/or gender (Duffy, 2006). These factors can act as barriers to disclosure and cause a reluctance to engage with services. An intersectional approach facilitates an understanding of how overlapping factors, such as homophobia, biphobia and transphobia, perpetuate abusive situations, and may prevent some elders from seeking support. It also facilitates an awareness that the context and experiences of abuse may be unique to their histories and identities. If this approach is not taken, many marginalized individuals' experiences of EA will fail to be uncovered, which in turn facilitates its continuance.

By drawing attention to the social and political contexts that reinforce power relations, intersectional approaches can help eradicate inequality (May, 2015), such as ageism. There is recognized value in eliminating ageist stereotypes. It has been shown that people who display a more positive self-image of ageing are more likely to recognize and report EA (Aday et al, 2017). In comparison, those who accept ageist stereotypes and cast themselves as unproductive, forgetful and a burden to society are less likely to disclose EA (Palmore, 2003). If an intersectional lens is not taken, older victims are likely to remain silent about their abusive situations. Moreover, intersectionality has the potential to advance social justice goals (Burgess-Proctor, 2006), which is more progressive than traditional feminist approaches because it challenges all inequalities, not just gender. Its application could therefore, for example, facilitate the implementation of the recommendations made by Age Platform (2017). These include engaging in a constructive discussion around a new UN convention on the rights of older people and mainstreaming a rights-based approach to ageing in all policy processes, legislative proposals and impact assessments. Developments such as these promote the rights of elders and may serve to empower them. In turn, this helps break down the inequalities that preserve abusive situations and prevents their resolution. This is beneficial because it may lead to a reduction in EA and/or empower individuals to act when it occurs.

Services and intersectionality

The benefits of using a framework that enables exploration of how age and ageism may impact on victims are highlighted when considering how services recognize and respond to EA. Ageist views and accompanying perceptions can affect the ability of professionals to recognize EA. Safe Lives (2016) found that some professionals disbelieve abuse occurs past 65, or assume medical conditions that derive from the physical and/or traumatic impacts of DA are instead connected to age-related concerns. Consequently, they often miss the connection between injuries and DA. Ageism and its associated stereotypes may also impact on how cases of sexual assault against older women are recognized. According to Connolly et al (2012), the ageist caricature encompasses a sexual myth that perceives older women as sexless, which renders them as unlikely targets of sexual violence. As a result, professionals find it hard to envisage that elders can be victims of sexual attacks (Bows et al, 2017). Consequently, rape and sexual violence against older women is less easy to comprehend, especially when it is compared with younger groups. Due to this, older survivors are even less likely to be believed. Taboos surrounding rape are also present for males, as Roberto et al (2014) argue that it is even harder to consider males as victims of sexual violence, especially older men. A failure to adopt an intersectional approach, which can be used to challenge institutional ageism, potentially leaves EA victims with no specialist support. This can have life-threatening consequences (Sharps-Jeffs, 2016).

Due to ageist stereotypes, many older female victims think that they will not be believed and that specialist services are only for younger women (Scott et al, 2004). These beliefs, combined with the various, often intersecting, barriers noted earlier, prevent older women from accessing appropriate services, leaving them vulnerable to dangerous environments (Safe Lives, 2016). Even when older women do access services, the failure to consider the relationship between age, gender and violence may result in many older survivors not receiving appropriate support (Scott et al, 2004). Consequently,

Sharp-Jeff (2016) argues that services should receive DA (domestic abuse) training that takes an intersectional approach. This would explore the multiple barriers and increased risks faced by particular groups, and include a focus on older people's experiences and their specific needs, alongside challenging institutional ageism. Services that fail to do so may leave many older survivors at risk and/or continue to fail to meet their support needs.

There is an absence of research examining older male victims (Melchiorre et al, 2016). Thus, little is known about their experiences of using services. However, given there is widespread belief that men are the perpetrators of DVA, any notion of them being victims is obstructed (Barber, 2008). Consequently, it is likely that services would be less likely to believe older male survivors and offer appropriate support. While EA research generally excludes males, Clarke et al (2016) found that practitioners from relevant statutory and third-sector groups rarely involved Criminal Justice agencies when responding to older male and female victims. Practitioners commonly assumed that facing the Criminal Justice System 'would be detrimental to the general health and wellbeing of the older person' (p 216). This view casts elders as a homogenous group and can arguably be construed as paternalistic and ageist. Such stereotyping fails to offer older victims the opportunity to have their voice heard through the Criminal Justice System. Although pursuing matters through Criminal Justice procedures may not always be the most appropriate course of action, professionals should not presume that older victims do not wish to face these. Instead, they should be consulted with, listened to and their views respected. As detailed later, intersectional analysis facilitates this because it recognizes that individuals have agency (Crenshaw, 1991) and are thus capable of making decisions.

Ageist constructions reinforce the common assumption that older people are particularly vulnerable (Jones et al, 2006). The association between vulnerability and old age mutually reinforces stereotypical ideas of old age itself (Pritchard-Jones, 2016). These constructions have manifold implications to the way support organizations treat older victims. When a person is classed as vulnerable this can lead to them being treated as incapable of decision making (Duffy, 2006). For example, Lonbay (2018) advocates that due to widespread ageism, older people are considered as inherently vulnerable. Consequently, when their abuse is reported to adult social services their opportunities to be engaged in adult-safeguarding processes are reduced, and rather than being empowered and involved, decisions are made on their behalf. Intersectional analysis recognizes that while there is unequal power, there is some degree of agency individuals can exert (Crenshaw, 1991). When an intersectional approach is taken within services, it should lead to marginalized people gaining more power over decisions that can affect their lives because they are no longer seen as passive victims (Chaplin et al, 2019). By challenging inherent perceptions of gender, age and other sites of inequality, an intersectional approach can encourage services to acknowledge the importance of older people as having choice and control over services they receive. Without this approach, it is likely that older victims will continue to be treated as powerless victims who require decisions to be made on their behalf, as opposed to being supported by professionals to pursue action.

Methodological benefits

Intersectional methodology is somewhat unexplored (Day, 2020). However, postulations on this are not wholly absent. Else-Quest et al (2016) discuss positivism, social constructionism and standpoint epistemology and analyse how compatible they are with an intersectional approach. It is outside the ambit of this chapter to explore these epistemologies and their merits, but it is advocated that social constructionism is well suited. It has recently been used to examine EA in rural and urban Zambia (Kabelenga, 2018). While a detailed account of social constructionism is beyond the parameters of this chapter, it is noteworthy that, somewhat akin to intersectional feminism, it takes a critical approach, and questions assumptions regarding gender, age, race and other inequalities. These are not biological and immutable; instead they are social constructs that can be challenged and changed (Hoffman, 1990). Exploring EA through intersectionality, as informed by social constructivist epistemology, thus provides a critical perspective that questions notions such as gender and old age by reflecting on how they are constantly being revised (Hall, 2014). As both reject the notion of homogenization, a standardized approach is avoided. Instead, it enables an articulation of the various cultural and ethnic backgrounds of the elder population and how these impact on abuse, leading to a more nuanced understanding of EA. If we do not take this combined approach, we are arguably left with an uncritical understanding of EA that fails to reveal the explicit and implicit assumptions about elders and obscures the essentialist notions that hide its root causes. In turn, this facilitates its continuance.

Feminist approaches and social constructivism have been interpreted as preferring research methods that allow individuals to express their experiences in their own words (Oakley, 1999; Ultanir, 2012). Combined, they could therefore be used to explore the lived experiences of EA victims. Often, people's stories are marginalized, suppressed and rejected in favour of dominant belief systems (Dickerson et al, 1996). Listening to their stories provides a challenge to the oppressive domains of knowledge construction and facilities change (Coale, 1994). Thus, it enables marginalized victims to have a voice, which can be used to challenge the inequalities that perpetuate and contribute to their abusive situations. Hall (2014) argues that a failure to listen to the voices of older victims further marginalizes this group. Further, it could lead to policy developments that take no account of the views of those affected. Hall (2014) also advocates that EA could be examined through a critical perspective (which intersectional feminism is), as informed by social constructivism. A continued failure to take this approach runs the risk of EA remaining largely hidden and obscures the broader social inequalities that perpetuate abusive situations and aids its continuance.

Conclusion

An intersectional approach enables a critical examination of the various inequalities that can increase the risk of EA and act as barriers to disclosure. This is beneficial for both older women and men because a fuller recognition of the intricacies of EA helps cast light on how social hierarchies place some elders more at risk than others, and what factors inhibit their ability to seek support. Due to its focus on power, it facilitates an awareness of the context and experiences of abuse, which are unique to individuals' histories and identities. It is thus fruitful for exploring how abuse against elders intersects with race, disability, sexualities and gender identities. If this approach is not taken, many marginalized individuals' experiences of EA will fail to be uncovered, which in turn facilitates its continuance. An intersectional lens also draws attention to the power structures that perpetuate abusive situations and act against their resolution. Without this framework, the inequalities that maintain EA, and possible solutions to it, could continue to be obscured.

Services should adopt an intersectional approach because it promotes acknowledgement that older people have choice and control over the services they receive. If this stance is not taken, it is likely older survivors will continue to be treated as powerless individuals who need decisions to be made for them. Further, an intersectional approach needs to be incorporated into training. Services that fail to do so potentially fail to challenge ageism and could continue to leave many older survivors at risk and/or fail to meet their support needs. This potentially has life-threatening consequences (Sharp-Jeff, 2016).

Intersectional analysis is beneficial because it can help eradicate inequality (May, 2015). A failure to eliminate myopic assumptions prevents elders from recognizing and reporting EA, which in turn leaves them at risk. Further, intersectionality offers a more progressive way to advance social justice goals (Burgess-Proctor, 2006), and could be used as an aid to implement measures that seek to empower older people. Without empowering measures, EA is likely to remain rife and victims may continue to stay silent.

Combining intersectionality with social constructivism is beneficial because it promotes methods that allow individuals to express their experiences in their own words. In turn, this helps challenge the oppressive domains of knowledge construction and facilities change (Coale, 1994). If policy makers and researchers continue to ignore older survivors' voices, they will be further marginalized. Moreover, a continued failure to take an intersectional approach that is informed by social constructivism runs the risk of EA remaining largely hidden and obscures identification of the broader social inequalities that help condone and maintain it.

Notes

[1] To remain faithful to the report, these terms have been used.
[2] To remain faithful to the research as it was conducted, this term has been used.
[3] To remain faithful to the research as it was conducted both black and African American are used.

References

Aday, R.H., Wallace, B. and Scott, S.J. (2017) 'Generational differences in knowledge recognition, and perceptions of elder abuse reporting', *Educational Gerontology*, 43(11): 568–81.

Adult Directors of Adult Social Services (ADASS) (2015) '*Adult safeguarding and domestic abuse. A guide to support practitioners and managers*', [online] www.local.gov.uk/sites/default/files/documents/adult-safeguarding-and-do-cfe.pdf

Age Platform Europe (2017) '*Victims' rights: let's not forget the victims of elder abuse!*', [online] www.ageplatform.eu/sites/defa ult/files/AGE per cent20position per cent20paper per cent20protecting per cent20victims per cent20of per cent20elder per cent20abuse.pdf

Anderson, M. and Collins, P.H. (2004) *Race, Class and Gender*, (5th Ed.), Belmount, CA: Wadsworth.

Barber, C.F. (2008) 'Domestic violence against men', *Nursing Standard*, 22(51): 35–9.

Blood, I. (2004) *Older Women and Domestic Violence: A Report for Help the Aged/hact*, London: Help the Aged, [online] www.ageuk.org.uk/documents/en-gb/for-professionals/communities-and-inclusion/id2382_1_older_women_and_domestic_violence_2004_pro.pdf?dtrk=true

Bows, H. (2018) 'Domestic homicide of older people (2010–2015): a comparative analysis of intimate – partner homicide and parricide cases in the UK', *The British Journal of Social Work*, 49(5): 1234–53.

Bows, H. (2019) 'Introduction', in H. Bows (ed) *Violence Against Older Women, Volume 1: Nature and Extent*, Switzerland: Palgrave Macmillan.

Bows, H. and Davies, P. (2019) 'Elder homicide in the UK (2010–2015): a gendered examination', in H. Bows (ed) *Violence Against Older Women, Volume 1: Nature and Extent*, Switzerland: Palgrave Macmillian, pp 131–59.

Bows, H. and Westmarland, N. (2017) 'Rape of older people in the United Kingdom: challenging the "real rape stereotype"', *British Journal of Criminology*, 57: 1–17.

Brandl, B. and Rozwadowski, J. (2003) 'Responding to domestic abuse in later life', Elder's Advisor, 5(1): 108–20.

Burgess-Proctor, A. (2006) 'Intersections of race, class, gender and crime: future directions for feminist criminology', Feminist Criminology, 1(1): 27–47.

Centre for Ageing Better (CFAB) (2019) 'Inequalities in later life', [online] www.ageing-better.org.uk/sites/default/files/2017-12/Inequalities per cent20scoping per cent20review per cent20full per cent20report.pdf

Chaplin, D., Twigg, J. and Lovell, E. (2019) 'Intersectional approaches to vulnerability reduction and resilience-building', Resilience Intel, 12 [online] https://cdn.odi.org/media/documents/12651.pdf

Coale, H.W. (1994) 'Using cultural and contextual frames to expand possibilities', Journal of Systemic Therapies, 13(2): 5–23.

Crenshaw, K. (1991) 'Mapping the margins: intersectionality, identity politics, and violence against women of colour', Stanford Law Review, 4: 1241–99.

Clarke, A., Williams, J. and Wydall, S. (2016) 'Access to justice for victims/survivors of elder abuse: a qualitative study', Social Policy & Society, 15(2): 207–20.

Connolly, M.T., Breckman, R., Callahan, J., Lachs, M., Ramsey-Klawsnik, H. and Solomon. J. (2012) 'The sexual revolutions last frontier: how silence about sex undermines health, well-being, and safety in old age', Generations, 36: 43–52.

Day, A.S. and Gill, A.K. (2020) 'Applying intersectionality to partnerships between women's organizations and the criminal justice system in relation to domestic violence', British Journal of Criminology, 60(4): 830–50.

Dickerson, V.C. and Zimmermann, J.L. (1996) 'Myths, misconceptions, and a word or two about politics', Journal of Systematic Therapies, 15(1): 79–88.

Duffy, F. (2006) 'A social work perspective on how ageist language, discourses and understandings negatively frame older people and why taking a critical social work space is essential', British Journal of Social Work, 47: 2068–85.

Edstrom, J., Kumar, S. and Shahrokh, T. (2016) 'Intersectionality: a key for men to break out of the patriarchal prison?', IDS Bulletin, 47(5): 57–74.

Else-Quest, N.M. and Hyde, J.S. (2016) 'Intersectionality in quantitaive psychological research: I. Theoretical and epistemological issues', Psychology of Women Quarterly, 40(2): 155–70.

Hall, M (2014) 'Elder abuse', in P. Davies, P. Francis and T. Wyatt (eds) Invisible Crimes and Social Harms, UK: Palgrave.

Help Age International (HAI) (2017a) 'Entitled to the same rights: What older women say about their rights to non-discrimination and equality, and freedom from violence, abuse and neglect', https://social.un.org/ageing-working-group/documents/eighth/EntitledsameRights-English.pdf

Help Age International (HAI) (2017b) *Violence against older women*', [online] www.helpage.org/what-we-do/rights/violence-against-older-women/

Hoffman, C. (1991) *An Introduction to Bilingualism*, London: Routledge, Longman Linguistic Library.

Jones, H. and Powell, J.L. (2006) 'Old age, vulnerability and sexual violence: implications for knowledge and practice', *International Nursing Review*, 53(3): 211–16.

Kabelenga, I. (2018) 'Elder abuse in rural and urban Zambia interview: study with community leaders', Dissertation, University of Lapland, [online] https://lauda.ulapland.fi/bitstream/handle/10024/63308/Kabelenga_Isaac_ActaE_239_pdfA.pdf?sequence=1&isAllowed=y

Kelly, L. (1998) *Surviving Sexual Violence*, Cambridge: Polity Press.

Krug, E.G., Dahlberg, L.L., Mercy, J.A., Zwi, A.D. and Lozano, R. (2002) *World Report on Violence and Health*, Geneva: World Health Organization.

Lazenbatt, A. and Devaney, J. (2014) 'Older women living with domestic violence: coping resources and mental health and wellbeing', *Journal of Clinical Nursing*, 1(1): 10–22.

Lonbay, S.P. (2018) '"These are vulnerable people who don't have a voice": exploring constructions of vulnerability and ageing in the context of safeguarding older people', *British Journal of Social Work*, 48: 1033–51.

May, V.M. (2015) *Pursuing Intersectionality, Unsettling Dominant Imaginaries*, New York: Routledge.

McGarry, J. and Simpson, C. (2011) 'Domestic abuse and older women: exploring the opportunities for service development and care delivery', *Journal of Adult Protection*, 13(6): 294–301.

Melchiorre, M.G., Di-Rosa, M., Lamura, G., Torres-Gonzales, F., Lindert, J., Stankunas, M., Ioannidi-Kapolou, E., Barros, H., Macassa, G. and Soares, J.J.F. (2016) 'Abuse of older men in seven European countries: a multilevel approach in the framework of an ecological model', *PLoS One*, 11(1): 1–28 [online] www.ncbi.nlm.nih.gov/pmc/articles/PMC4718635/

Minocha, S., Hartnett, E., Dunn. K., Evans, S., Heap, T., Middup, C.P., Murphy, B. and Roberts, D. (2013) 'Conducting empirical research with older people: designing for – and with – vulnerable people', [online] http://oro.open.ac.uk/36592/1/Minocha_DFWVP2013.pdf

Mowlam, A., Tennant, R., Dixon, J. and McCreadie, C. (2007) *Mistreatment and Abuse of Older People: Qualitative Findings*, London: Comic Relief and Department of Health.

Nash, J. (2008) 'Re-thinking intersectionality', *Feminist Review*, 89: 1–15.

National Health Service (NHS), England (nd) '*Improving care for older people*', [online] www.england.nhs.uk/ourwork/clinical-policy/older-people/improving-care-for-older-people/

Naughton, C., Drennan, J., Treacy, P., Lafferty, A., Lyons, I., Phelan, A., Quin, S., O'Loughlin, A. and Delany, L. (2010) *Abuse and Neglect of Older People in Ireland: Report on the National Study of Elder Abuse and Neglect*, Dublin: HSE and UCD.

Nerenberg, L. (2002) 'A feminist perspective on gender and elder abuse: a review of the literature', *National Committee for the Prevention of Elder Abuse*, [online] www.researchgate.net/profile/Lisa_Nerenberg/publication/ 237400086_A_Feminist_Perspective_on_Gender_and_Elder_Abuse_ A_Review_of_the_Literature/links/00b4953b562b4868c5000000/A-Feminist-Perspective-on-Gender-and-Elder-Abuse-A-Review-of-the-Literature.pdf

NHS Digital (2019) 'Safeguarding Adults: England, 2018–19', [online] https://digital.nhs.uk/data-and-information/publications/statistical/ safeguarding-adults/annual-report-2018-19-england

Oakley, A. (1999) 'Paradigm wars: some thoughts on a personal and public trajectory', *International Journal of Social Research Methodology*, 2(3): 247–54.

O'Brien, R.B. (2016) 'Intersectionality and adolescent domestic violence and abuse: addressing "classed sexism" and improving service provision', *International Journal of Human Rights in Healthcare*, 9(3): 161–73.

Office for National Statistics (ONS) (2018a) *'Living longer: how our population is changing and why it matters'*, [online] www.ons.gov.uk/ peoplepopulationandcommunity/birthsdeathsandmarriages/ageing/ articles/livinglongerhowourpopulationischangingandwhyitmatters/ 2018-08-13

Office of National Statistics (ONS) (2018b) *'Estimates of the population for the UK, England and Wales, Scotland and Northern Ireland'*, [online] www. ons.gov.uk/peoplepopulationandcommunity/populationandmigration/ populationestimates/datasets/populationestimatesforukenglandandwaless cotlandandnorthernireland

Office for National Statistics (ONS) (2019) *'Domestic abuse victim characteristics, England and Wales: year ending March 2019'*, [online] www.ons.gov.uk/ peoplepopulationandcommunity/crimeandjustice/articles/domesticabus evictimcharacteristicsenglandandwales/yearendingmarch2019

O'Keefee, M., Hills, A., McCreadie, D., C., Scholes, S., Constantine, R., Tinker, A., Manthorpe, J., Biggs, S., and Erens, B. (2007) *UK Study of Abuse and Neglect of Older People Prevalence Survey Report*, Prepared for Comic Relief and the Department of Health.

Palmore, E.B. (2003) 'Ageism comes of age', *Gerontologist*, 43: 418–20.

Penhale, B. (2003) 'Older women, domestic violence, and elder abuse: a review of commonalities, differences, and shared approaches', *Journal of Elder Abuse and Neglect*, 15(3–4): 163–83.

Penhale, B. and Parker, J. (1999) 'Elder abuse and older men: towards an understanding', COE 1999, European Council.

Pritchard. J. (2000) *The Needs of Older Women: Services for Victims of Elder Abuse and Other Abuse*, Great Britain: Policy Press.

Pritchard-Jones, L. (2016) 'The good, the bad, and the "vulnerable older adult"', *Journal of Social Welfare and Family Law*, 38(1): 51–72.

Rahman, M, and Jackson, S. (2010) *Gender and Sexuality Sociological Approaches*, Cambridge: Polity Press.

Roberto, K.A., McPherson, M.C. and Brossoie, S.J. (2014) 'Intimate partner violence in late life: a review of the empirical literature', *Violence Against Women*, 19(2): 1538–58.

Safe Lives (2016) *Safe Later Lives: Older People and Domestic Abuse*, London: Age UK.

Scott, M., McKie, L., Mortan, S., Seddon, E. and Wosoff, F. (2004) *Older Women and Domestic Violence in Scotland: And for 39 Years I got on with it*, Edinburgh: Health Scotland.

Sharp-Jeffs, N. and Kelly, L. (2016) 'Domestic homicide review (DHR) case analysis: report for standing together against domestic violence', [online] www.sistersforchange.org.uk/wp-content/uploads/2019/03/105-DHR-analysis-report.pdf

Stanko, E. (1990) *Everyday Violence: How Women and Men Experience Sexual and Physical Violence*, London: Pandora Press.

Ultanir, E. (2012) 'An epistemological glance at the constructivist approach: constructivist learning in Dewey, Piaget, and Montessori', *International Journal of Instruction*, 5(2): 1308–470.

Westwood, S.L. (2018) 'Abuse and older lesbian, gay, bisexual and trans (LGBT) people: a commentary and research agenda', *Journal of Elder Abuse and Neglect*, 31(2): 97–114.

Women's Aid (2019) *The Domestic Abuse Report 2019: The Economics of Abuse*, [online] www.womensaid.org.uk/wp-content/uploads/2019/03/Economics-of-Abuse-Report-2019.pdf

Women's Budget Group (WBG) (2018) *The Female Face of Poverty: Examining the cause and consequences of economic deprivation for women*, [online] http://wbg.org.uk/wp-content/uploads/2018/08/FINAL-Female-Face-of-Poverty.pdf

Woody, I. (2014) 'Aging out: a qualitative exploration of ageism and heterosexualism among African American lesbians and gay men', *Journal of Homosexuality*, 61(1): 145–65.

World Health Organization (WHO) and International Network for the Prevention of Elder Abuse (INPEA) (2002) '*Missing voices: views of older persons on elder abuse*', [online] https://apps.who.int/iris/bitstream/handle/10665/67371/WHO_NMH_VIP_02.1.pdf;jsessionid=E1FB70F7D443A761629812FBD6AB548F?sequence=1

Yon, Y., Ramiro-Gonzalez, M., Mikton, C.R., Huber, M. and Sethi, D. (2018) 'The prevalence of elder abuse in institutional settings: a systematic review and meta-analysis', *The European Journal of Public Health*, 29(1): 58–67.

Yon, Y., Wister, A.V., Mitchell, B. and Gutman, G. (2014) 'A national comparison of spousal abuse in mid-and old age', *Journal of Elder Abuse & Neglect*, 26(1): 80–105.

Yuval-Davis, N. (2006) 'Intersectionality and feminist politics', *European Journal of Women's Studies*, 13(3): 193–2.

13

Intersections of LGBTQ+ Social Spaces Using Gender Analysis and the Social Model

Lisa Overton and Joshua Hepple

Introduction

Social spaces, while complex, have been noted as key to finding community, relationships and identity for lesbian, gay, bisexual, transgender and queer (LGBTQ+) people (Overton, 2014; Formby, 2017; Hepple, 2017). However, these social spaces do not exist in a vacuum and operate within existing normative frames that construct some bodies as deviant by their very existence. This chapter draws on two examples from the respective authors about negotiating social spaces – around and within – using an intersectional framework and engaging with gender analysis and the social model of disability (UPIAS, 1976).[1] Drawing on intersectionality, as coined by Crenshaw (1989), we illustrate how multiple layers of identities, experiences and processes, when taken together, demonstrate how groups of people experience and move about in the world, in a complex web of agency, victimhood, fear and resourcefulness. Overton's research draws out the complexities of negotiating public spaces such as streets surrounding LGBTQ+ social spaces and public routes home in New Orleans for femme-presenting and queer-presenting women, revealing that fear and a sense of danger are a constant backdrop, whereas the social venue itself as an LGBTQ+ venue is seen as safe and welcoming – unproblematic. Hepple's autoethnographic account draws on his experiences as a gay, disabled man, highlighting that gay social spaces also operate within exclusionary frameworks that can create both fear and danger when seeking pleasure. Combined, this chapter takes two different LGBTQ+ contexts to demonstrate that applying an intersectional lens can reveal the fault lines that exist in spaces that are meant to be 'inclusive' but are actually more complex in reality.

Defining spaces

This chapter is centred within and around LGBTQ+ social spaces, specifically pubs, bars and clubs. This also includes spaces surrounding streets and transport intersections. By examining these social spaces using an intersectional lens, we show how non-normative bodies negotiate a complex web of pleasure and danger due to always being positioned as peripheral. Through this lens, as 'members' of LGBTQ+ communities ourselves, we examine how 'different' bodies experience, negotiate and ultimately live in spaces not designed for us, where our bodies can feel like sites of power and where our sexualities are positioned within the grotesque (Russo, 2009; Kafer, 2013; Bogden, 2014).

We use intersectionality to examine trends between sexuality, disability and different kinds of bodies. For example, when a space that is inclusive for one identity, such as a gay bar, is not inclusive for all, and does not cater for someone with an impairment, that individual is further disabled; and when a space is seen as LGBTQ+ 'safe' but women fear the threat of male violence in the surrounding streets, that risk can prevent her from accessing this social space. Despite the fear and concern that social spaces might not be as safe or welcoming as they could be, we show how these feelings and fears are negotiated.

Physical spaces have long been discussed by disability and gender scholars (Stanko, 2013; Shakespeare, 2014; 2017). The social model of disability problematizes physical space in that it is not individuals that are disabled but the spaces themselves that are disabling (UPIAS, 1976). In other words, people are disabled by the absence of adaptions in society. Space itself as disabling is an interesting lens as it forces us to consider how the built environment is not accessible to all in the same way. Physical spaces, then, construct a range of people as deviant, placing them outside of the norm.

Non-normative bodies

Our bodies are constructed by gender norms and those that deviate from ideal standards are seen as non-normative (Butler, 1990; Covino, 1996; Jagose, 1996; Freund, 2001; Evans and Lee, 2002; Bias, 2021). Disabled people have been constructed as 'less than' (Hubbard, 1997; Freund, 2001) and disability has been conceptualized as 'in addition to' rather than integral and part of the body. This is reflected in terminology like 'people with disabilities' rather than 'disabled people' (Shakespeare, 2014). This suggestion that disability is inherent to the body is now seen as regressive and fails to understand wider barriers (UPIAS, 1976; Shakespeare, 2017).

The medical model of disability suggests that barriers can only be overcome by individuals seeking medical attention for their impairments. In other words, someone can only overcome their disability if they seek medical intervention to remove their impairment. Within this, there is often an overemphasis of bodily capability through 'overcoming' with positive attitude and persistence. This is not necessarily always a helpful way of viewing impairments. Hepple very much acknowledges that he has cerebral palsy and defines as a disabled man. However, he will also take various medications for his involuntary movements so that he can concentrate on other parts of his life. This does not undermine his disabled identity, yet also lets him live a more fulfilling life. While cerebral palsy has very much shaped Hepple's identity and life experience, it is not the only part of who he is. Should there be medical intervention that can make him more comfortable in other areas of his life, this does not reduce his disabled identity.

However, as Young (2014) has explained, this is dangerous territory and is also 'inspiration porn'. This disempowers those who have no medical cure and, more importantly, rejects the concept of the person as they are.

While language and philosophy around the social model is now intrinsically embedded within disability activism, it was only in 1976 when a group of disabled activists joined together to reject the notion of the medical model and acknowledged that they were disabled by their environment before they were disabled by their bodies and impairments. A group called United People with Impairments Against Segregation (UPIAS) came up with the following definition: 'it is society which disables physically impaired people. Disability is something imposed on top of our impairments, by the way we are unnecessarily isolated and excluded from full participation in society' (1976, p 4).

This definition reinforces the idea that disability is external to the individual and not primarily related to someone's physical impairment. This theory goes beyond physical barriers and explores society's systems, processes and attitudes. For example, someone may be unable to book a doctor's appointment or interact with their bank if they have a speech impairment and are unable to email because the surgery and bank only operate over the phone.

Society cannot eradicate every disadvantage that is caused by an impairment; for example, a wheelchair user could never become a firefighter and someone who is blind could never drive an ambulance. Further, impairments can cause pain and have other debilitating repercussions such as IBS and chronic fatigue, but this does not undermine many of the important aspects of the social model. Where society can eradicate barriers so that people with impairments can interact equally, it always should strive to do so.

In 2011 the World Health Organization promoted the notion of the bio-social-pyscho model of disability, which acknowledges all of the different factors that could make someone disabled and therefore bring the medical and social aspects into play at the same time (World Health Organization, 2011), though there are criticisms of this approach (Inclusion London, nd). Additionally, Shakespeare (2017) has critiqued the social model in the way that one can acknowledge that society cannot eradicate physical necessities such as the benefits of running or performing physical activities. However, this does not undermine the importance of having accessible, level access spaces for wheelchair users and listening to the requirements of other impairment groups when designing spaces for everyone.

Solomon (2014) writes extensively on identity and perceived barriers that should be overcome and how they relate to life experience, arguing that too much emphasis on the body removes the societal disabling factors. Using the example of dwarfism, Solomon shows that some fully embrace their identity, whereas others are constantly trying to reduce their impairment and possibly engage with experimental medicine. While it would be wrong to remove any individual agency to reject impairment as a part of one's identity, when a minority group is already divided, Solomon (2014) recognizes the frustration on both sides. Young (2014) provides an interesting take on medicine in the way that those with dwarfism very much saw this as part of their identity and therefore rejected any medical offers that could 'cure' them. This is an example of how people with dwarfism want to claim that as part of their overall identity and embrace it within their own culture. One can compare this with the Deaf Society where people who identify as deaf see themselves as a cultural minority and actively use British Sign Language as their primary means of communication. They do not see themselves as any different to those who are not deaf and have no desire to have their hearing restored, if that were possible, as that would shift their overall life experience.

These examples show how our very identities are debated from the 'inside' and the 'outside'. Relatedly, queerness has been constructed as abnormal, as a disease and as a dangerous, socially unacceptable peculiarity that must be hidden or cured. For example, homosexuality was diagnosed as a mental health condition by the World Health Organization until 1992 (Holzhacker, 2014). LGBTQ+ people have also been constructed as 'abnormal' (Jagose, 1996; Wilchins, 2017), then paradoxically as a coherent, unified group through organizations such as the International Lesbian, Gay, Bisexual, Trans and Intersex Association (IGLA) as well as in opposition, even waging war between identities seen between Stonewall and 'gender-critical' feminists on the 'inclusion' of trans identities within their agenda (Hines, 2019; McLean 2021). LGBTQ+ people continue to be punished through societal ostracization preventing them from accessing health and employment to 'corrective' rape and death (World Bank, 2015). There is also a lack of commitment to recognize diverse gender identities, as evidenced with the refusal of the UK government to recognize gender non-binary people (Parker, 2015), demonstrating further that depending on which 'letter' you claim in the LGBTQ+ acronym depends on how far you have been accepted into normative society and further problematizes who is 'included' in a range of spaces.

Methodology

We have applied intersectionality as a lens through which to explore the complexities of 'inclusive' space for LGBTQ+ people focusing on entertainment venues of pubs, bars and clubs. For Hepple, this has involved an experiential, autoethnographic approach drawing and reflecting on his media contributions and own experiences. Overton, on the other hand, has reflected upon life history interviews and field notes that emerged from her research about 'growing up post-Hurricane Katrina' focusing on a subgroup-group of 'gender performance artists', The Kings. The data here includes stories from both audience and performers and broadly defined as part of LGBTQ+ communities in New Orleans who engage with 'queer' entertainment spaces, particularly The Kings' weekly drag king performance show at a bar in the French Quarter in 2011–12. All participants and venues have been anonymized to protect identities, and the project received ethical approval from the School of Health and Social Science at Middlesex University.

As part of our epistemological considerations thinking through intersectional identities, we take a critical perspective upon acronyms and monikers used to describe sexual identities. There is much contestation over abbreviations and even with best efforts, certain groups can be excluded. Our interpretation suggests that queer is anyone who may not 'fit' the mould as traditionally heterosexual rather than a term that is actively used. At the same time, we realize that consistency for the purpose of this chapter is necessary and so we will use 'LGBTQ+' as our general term throughout.

Movements based around sexual identities have used different methods to promote inclusion over the years, often 'adding' letters to the acronym. For example, it was only in 2007 that Stonewall incorporated the 'T' and began emphasizing trans inclusion within wider society. Historically, these movements attempted an assimilation approach to inclusion with 'we are just like you' discourses. However, a queering approach that emerged through Queer Theory took on a more confrontational view, problematizing 'normativity' with the message that 'we are everywhere' (Litwack, 2018, p 336). Many may be familiar with the phrase 'we are here, we are queer, get used it to it', for example. However, the lived realities of the everyday for LGBTQ+ people comprise of intersectional identities moving through physical spaces that are themselves policed by intersections of normativity, and as our chapter will show, theory can only go so far when faced with what can be very real dangers and challenges of being 'out' and 'proud'. 21st-century discourses attempted to suggest that 'we are born this way', suggesting queer is as 'natural' as straight, but leaving little room for nuance and ignoring bodies of work that suggest that sexualities can develop and change over time. All sexualities can be read as queer in some way in that few sexual identities and relationships measure up to normative standards in reality. That said, LGBTQ+ is widely accepted as a standard acronym although there are discrepancies. Stonewall continue to use LGBT, others who are engaged with the Yogyakara Principles firmly promoted by Narrain (2016) use 'SOGI' (Sexual Orientation and Gender Identity), now SOGIESC (the ESC bringing in Expression and Sex Characteristics) (Narrain, nd), and UN discourse engages with Sexual and Gender Minorities as a term (O'Malley, 2018). Furthermore, the lines between assimilation approaches and Queer Theory-inspired confrontational challenge approaches are much more blurred. For example, Stonewall (2017), who originally advocated for assimilation goals like gay marriage, now also run the 'Get Over It' campaign launched in 2007 that can be read as taking a 'queer' approach, including the slogan 'Some people are gay/trans/bi/lesbians/queer. Get over it.'

Understanding the nuances and differences from within LGBTQ+ movements is an important aspect of our epistemological position as it demonstrates that even within LGBTQ+ communities, experiences and groups differ. We need to be mindful that while acronyms are useful to bring diverse sexual identities together, our identities will not be experienced in the same way as other LGBTQ+ people, acknowledging other elements of identity beyond the 'traditional' intersections such as race, gender, class and disability. We take the view that throughout the chapter our two case studies often do not fit neatly into broad categories, and we encourage others to embrace the messiness of an intricate intersectional lens to explore the latticework of multiple identities (Pryse, 2000).

Non-normative bodies and public space: experiences from New Orleans

Women's bodies have long been positioned as sites to produce gendered discourses of power at national and community levels (Yuval-Davis, 1997; Ahmed, 2002; Evans, 2002). This means that women can experience their own bodies as non-normative through a self-conscious awareness that their bodies in public spaces take on other meanings and can invite unsolicited attention and fear of male violence. Fear of male violence is a structural gender inequality that affects most societies across the world (WHO, 2021). It should also be clarified here that we are referring to the fear of cisgender male violence embedded in cultures and societies and has been conceptualized within a reframing of traditional patriarchy, into what Bradshaw et al (2017) have called 'super normal patriarchy'.

Overton's research explored 'straight' and LGBTQ+-identifying young women and gender diverse people who grew up after Hurricane Katrina seven years after the event itself. Through life history interviews, Overton explicitly looked at gendered and sexual identities, or 'gendered sexualities', to highlight that both are intrinsically connected. One of the core findings was that while the disaster resulting from Hurricane Katrina revealed and amplified specific issues, young, queer-identifying and 'straight'-identifying women, and gender diverse people, often felt that negotiating public spaces, especially at night, incited fear and concern over their safety because of the threat of male violence against them, disaster or not. In fact, some women-identified participants felt that even though they should not have to put up with this threat, they had to accept it, as illustrated here by Rita, a bi-identifying woman:

'I've been cat called and all that and if I'd have been alone I would have been more scared than if I'd have been in a group. I look like a bad ass, I think my size too it means people are less likely to bother me. As much as I hate it, it is something I have to put up with as a female. It's sad there's not education to teach men it's not OK to talk like that. I don't feel like it increased post-Katrina but I wasn't here long enough before so I wouldn't know.' (Rita)

While Rita highlighted she was not in New Orleans long enough to comment on embedded cultures of violence pre-Katrina, it was long enough to be able to say that her experiences of feeling afraid of male violence did not differ, highlighting, as Jessica does later on, that being a woman in public spaces feels risky. Rita also mentions that her body size is bigger than average and her look as "bad ass", both of which help to keep her protected, further signposting to subtle deviances from the heteronormative body that can desexualize – in this case with positive results. However, for other 'deviances' such as 'looking' like a lesbian or being seen in lesbian public spaces, women's bodies were hypersexualized. Here, we can draw parallels with disabled peoples' experiences of public spaces and links to the perception of the desexualization and hypersexulization of disability, which we will discuss further in this chapter. What is important to point out are these micro-intersectional elements within identities such as LGBTQ+. That is, sexuality, for example, is not one intersection but can include multiple or micro-intersections within it. What was clear was that when sexuality intersects with gender and youth, perception of male violence changed for the participants. This viewpoint is illustrated by Jessica, who was in her late teens at the time of Katrina and in her 20s at the time of the interview:

'Violence has always been a threat in New Orleans but I feel like now that I am more out in the world it's something I have to watch out for whereas when I was younger I was either with my mum and sister or my dad and there are corrupt cops out there too and it's sad because you're looking at these people as people who protect you and make you feel safe so who are you supposed to rely on to feel safe? A guy? Yourself?' (Jessica)

Being 'out in the world' for Jessica is twofold. On the one hand, it means being able to be independent instead of under the protection of parents when she was a teenager and, on the other hand, it means being 'out' as a lesbian. For young women, queer and straight, the fear of violence may be linked to increased autonomy, visibility as a 'woman' and/or visibility as LGBTQ+.

As generally 'deviant' simply by being women, women's bodies sit complexly within this framework, experiences which become more complex when considered in intersection with queer, disabled or racial/ethnic identities. In the research, most participants in this subgroup were white except one who identified as African American and one who identified as Hispanic. Beaux, who identified as African American, felt their relative affluence afforded them a greater degree of privilege and did not feel disadvantaged by their race, but further research is needed around the intersections between LGBTQ+ social space with gender, race, social class and disability, not least because black people are more likely to experience police violence in public spaces than whites, to explore the impacts of social class and affluence (Schwartz and Jahn, 2020; GLA, 2021).

The pub and the drag kings

Drawing on the previous section, we now consider the intersection between gender, sexuality, public space and the fear or threat of violence using the stories of queer-identifying women as both performers and patrons of a weekly 'drag king' show in New Orleans' French Quarter. This area is locally recognized as the 'gay south', predominantly made up of bars for gay men with few 'mixed' spaces for lesbian, gay, bisexual, trans and queer plus people. The Kings' show takes place in a mixed space, the pub, but the show itself is on a LGBTQ+ women and trans/non-binary night and at the time was the only space of its kind. The research findings propose that the intersection of gender and sexuality has a double impact on the perception of risk of gender-based violence. Several queer-identifying participants identified sexuality as a factor in feeling unsafe in public spaces around gay social space venues. Jessica elaborates that "I never go to my car on my own in Quarter at night. Like after a show or anything, it's just not worth the risk."

Going out alone is seen to be a 'risk' at night, even in areas like the French Quarter which, as highlighted earlier, is LGBTQ+-friendly and is also often very busy; however, neither of these made Jessica feel safe enough to warrant doing something that during the day would be mundane such as going to her car. Thinking 'sensibly' in terms of ensuring you are not alone as queer and as a woman because of the fear and threat of violence is prevalent in almost every culture (Stanko, 2013). Younger women are most at risk (WHO, 2021) yet worryingly, young women still place a significant degree of responsibility on themselves, as illustrated by Harrie: "I feel more conscious of it especially when I'm in drag, like you feel more exposed to it when you go out at night." Simply being out at night seems to be enough to implicate a young woman if she were to be attacked but being a young woman in 'drag' costume increased these participants' fears. For Harrie, whose drag persona is based around rap culture and explicitly masculine, she felt particularly vulnerable and more conscious of being targeted not just for her youth and gender, but also because she was dressed in a non-normative gender role: as masculine. Her experience highlights that when identities intersect, they can create a unique positioning that could have specific consequences for those who identify within that group.

LGBTQ+ social space was perceived by young women as safe overall, and moreover as space to find and create community, build friendships, romantic relationships, to be and discover the 'self'. Queerness and deviance were the norm at the Tuesday night midnight show for The Kings of New Orleans and their audience members. This space provided much-needed solace post-Katrina, where young queer people had been confined in evacuation lodgings that could place them in unsupportive environments, and where their 'chosen family' and 'safe spaces' based on LGBTQ+ identities were not accepted or fully understood. Despite the recovery efforts from October 2005, The Kings never missed a midnight show. The knowledge that this space was always there for them enabled LGBTQ+-identifying young women and gender diverse people to have a space to go. In these spaces, participants found community, as Betty explains: "I learnt about the term pansexual from Jessica, and I realized that's what I am. I learned to be myself when I joined The Kings."

This space gave young women the power to change their lives, through embracing their queer identities. The Kings, through embracing a range of queer identities and diverse sexualities, created a space to feel and be included in a community where non-normative embodiment is at the centre, where the grotesque is celebrated and challenged. Risk and danger exist on the 'outside' in the public spaces of streets that have to be negotiated in order to access space that feels safe. However, while this group of queer young women in this particular space felt a sense of community, not all LGBTQ+ social spaces offer the same opportunities. In the next section,

Hepple's autoethnography reflects on the intersections of gender, sexuality and disability.

Reflections on G-A-Y nightclub and being a gay disabled man

When gender, sexualities and disability intersect, structural inequalities are revealed. If a disabled person is congratulated for doing something that a non-disabled individual may do daily, a power imbalance is created. There are connections between objectification and inspiration porn, because the non-disabled individual has decided that the activity of the disabled person is worthy of praise. In a similar manner, often individuals with physical impairments are congratulated for entering sexual spaces. Hepple recalls experiencing praise for entering sexualized spaces such as G-A-Y nightclub in London. While there may not have been bad intent, this attention is misguided and infantilizing.

Consequently, the disabled clubber is denied the ability to interact on an equal level with non-disabled patrons, as they are seen as a figure of inspiration. This infantilization leads on to desexualization. In other words, when anyone in a nightclub wants to be acknowledged and appreciated as having the capacity to have consensual sex and when the pressure and attention moves on to the very fact that they are in the nightclub, the energy and conversation can become demeaning. The disabled individual may well want to flirt or have intellectual conversations with a hopeful sexual partner and when this is received with condescending praise the disabled person feels disempowered. The lack of agency given to this disabled person can be extremely demoralizing given that it removes all sexual and romantic possibilities from that individual (Lee et al, 2020). While sexual objectification can be harmful and disempowering, infantilization can be equally as dangerous. Many people enjoy appreciation and consensual attention based on appearance. Non-disabled people often become so preoccupied by the medical impairment of disabled people that they ignore the person. Hepple's wheelchair often attracts more attention than he does.

Infantilization in clubs and the general desexualization of disabled people could lead on to fuel perceived vulnerability and victimization of those who may be susceptible to hate crimes. When the capacity to love, form relationships and have sex is removed from disabled people, they become targets for attack, as a large part of human experience is removed (Richardson et al, 2013). It can be easy to see why disabled people can be targets of hate crimes. In many cases, their bodies will be physically compromised, which may put them in a vulnerable situation if under physical threats or attack (Quarmby, 2011). Many disabled people will have to live with their physical impairment throughout their lives; however, this chapter argues that the overmedicalization of disability can unnecessarily create even more vulnerability that lowers disabled people's standing in society (Roulstone and Mason-Bish, 2015).

Exclusion from sexual spaces

Some venues argue that they do not need to improve access given that they do not have disabled customers. Hepple and Glass have written about challenging bar owners on their lack of access and found that there is general apathy towards appealing to disabled customers (Glass, 2020). Not only is this unfair on the disabled man who wants to go to a gay bar with his friends but the lack of disabled people in sexualized spaces is arguably one of the most othering and disabling notions as set out in the social model. The human capacity to love, be intimate with and have consensual sex with other people is at the heart of human experience and if disabled people are not visible in these environments, then their position in society is diminished (Shakespeare et al, 1996; Richardson et al, 2013). Shakespeare (2014) notes that this form of marginalization can be applied to both queer and disabled people, as the non-disabled person is seen as the default 'ordinary' (or normative) position, whereas the disabled person is seen as other. He compares this analogy to the standard heterosexual man as the norm, which he suggests automatically implies that anyone who has any type of queer sexual expressions is deemed to be other and possibly deviant. In turn, this results in multiple marginalization for those who are disabled and queer (Shakespeare, 2014).

Grindr and sexual agency in cyberspace to IRL space

When non-disabled people are afraid to talk to those who have a speech impairment, those impaired individuals are silenced. Sex is ultimately a very intimate way of communication and when we are afraid to talk to those who may be different from ourselves, we are automatically 'othering' them and making certain communities and groups ostracized and left to feel different and lonely. In turn, this can stigmatize disabled people further, increase a perception of vulnerability and, sadly, they may then become easy targets of crime.

In 2016, Hepple wrote in *The Guardian* about his sexual experiences of using Grindr as a disabled man (Hepple, 2016). His physical impairments mean that he cannot masturbate and this in itself is a good way of demonstrating the interplay between the social and medical models of disability. In other words, due to the severity of his movements, it would be impossible to create any type of independent way that Hepple could perform this action, rather like eating or using the toilet, which also require assistance. Hepple (2017) blogged about how this compares with his experiences in person in a club in terms of interacting with people, in response to a debate about the closure of various queer spaces. Hepple argues that online apps can put everyone on to some safer and better level playing field.

When Hepple uses apps such as Grindr to introduce himself, he is able to use words to convey his personality far faster than he ever could in a club, speaking to someone. This is not just because of the practical difficulties of understanding someone with a speech impairment but because he knows that Grindr can help him communicate equally without misconceptions. In other words, people are often startled by the physical presentation of his cerebral palsy and are nervous around him socially in physical environments. Hepple can choose what he discloses when on the app and can control the situation. While many Grindr users often feel rejected from the immediate block feature, Hepple takes comfort in the fact that he can act anonymously as well as being able to end communication with one button should a conversation become difficult or unwanted. In other words, while it can be painful to be rejected in such a blunt direct manner, there is no possibility of unwanted stalking or attention from the other person and the contact can come to an immediate end. This can be compared with those awkward conversations in clubs when one person is unable to pick up on hints that the other person is not interested.

Sexual autonomy and agency are fundamental to the human condition. Equal pay, access to social security and having the right physical adjustments in place are important, yet it is proposed that all of these adjustments may fall into place more naturally once disabled people are fully acknowledged as independent human beings. This starts with sexual agency and can be compared with the rights of women for birth control and independent autonomy over their bodies. Notwithstanding that some disabled people have intellectual impairments and those impairments must be considered when we look at issues such as consent, many people who solely have physical impairments have no more issues around capacity to consent as their non-disabled peers. One should not dismiss the extra needs that disabled people may have, yet when one focuses on perceived vulnerability rather than agency, disabled people automatically become burdens on society. One no longer sees the contribution that they could make should they live in an environment where all of their impairments are catered for. This implicit narrative suggests disabled people are therefore unable to have agency, something which is compounded by barriers to social space as well as barriers in perceptions.

Conclusion

Accessing social spaces is an act to seek out pleasure but this pleasure goes hand in hand with danger, even in spaces that proclaim to be inclusive. This produces a complex web encompassing agency and victimhood, fear and resourcefulness. Non-normative bodies are always placed on the periphery in some way. For Overton's research participants, this was through 'public' spaces but not within the LGBTQ+ venue itself. For Hepple it was presented through his own lived experience as a gay man with cerebral palsy. The overt policies and lack of access to some extent validated and perpetuated some of the stigma and isolation he felt as a disabled man. When multiple non-normativities are occupied, the periphery can still exist, even in spaces that are meant to challenge the centre.

Hepple and Overton's works show independently that social spaces are important elements of LGBTQ+ identities in different ways. Hepple's work expands the notion of space further than the physical through an examination of Grindr. Overton's research about queer young women in New Orleans who are 'drag kings' shows how transgressing traditional gender norms in terms of dress and appearance changes the way young women view social space but, ultimately, that public space is experienced in a gendered way, drawing out underlying fears of violence based on sexuality or gender. Hepple's experiential analysis highlighted how the 'layers' of identities create both vulnerabilities and opportunities for gay, disabled, young men. What we show, through taking the reader on a journey through the intersections of space, gender, sexuality and disability, is that one identity is not more important than the other but rather must be taken in intersection together. The way bodies 'differ' from the norm of white, able-bodied male can create exclusions, dangers and vulnerabilities. These have to be negotiated differentially in order to access spaces of pleasure, often through creative and wilful push-through.

Note

[1] For the avoidance of doubt, by disability the authors mean the wider societal barriers, and by impairment the authors are referring to the inherent medical condition.

References

Ahmed, S. (2002) 'Racialized bodies,' in M. Evans and E. Lee (eds) *Real Bodies: A Sociological Introduction*, London: Palgrave, pp 46–63.

Bogdan, R (2014) *Freak Show: Presenting Human Oddities for Amusement and Profit*, Illinois: University of Chicago Press.

Bradshaw, S., Linneker, B. and Overton, L. (2017) 'Extractive industries as sites of supernormal profits and supernormal patriarchy?' *Gender & Development*, 25(3), pp 439–54.

Butler, J. (1990) *Gender Trouble: Feminism and the Subversion of Identity*, New York: Routledge.

Covino, D.A. (1996) *The Abject body: Toward an Aesthetic of the Repulsive*, Chicago: University of Illinois.

Crenshaw, K. (1989) 'Demarginalizing the intersection of race and sex: a black feminist critique of antidiscrimination doctrine, feminist theory and antiracist politics', *University of Chicago Legal Forum*, 1(8): 139–67.

Evans, B., Bias, S. and Colls, R. (2021) 'The dys-appearing fat body: bodily intensities and fatphobic sociomaterialities when flying while fat', *Annals of the American Association of Geographers*, 111(6): 1816–32.]

Evans, M., and Lee, E. (eds) (2002) *Real Bodies: A Sociological Introduction*, London: Palgrave.

Formby, E. (2017) *Exploring LGBT Spaces and Communities: Contrasting Identities, Belongings and Wellbeing*, London & New York: Routledge.

Freund, P. (2001) 'Bodies, disability and spaces: the social model and disabling spatial organisations,' *Disability & Society*, 16(5): 689–706.

Greater London Authority (GLA) (2021) *London's Diverse Population Dataset* [online] https://data.london.gov.uk/dataset/london-s-diverse-population

Glass, D. (2020) *United Queerdom*, London: Zed Books.

Hepple, J. (2016) 'If you're a disabled, gay twentysomething, Grindr is a godsend,' *The Guardian*, [online] www.theguardian.com/commentisfree/2016/dec/01/disabled-gay-twentysomething-grindr-cerebral-palsy

Hepple, J. (2017) 'Sex and inaccessible queer venues,' *Huffington Post* [online] www.huffingtonpost.co.uk/joshua-hepple/sex-and-inaccessible-quee_b_17344284.html

Hines, S. (2019) 'The feminist frontier: on trans and feminism', in T. Oren and A. Press (eds) *The Routledge Handbook of Contemporary Feminism*, London: Routledge, pp 94–109.

Holzhacker, R. (2014) '"Gay Rights are Human Rights": the framing of new interpretations of international human rights norms,' in G. Andreopoulos and Z.F. Kabasakal Arat (eds) *The Uses and Misuses of Human Rights*, New York: Palgrave Macmillan, pp 29–64.

Hubbard, R. (1997) 'Abortion and disability: who should and who should not inhabit the world', in L. Davis (ed.), *The Disability Studies Reader*, London: Psychology Press, pp 93–104.

Inclusion London (nd) 'The social model of disability', [online] www.inclusionlondon.org.uk/disability-in-london/social-model/the-social-model-of-disability-and-the-cultural-model-of-deafness/

Jagose, A. (1996) *Queer Theory: An Introduction*, New York: NYU Press.

Kafer, A. (2013) *Feminist, Queer, Crip*, Indiana: Indiana University Press.

Lee, S., Fenge, L.A. and Collins, B. (2020) 'Disabled people's voices on sexual well-being', *Disability & Society*, 35(2): 303–25.

Litwack, E. (2018) 'Getting around: globalization and transnationalism', in M.J. Murphy and B. Bjorngaard (eds) *Living Out Loud: An Introduction to LGBTQ History, Society, and Culture*, New York: Routledge, pp 333–72.

McLean, C. (2021) 'The growth of the anti-transgender movement in the United Kingdom. The silent radicalization of the British electorate', *International Journal of Sociology*, 51(6): 473–82.

Narrain, A (2016) '*The Yogyakarta principles on sexual orientation and gender identity: marking ten years of SOGI jurisprudence*', [online] https://arc-international.net/blog/the-yogyakarta-principles-on-sexual-orientation-and-gender-identity-marking-ten-years-of-sogi-jurisprudence/

Overton, L.R.A. (2014) 'From vulnerability to resilience: an exploration of gender performance art and how it has enabled young women's empowerment in post-hurricane New Orleans', *Procedia Economics and Finance*, 18: 214–21.

O'Malley, J., and Holzinger, A. (2018) '*Sexual and gender minorities and the sustainable development goals, United Nations Development Programme*', [online] www.undp.org/sites/g/files/zskgke326/files/publications/SDGs_SexualAndGenderMinorities.pdf

Parker, J. (2015) 'I'm non-binary and transgender – but the government can't officially recognise me', *The Independent* [online]www.independent.co.uk/voices/i-m-nonbinary-and-transgender-but-the-government-can-t-officially-recognise-me-10505570.html

Pryse, M. (2000) 'Trans/feminist methodology: bridges to interdisciplinary thinking,' *NWSA Journal*, 12(2): 105–18.

Quarmby, K. (2011) *Scapegoat: Why We are Failing Disabled People*, London: Portabello Books.

Richardson, N., Smith, C. and Werndly, A. (2013) *Studying Sexualities: Theories, Representations, Cultures*, Hampshire & New York: Palgrave Macmillan.

Roulstone, A and Mason-Bish, H (eds) (2015) *Disability, Hate Crime and Violence*, London: Routledge.

Russo, M. (2009) *The Female Grotesque: Risk, Excess and Modernity*, London: Routledge.

Schwartz, G.L. and Jahn, J.L. (2020) 'Mapping fatal police violence across US metropolitan areas: overall rates and racial/ethnic inequities, 2013–2017', *PloS one*, 15(6): e0229686.

Shakespeare, T. (2014) *Disability Rights and Wrongs Revisited*, London & New York: Routledge.

Shakespeare, T. (2017) *Disability: The Basics*, London & New York: Routledge.

Shakespeare, T., Gillespie-Sells, K. and Davies, D. (1996) *The Sexual Politics of Disability: Untold Desires*, London: Cassell.

Solomon, A. (2014) *Far from the Tree: Parents, Children and the Search for Identity*, New York: Scribner.

Stanko, E. (2013) *Intimate Intrusions (Routledge Revivals): Women's Experience of Male Violence*. London: Routledge.

Stonewall (2017) '*Get Over It campaigns*', [online] www.stonewall.org.uk/our-work/campaigns/get-over-it

UPIAS (1976) *Fundamental Principles of Disability*, London Union of the Physically Impaired Against Segregation, [online] https://disability-studies.leeds.ac.uk/wp-content/uploads/sites/40/library/Oliver-in-soc-dis.pdf

Wilchins, R. (2017) *TRANS/gressive: How Transgender Activists Took on Gay Rights, Feminism, the Media & Congress ... and Won!*, Riverdale, NY: Avenue Books LLC.

World Bank (2015) *Sexual Minorities and Development: A Short Film* [online] www.youtube.com/watch?v=IjVhAsgfqME&t=6s

World Health Organization (WHO) (2011) *World Report on Disability*, Geneva: World Health Organization.

World Health Organization (WHO) (2021) 'Violence against women prevalence estimates, 2018: global, regional and national prevalence estimates for intimate partner violence against women and global and regional prevalence estimates for non-partner sexual violence against women', Geneva: World Health Organization, on behalf of the United Nations Inter-Agency Working Group on Violence Against Women Estimation and Data (VAW-IAWGED); 2021. Licence: CC BY-NC-SA 3.0 IGO.

Young, S. (2014) '*I'm not your inspiration, thank you very much*', TEDTalks, YouTube, [online] www.youtube.com/watch?v=8K9Gg164Bsw&t=29s

Yuval-Davis, N. (1997) 'Women, citizenship and difference', *Feminist Review*, 57(1): 4–27.

14

Conclusion: Where Next for Intersectional Criminology?

Ben Colliver and Jane Healy

Introduction

In this chapter, we take the opportunity to draw together some of the common themes and areas of crossover produced by the individual contributors. We also reflect on some of the key issues identified throughout the book that warrant further investigation, utilizing an intersectional framework to enhance our understanding of such relevant topics. Our aim is to centre criminological and Criminal Justice research that is conducted and analysed intersectionally, work that often remains on the margins of criminology in the UK. The chapters presented offered a multi-directional analysis of power and oppression. This conclusion begins by reflecting on the six core ideas of intersectional frameworks as outlined by Hill Collins and Bilge (2016). In doing so, we conceptualize how these six objectives have manifested within the chapters presented in this edited collection. We explore how issues of social inequality, power, relationality, social context, complexity and social justice have been addressed within each of the chapters. We close this chapter by reflecting on the relative lack of intersectional, criminological research in the UK, which is a common thread throughout all of the chapters presented in this edited collection. As such, we call for further intersectional work to be conducted. Despite Hill Collins and Bilge (2016, p 87) arguing that 'within the neoliberal university, intersectionality has been invited to settle down within, instead of unsettling, the established frames of knowledge production and dissemination', we propose that this is yet to happen within British criminology. Rather, intersectional analyses and frameworks remain marginalized within the discipline.

Social inequality

The first core concept relating to intersectionality is social inequality (Hill Collins and Bilge, 2016). As the chapters in this collection have demonstrated, social issues and oppression are not usually caused by a single issue. As Hill Collins and Bilge (2016, p 26) point out, 'using intersectionality as an analytic tool encourages us to move beyond seeing social inequality through race-only or class-only lenses'. For example, Finnegan's chapter draws upon the intersection of age, gender and class to provide a more critical reading of how older people experience abuse, and how these experiences may be compounded by multiple marginalizations. Likewise, Duffus' chapter draws upon inequalities along the lines of class and gender to offer a more complex understanding of how social inequalities intersect and impact people's experiences within the probation service.

What is clear throughout the chapters is that it is rare to see one form of social inequality impacting people's experiences. Rather, this collection has evidenced the need for researchers to adopt an intersectional analytic framework to consider how multiple inequalities interact and result in heterogeneous experiences. It is clear that social inequalities are of crucial importance at all stages of the Criminal Justice System, for victims and people who have offended.

Power

Hill Collins and Bilge (2016, p 26) contend that 'people's lives and identities are generally shaped by many factors in diverse and mutually influencing ways'. As such, issues of oppression are not purely singular, but rather different forms of oppression obtain meaning and value from each other. This is evidenced throughout the chapters presented within this collection. For example, Colliver demonstrates how issues of anti-religious sentiment and racism often co-exist in trans-inclusive spaces. Hill Collins and Bilge (2016) also suggest that research that considers global power relations, including issues of nationalism and neo-liberalization, provides more thorough understandings of social inequality. This can be seen within McBride and James' chapter, which situates issues of hate within a neo-liberal context, offering a structurally situated reading of the experiences of transgender people and gypsies and travellers.

It is also evident that power operates at different levels, including structural, political and interpersonal. Appreciating these various layers of power allows us to challenge broad, homogenizing labels and problematize these labels by considering the perspectives of those who are so labelled. Marshall's chapter problematizes the label 'victim of exploitation' and interrogates the ways in which those who are labelled negotiate both interpersonal power and structural power, drawing on notions of 'constrained choices'. On the other hand, Levell critiques the use of the label 'gang-involved', highlighting the political and structural power agencies that have a vested interest in producing and applying labels and the role of class and race in the production of such labels. Both of these chapters situate their findings within a multitude of power hierarchies, and draw upon an intersectional analysis to explore how power is negotiated.

Relationality

The third aspect of intersectionality that Hill Collins and Bilge (2016) identify is 'relationality'. In this sense, rather than focusing on the differences between varying forms of oppression, we must focus on the interconnectedness of these oppressions. Relating this to issues of power, they argue that this is not a static concept, but is based on relationships. Healy's chapter explored the relationship between gender and disability, and draws on issues of power in relation to the policing and reporting of disablist hate crime. Here we see how stereotypes held by those in relative power impact the experiences that victims have when navigating the Criminal Justice System. By the same token, Pickles explores the 'tapestry of social violence', rooting identity-based violence within historical, political, social and cultural contexts. His chapter draws on ideas of 'collectivism' and relationships as being fundamental in aiding radical healing. Here, we are able to see that relationality extends beyond our understanding of intersectional oppressions, but is also vital in responses to oppression and victimization.

Social context

All of the chapters included in this collection place issues of crime and Criminal Justice within their social, political and cultural context. As such, the authors demonstrate that utilizing an intersectional analysis involves 'contextualizing one's arguments, primarily by being aware that particular historical, intellectual, and political contexts shape what we think and do' (Hill Collins and Bilge, 2016, p 28). It is therefore essential to note that the chapters presented in this collection are time- and place-specific, contextualized within the political, social and cultural context of the UK. Therefore, the discussions and implications of this collection may not traverse international and global contexts.

What is evident throughout the book is that there exists a political, social and cultural climate in which 'difference' is often positioned as 'less than', therefore legitimizing hate crime, marginalization and oppression. The chapters that have explored various aspects of the Criminal Justice System have presented a social and political context in which more punitive responses to crime have taken a hold. Those exploring identity-based violence and hate crime have underlined the othering of victims and communities. In this context, the authors have been able to explore the disproportionate impact these punitive responses have on those who may be the most politically, economically and socially marginalized.

Complexity

Hill Collins and Bilge (2016) argue that intersectionality is an inherently complex concept. Issues of power, context, inequality and relationality mean that intersectionality is not a straightforward concept to engage with. The challenge involved in applying an intersectional framework is demonstrated throughout the chapters, evidenced by the different ways in which authors engage with the concept and apply it within real-world research. However, what is clear is that intersectionality as a complex, critically analytical concept offers us the opportunity to more fully engage with and analyse social power structures, their formation and maintenance, and how these structures enable and legitimize oppression. Hepple and Overton's chapter explored the complex relationships that exist between individuals, spaces and communities and how individual identities are negotiated within the context of different spaces.

Throughout this edited collection, the complexity of intersectionality is compounded by the complexity of identities, experiences and lived realities. A common complaint throughout this book is that previous research has often adopted a one-dimensional approach to investigating identities, and resultantly we have no choice but to engage with oversimplistic understandings of people's experiences of crime, victimization and offending. In the chapters exploring hate crime, the contributors detail how oppression is rarely experienced along one axis; rather, the complexity of varying identity characteristics creates intricate and unique experiences of hate.

One of the key criticisms of intersectionality is that it perpetuates 'identity politics' that cultivates separatism (Hill Collins and Bilge, 2016). However, what becomes apparent through the chapters in this collection is that adopting an intersectional analysis enables us to consider the similarities, overlaps and relationships between different hierarchies of power, and the material impacts these hierarchies have on people's experiences. Adopting an intersectional analysis also has symbolic, political and social importance. It has been claimed that intersectionality is too focused on separatist identity politics (Ehrenreich, 2002; Mitchell, 2013). However, it is only those who already hold the most social power that benefit from suppressing identity politics. Those members of our society and communities who are most marginalized, and experience a matrix of oppression as a result of various intersecting power hierarchies, cannot benefit from single-axis frameworks that do not fully appreciate the complex nature of power.

Social justice

While Hill Collins and Bilge (2016) claim that aiming for social justice is not a requirement for adopting an intersectional analysis approach, they also contend that there is a commonality between those who embrace intersectionality and those who centre social justice. This is evident throughout this collection, in which all of our authors engaged in research are pursuing a fairer, more just representation of people's experiences of oppression, crime and victimization. Many of the issues and concerns presented throughout this collection such as minority groups' experiences of the Criminal Justice System, victims of hate crime or elder abuse are central to challenging the status quo and creating a fairer society. Part I of this book, which charts the development of intersectionality, and also considers the role of Britain's colonial legacy, emphasizes the importance of acknowledging and appreciating historical developments. It is only in doing so that we can fully understand the development of social injustice and people's experiences, and develop tools, policies and resources to truly challenge these injustices.

The lack of intersectional research

Moving away from the six core aspects of intersectionality, one of the dominant threads that runs throughout each of the chapters in this edited collection is the lack of existing intersectional work within criminology. While there is some important research emerging in criminology that utilizes an intersectional analysis (Couture-Carron, 2017; Logie et al, 2017; Sun et al, 2018), British criminology has been slow in adopting this approach (Parmar, 2017). This view is reiterated throughout the chapters in this collection. All authors highlight the lack of existing research that utilizes an intersectional framework or analysis within their respective fields. As such, this collection offers a new and contemporary overview of innovative research that is currently being conducted. As mentioned, criminological inquiry has a tendency to apply a single-axis framework when investigating issues of criminal justice, victimization and offending. Resultantly, it remains that criminology in the UK has significant work to do in order to fully appreciate the experiences of people who may experience oppression and marginalization.

Fluidity of identity

Another key message that runs across the chapters in this collection is that identities are fluid. Consequently, it can be detrimental to conceptualize identity categories as static, fixed and stable. Moran and Sharpe (2004, p 400) argue that research often considers identity under broad categories of race, gender and so on, and as a result overlooks 'the differences, the heterogeneity, within what are assumed to be homogenous identity categories and groups'. It is therefore essential to consider the fluid nature of identity, and to appreciate that identities are multiple, and our own understanding of our identity may not be the same as others' perception of our identities (Wetherell, 2009). As individuals with complex identities, we may experience others imposing a master identity upon us (as discussed by Colliver), or we may seek to emphasize a particular aspect of our identities within certain spaces and contexts (as many of the contributors highlight). It is therefore vital that we employ multi-directional analyses when researching important issues around Criminal Justice. Failing to do so arguably results in simplistic and reductive understandings of our identities and experiences.

Conclusion

As the first edited collection that explores intersectionality within criminology in the UK, this compilation showcases contemporary criminological research that utilizes an intersectional framework and analysis. In these chapters, authors have demonstrated the importance to future research of adopting this approach, from a theoretical *and* conceptual perspective. We therefore hope that this collection inspires and encourages researchers to employ an intersectional framework within their own criminological research to engage with the complexities associated with power relations, social contexts and inequalities. In doing so, our discipline will be more fully engaged with the social realities of our communities and our participants, and how they are experienced and responded to, and offer a more realized and honest account of crime, Criminal Justice and victimization.

References

Couture-Carron, A. (2017) 'One size doesn't fit all: dating abuse against women from the perspective of South Asian Muslim youth in Canada', *Journal of Interpersonal Violence*, 32(23): 3626–47.

Ehrenreich, N. (2002) 'Subordination and symbiosis: mechanisms of mutual support between subordinating systems', *UMKC Law Review*, 71(2): 251–324.

Hill Collins, P. and Bilge, S. (2016) *Intersectionality*, Cambridge: Polity Press.

Logie, C.H., Daniel, C., Ahmed, U. and Lash, R. (2017) '"Life under the tent is not safe, especially for young women": understanding intersectional violence among internally displaced youth in Leogane, Haiti', *Global Health Action*, 10(2): 1270816–1270816.

Mitchell, E. (2013) 'I am a woman and a human: a Marxist-feminist critique of intersectionality theory', *The North Star*, [online] www.thenorthstar.info/?p=11425

Moran, L. and Sharpe, A. (2004) 'Violence, identity and policing: the case of violence against transgender people', *Criminal Justice*, 4(4): 395–17.

Parmar, A. (2017) 'Intersectionality, British criminology and race: are we there yet?', *Theoretical Criminology*, 21(1): 35–45.

Sun, S., Crooks, N., Kemnitz, R. and Westergaard, R.P. (2018) 'Re-entry experiences of black men living with HIV/AIDS after release from prison: intersectionality and implications for care', *Social Science & Medicine*, 211: 78–86.

Wetherell, M. (2009) *Theorizing Identities and Social Action*, London: Palgrave Macmillan.

Index

References to figures appear in *italic* type.

www.ingramcontent.com/pod-product-compliance
Lightning Source LLC
Chambersburg PA
CBHW070618030426
42337CB00020B/3841